ONE

HUNDRED

NAMES

FOR

LOVE

ONE
HUNDRED
NAMES
FOR
LOVE

A STROKE, A MARRIAGE,
AND THE LANGUAGE
OF HEALING

DIANE
ACKERMAN

W. W. NORTON & COMPANY

NEW YORK LONDON

Excerpt from "The Oven Bird" from *The Poetry of Robert Frost*, edited by Edward Connery
Lathem. Copyright 1916, 1969 by Henry Holt and Company. Copyright 1944 by Robert Frost.
Reprinted by arrangement with Henry Holt and Company, LLC. Excerpts from *Life With Swan*
by Paul West reprinted with the permission of Scribner, a Division of Simon & Schuster, Inc.
Copyright © 1999 by Paul West. All rights reserved.

For information about permission to reproduce selections from this book,
write to Permissions, W. W. Norton & Company, Inc.,
500 Fifth Avenue, New York, NY 10110

For information about special discounts for bulk purchases, please contact
W. W. Norton Special Sales at specialsales@wwnorton.com or 800-233-4830

Manufacturing by Courier Westford
Book design by JAM Design
Production manager: Anna Oler

ISBN 978-0-393-07241-9

W. W. Norton & Company, Inc.
500 Fifth Avenue, New York, N.Y. 10110
www.wwnorton.com

W. W. Norton & Company Ltd.
Castle House, 75/76 Wells Street, London W1T 3QT

1 2 3 4 5 6 7 8 9 0

For P-Wombat and L-Wombat

PART ONE

THE CARTOGRAPHY OF LOSS

TRAILING PLASTIC TUBES, PAUL MADE HIS WAY ACROSS THE room, steeped in twilight, and I was struck by how the body sometimes looks like the sea creature it is, a jellyfish with long tentacles, not really a fish at all but a gelatinous animal full of hidden symmetries, as well as lagoons and sewers, and lots of spongy and stringy bits. But mainly salt water. Lugging tubes and cables, he had joined the hospital's bloom of deep-sea creatures. But all that would soon change because he'd been cleared to leave the following morning, though he'd still be taking potent antibiotics.

"We escape at dawn!" he stage-whispered over his shoulder in a British sergeant-major voice. The prospect made us both a little giddy.

For three weeks, he'd languished in this high-tech cove, with a kidney infection that had waxed systemic, one of those staph bugs older than sharks or ginkgo trees, and I'd camped out with him lest he trip over the leashes dripping fluids into or out of him.

I'd been on book tour for *An Alchemy of Mind* when I learned Paul had to be hospitalized, and curtailed my travels to fly straight home. But the magic and glory of the brain was still very much on my mind, so, lounging in a visitor's chair, propped up on pillows,

I passed the time browsing back issues of *Cerebrum* and *Brain in the News*. From my thermos, I poured us cups of the hot grain drink Roma, which smelled of chicory and graham crackers.

After all, we'd been down this wharf before, too many times. Twenty years earlier, when he was only fifty-five years old, Paul had battled a devastating heart arrhythmia that nearly killed him. After months of my sensing that something wasn't quite right— the jazz I heard in his chest when we curled up in bed; how pale and clammy he sometimes grew, especially after meals—I'd finally convinced him to see a doctor by insisting it was the *only* thing I wanted for Christmas, the gift of being able to set my mind at ease. A friend had recommended a superb and kind cardiologist in a nearby city, whose verdict was that Paul needed a pacemaker to chime in whenever his heart paused too long between beats. Otherwise he might suddenly pass out, maybe for good, just as his father had from the same malady in his seventies. For Paul, that meant a weeklong hospital stay in Syracuse, the first of many such trysts, and Paul lamenting, broken-spirited: "I used to be such a lion."

When he woke up, after a four-hour surgery during which his heart had twice spat out a pacemaker wire, cleverly insinuated down veins and lodged in the heart muscle, I'd greeted him with my best hundred-watt smile, and holding a stuffed lion.

Ever since that day, we'd driven the hour-and-a-half over wintry, dimly lit roads for checkups, pacemaker tests, and echocardiograms, always anxious, then relieved, and sometimes edgy again, living a predictably uncertain life, much like the "regular irregularity" of his arrhythmic heart.

Other medical escapades followed, like the time when routine lab work revealed a blood sugar level of 800 (normal is around 100), signaling diabetes, and a new regimen began of blood-sugar tests, a special diet, and three more pills. Or when Paul's blood pressure kept soaring, and we had to drive that glassy road to Syracuse again and again, to monitor and reblend his cocktail of medicines. Or the days he fretted in the hospital in Ithaca, receiving IV antibiotics for cellulitis, an infection of his body tissue that began innocently, at a small scratch on his toe, but quickly launched a dangerous campaign up his foot and leg.

This time, a systemic infection was scary enough, but not as harrowing as what we'd been through before. Since the hospital was likely to be our home for a few weeks, we had settled in as best we could. I provided a pantry of canned goods and snacks on a corner table, scented soap and favorite comb in the bathroom, cozy slippers, my knitting, and a library of books along the windowsill. Paul adapted in his own inimitable way: he grew so bored that he wrote a complete sonnet cycle about the Egyptian god Osiris.

The past three weeks had been alternately calamitous and withering, as Paul battled the staph infection and also kidney stones that had to be shattered with laser strikes, and I'd felt picked over by the gulls of worry. The inescapable din of shifts changing, trolleys rattling, visitors streaming, and machines pinging had played havoc with my peace of mind. At least I'd been able to come and go, while Paul felt bedfast and caged almost to the point of frenzy. Every evening we watched the setting sun's hallelujahs beyond the sealed window and ached to go home. I looked forward to our being alone together again and at ease, among native routines, with hour upon hour of unfailing quiet.

THEN THE LIGHTNING strike. Paul shuffled out of the bathroom and stood at the foot of the bed, eyes glazed, his face like fallen mud. His mouth drooped to the right, and he looked asleep with open eyes that gaped at me in alarm.

"What's wrong?"

He moved his lips a little, making a sound between a buzz and a murmur. For a moment I had the odd thought he might have a mouthful of bees. Then my spine filled with ice, and I felt as if the floor dropped twenty feet. A decade before Paul had had a Transient Ischemic Attack (TIA), a brief stoppage of blood flow to the brain, igniting strokelike symptoms that pass, but often predict a true stroke. I recognized its burred speech and rigid face. *Anything but that!* I thought, struggling to comprehend. *Not now! Not again!*

"Are you having a stroke?" I finally found the words to ask. But he didn't need to answer. I could feel my head shrinking tighter, as I leapt to my feet and frantically guided him into my chair. Then I grew suddenly numb and thought: *This can't be happening! Stay calm! Figure out what to do! Maybe it's just another TIA, like last time— a nightmare, but not the end!*

I ran for help, sighted a nurse, and blurted out: "I think my husband's having a stroke!" And together we rushed back to the room, down quaking corridors, and found Paul sitting like a stone pharaoh—hands in his lap, expressionless, staring straight ahead.

"Please get a doctor, get a doctor!" I pleaded. "If it's a stroke and he needs to be given tPA, there isn't much time!" I knew of tPA, the miracle clot-busting drug that can sometimes reverse a stroke if it's given during the first three hours. *TPA*—the letters sounded like a dead ringer for *abracadabra.*

She paged a doctor, and began asking Paul questions I didn't hear, taking his blood pressure, temperature, and pulse matter-of-factly, as if nothing mind-bending were happening, nothing like the detonation of a virtuoso brain, nothing like the collapse of our whole world. His blood pressure was high, and he couldn't grip with his right hand. *Too slow, too slow!* I thought.

Still time, still time, I kept telling myself, with an eye on the clock. I hugged Paul tight, as if I could staunch some wound, and tried to reassure him. But it sounded false as I said it. How could I comfort him when he was colliding at speed with himself? All I could do was hold him, even if he didn't respond. Sitting limp and hollow-eyed, he seemed to be in another solar system. Suddenly he looked at me, full of wordless horror, and I knew he knew what was happening.

A doctor on duty rushed in, methodically brisk, checked the vitals on the clipboard, and seemed shockingly calmer than I was, a member of another species.

"Can you smile?" he asked Paul.

He couldn't.

"Can you speak to me, tell me where you are?"

He couldn't.

"Can you raise your arms?"

He couldn't.

"Look at this pen," the doctor said, moving it slowly from left to right across his line of sight. "Can you follow it with your eyes?"

He couldn't.

Sirens started wailing inside me. I knew those four quick diagnostic tests for stroke, and Paul had flunked.

Don't leave me, I silently pleaded. Instead time and space did, rotating around both of us, and I felt tippy, as if I were on shipboard in a bow-cracking storm. The bed's stainless steel began frying sparks, the walls curved into a bowl, and the nurse's voice scratched like an old-fashioned Victrola needle.

As for Paul, he later told me that he'd felt assaulted by things bright and metallic, a twitch in every fiber of his being, bouncing pulses, weird ringing in his ears. There were odder phenomena too, from a shaking sound in his head to a noise like crumbled tea leaves from somewhere in his lumbar region. Also a belfry of quiet tinkling that roamed around his head. As his world tried to right itself between earth and heaven, he felt the presence of a wispy halo, making him wonder if he'd become one of the elect. Whenever the belfry sounds decreased for a slim moment it drove him mad with delight. *The dark night of the merry-go-round* flashed through his mind. In his mouth, a taste balsamic and crude, which he fixed upon with all the rapture of a man touching a toothache in the night.

His fingers, partially deprived of sensation, felt waxlike, dull, opaque, brutalized, and wouldn't respond. His whole body defied touch, as his flesh converted to something stiffer. It wasn't an unpleasant sensation, just different. He felt somewhere, without thinking the words: *What's happening? I'm alive. Sort of.* A British policeman's stern baritone demanded: *What's all this here?*

Then the unfamiliar doctor asked me a streak of questions, and suddenly coming back from a great distance, in a shaky voice I described the events and tried to fill him in on Paul's medical history as quickly as possible. He wrote cryptic notes on a chart in a slow loopy scrawl, the pen scraping like a quill across my jangled nerves. But there was no way he could assimilate all that was happening to this one particular soul—a heart patient he'd never met before, a brilliantly strange mind, let alone my sweetheart and life's companion.

What were Paul's eyes fixed upon with that blank stare? I had the distinct sense that he wasn't seeing at all, at least nothing in the outside world, but down the wrong end of a telescope, peering at the red and yellow shambles behind his eyes.

Tearfully brittle, my world still spinning, I left Paul with the doctor and rushed into the hallway, where, talking into the tiny perforations of my cell phone, I delivered the news to Dr. Ann, our beloved M.D. and friend. Dr. Ann is one of the last old-time family doctors, who visits her patients in the hospital every day, and often becomes part of their extended family. Her voice sharply focused yet intimately sad, she explained that since Paul was on Coumadin, an anticoagulant for his heart, he couldn't take tPA. I'd also heard of clinical trials using vampire-bat saliva after a stroke, and Paul would have loved the idea of medical rescue by vampire bats. But Coumadin would put the vampire-bat saliva off-limits, too. For him, there was no silver bullet. She assured me that it was still too early to know if the symptoms would be permanent. Meanwhile, she promised to muster a team of specialists and order a battery of tests.

An hour later, out of Paul's earshot, a neurologist holding a CAT scan told me a tale of a tragedy whose likely outcome I heard but tried not to imagine, as if by not picturing it I could magically prevent it. The films in his hand showed a ravaged brain: Paul had a small wasteland in the left middle frontal gyrus (a *gyrus* is a bump or a ridge); dead zones in the right and left parietal lobes; swaths of weakened brain cells elsewhere. While my eyes trusted the images, my mind fled to the edges of the hall and tried to slide under the paint, shell-shocked, desperately fending off the news. Silently, I screamed, *No, no, no, no, no, no no!*, hoping somehow to parry reason. It was no use. The images weren't a diagnosis, but I grasped their implications well enough to half extinguish hope. What worried me the most was the damage in Paul's left hemisphere to the key language areas and the fibers connecting them: a withering nightmare.

For Paul, the wordsmith I loved, the most likely culprit was a large clot infused with bacteria from his kidney infection. Shaken loose by his irregular heartbeat, it had traveled to his brain and lodged in his middle cerebral artery, stopping the river of blood that supplies nourishment to a vast terrain of hills and ridges. I found myself imagining the havoc nonetheless, though I had to limn it in my mind's eye, and pretend it was a rural landscape at a distance, not human, not intimate. At exactly the same time, with wincing clarity, I knew the truth. In nonretractable moments, whole networks of neurons had died, a lifetime's verbal skills, knacks, memories.

What had vanished? RAF days on the Isle of Man, when he and his pals had flown to London for lunch, and kept mum about Prince Philip's night flights to visit a bevy of girlfriends? Our Floridian sojourns? The model airplanes of his boyhood, with which he single-handedly won the war? Would he remember his own books? His sister? Our history?

CHAPTER 2

WE HAD FALLEN IN LOVE AT PENN STATE, IN THE EARLY 1970s, when I was a flower-child undergraduate and he a professor with yards of education, wavy brown hair, and a classy English accent. Somehow, though just a sophomore, I'd signed up for his graduate Contemporary British Literature course. There I perched in a back corner, surrounded by the familiar last-row smells of sweaty overcoats, chalky erasers, smoky-caramel leather-bounds, musty old paperbacks and cloth-bounds redolent with mildew and book lice, tart newly inked fare, more acidic editions printed on European papers. A few students had deckle-edged novels, whose virgin pages forced a reader to muscle in and possess them, slicing pages open with worldly-wise aplomb. Fascinated by the discussions, I rarely said a word, since I felt completely out of my depths. But Paul and I talked gamely about literature and life during his office hours, and he responded well to my poetry. For several semesters afterward, I kept bumping into him on campus or in town. On our first real date, we had drinks at his house, talking nonstop until dawn—and I stayed for forty years.

Some said we had absolutely nothing in common. Paul and I came from distinctly different cultures, generations, and ethnic backgrounds. We flew to different nations when we dreamt—mine were anxiously American, his were a fabulist's rural England. American culture was the backdrop I grew up with, but because Paul discovered it as an adult, he never took its oddities (such as eating corn on the cob) for granted. Eighteen years older than I, he grew up in an English village during WWII, listened to swing music, and had memories of being bombed. I was a baby boomer, steeped in Beatles-era rock 'n' roll. My father owned a McDonald's. When it came to literary style, we both preferred the opulent to the sparse. We prized books brimming with poetic descriptions, offbeat characters, and picturesque ideas. But our taste in other things varied. He relished bold and flamboyant designs; I preferred the intricate, ambiguous, delicate.

Paul patrolled the darker recesses of the night—writing in a semi-trance, or watching tapes of cricket matches—until retreating to slumber at last at 5 or 6 a.m. Songbirds migrate at night, and in my imagination I twinned his restlessness with their lunar flights. I, on the other hand, was bewitched by daylight. I woke at dawn and greeted him with a gentle *tag, you're it* hand slap before he climbed into bed. He always waited for me to wake before he went to sleep, so that he could kiss me good morning and good night. He called our relay "the Changing of the Guard," and did a fair (if nakedly dangling) imitation of the Queen's stiff-legged soldiers in tall black hats and red jackets marching in front of Buckingham Palace.

Drowsily heading into the kitchen to make a cup of tea, I knew I'd find a little hand-scrawled love note awaiting me, a gung-ho welcome to the world again after a nighttime away, which he'd attached to the refrigerator door by a magnetic bat, alligator, whale, lion, wolf, flower, or airplane, depending on his mood. A new note appeared almost every day for decades. Instead of signing his notes, he would draw himself with curly hair, svelte shape, pointed feet, full-stop eyes, and delirious smile. It was his version of a cartouche or a royal seal, meant to keep me company until he awoke at noon. Sometimes I accused him of being a maggoty-headed misanthrope, who haunted the wee hours to avoid having a social life. But I supposed his circadian rhythms were simply off-kilter because he had been a night owl since childhood.

Working from home meant we could vary snack and coffee breaks, change our desks or view, goof off, drink on the job, even spend the day in pajamas, and often meet to gossip or share ideas. On the other hand, we bossed ourselves around, set impossible goals, and demanded longer hours than office jobs usually entail. It was the ultimate "flextime," in that it depended on how flexible we felt each day, given deadlines, distractions, and workaholic crescendos.

Our studies offered a good example of our essential natures. Paul's was a pack rat's haven: balsa airplanes; eight pairs of cheap, dusty sunglasses (all aviator style); a windup miniature skull; a plastic six-shooter; his father's WWI medals, framed; a do-it-yourself Egyptian mummy-making kit; a Cockney rhyming dictionary; a collage he'd made that blended paint with flattened wads of green chewing gum, used matchsticks, and labels from a box of La Tropical cigars; boxes of crayons and colored pencils; a never-used soap lion; a blue and white Amazonian mask; classical CDs stacked unevenly, like geological strata, on every free ledge; a gray filing cabinet full of old clothes he hated to part with; crumpled manila folders fat with letters; tall heaps of books, papers, research materials—all the curious *accumulata* of a bustling novelist's life. One needed a guide dog and map to navigate the room. Possibly it reminded him of the craggy English moors.

In the cork-lined alcove where he typed, there were no windows to usher in the outside world, no daylight. "I don't need nature," he once told me. "I can create it." He never touched a computer. On an old blue-and-gray Smith Corona—a classic, leaden typewriter with long strike arms, noisy carriage, and well-worn, begrimed keys—he furnished one lavish fictive world after another and inhabited them with a cavalcade of engagingly kooky people, producing dozens of books during our years together. When he was dubbed a Chevalier of the Order of Arts and Letters by the French government, I pronounced him "Chevy," which became one of his nicknames.

My study, on the other hand, was all windows festooned with bright floral drapery. Stained-glass magnolias framed a bay window, beyond which a large old real magnolia swelled. A tall curiosity cabinet of shelves held pottery "storyteller" dolls from Indian pueblos, the "Oldest Bird House on Earth" built from local fossils, framed photographs of family and friends, a miniature Frank Lloyd Wright window, carved jade monkeys and flowers I inherited from my mother, and a mannequin hand, whose pose I often changed. A computer with a large sleek monitor presided over the desk, and a laptop waited in the bay window. Tattered, faded, ripped-out newspaper and magazine clippings filled a series of wooden filing cabinets and overflowing three-ring binders I affectionately called my "portable universe," a repository of things I found curious. The walls had been painted the yellow of spring light in the forest, and oriental area rugs softened an oatmeal-colored wooden floor. Photos of monk seals, bats, and other endangered animals I'd worked with graced the walls. I worshipped nature, roamed the world of nonfiction, biked most days, and shmoozed a lot with friends. Paul could easily accommodate violence and evil into his imagination, work, and sensibility. I couldn't; I didn't even like movies to end unhappily.

Paul had a different kind of memory from mine, an almost perfect recall—his dark past (wars, poverty, early marriage, years of turmoil) was a country he could homestead. I preferred Zen's idea of living mindfully in the moment. I was more concerned with social issues than he, and felt drawn to volunteer work in the community. His sense of community wasn't local; it spanned seas and eras.

In our writing lives, Paul was a born phrasemaker, and I loved phrases, too; but we didn't construct them in the same way. His were more flamboyant and allusive, such as describing Oxford dons as "noetic pharaohs" and old bread as "sprouting its beard." To a large extent he searched for arresting images as fishhooks to pull up all sorts of thrashing memories. I used imagery more for defining experience. Indeed, that's one key way in which our creative processes differed.

He was without exception the most deliciously quirky person I'd ever met, a classic British eccentric of myth and legend, right out of a P. G. Wodehouse novel. He wouldn't touch or be near fresh fruit, beets, cucumbers, or tomatoes. He didn't leave the house much; instead he was abundantly happy to talk with friends in letters or on the phone. He hated wind, rain, snow—truly, any weather if not sunny and mild. He didn't like wearing clothes, and cheerily strolled around the house and yard like one of Dubuffet's naked pink men. Because society requires clothes he did make concessions: in the summer he wore swim shorts and a blue short-sleeved shirt when we went out, and in the winter he wore a velour jogging suit in unvarying shades of black, gray, or blue. But never, ever socks. At least once he flew home to England lugging a ream of typing paper, which he sat on, "to soften it up."

One day, when we were out driving, he asked me rather urgently to close the sunroof.

"Why?" I asked.

"I don't like space above me," he said. I smiled. This was a new one.

"You know, dear," I replied as evenly as possible, "if you're very lucky, you're going to have space above you for a long time on this planet." Then I closed the sunroof anyway.

I found his eccentricities novel and amusing, in part because they weren't an affectation but grew naturally, like crystals, in the cave of his personality. They sprang unconsciously from a childhood in an English coal-mining town; early absorption of its customs and values; and a deeply eccentric family, in which it was typical to pay a call on relatives only to find aunts, uncles, and cousins all napping naked in the living room with open books covering their privates. The unique society of his brain cells was more than a little different from my own mental colony, but we granted one another most-favored nation status.

When asked about the secret to our decades-long duet, I some-times teased that we stayed together for the sake of the children—each was the other's child. And we were both wordsmiths, cuddle-mad, and extremely playful. But who can say why two people become a couple, that small principality of mutual protection and regard? Couples are jigsaw puzzles that hang together by touching in just enough points. They're never total fits or misfits. In time, a pair invents its own commonwealth, complete with anthems, rituals, and lingos—a cult of two with fallible gods. All couples play kissy games they don't want other people to know about, and all regress to infants from time to time, since, though we marry *as* adults, we don't marry adults. We marry children who have grown up and still rejoice in being children, especially if we're creative. Imaginative people fidget with ideas, including the idea of a relationship. If they're wordsmiths like us, they fidget a lot in words.

So our household had been saturated in wordplay. We relaxed with "Cheater's Scrabble," in which we combined several sets, didn't feel confined by the edges of the board; accepted puns, phrases, and foreign terms; and played not to win but to tie. It seemed more cordial that way. "RareJaponesquedstool" morphed into "RareJaponesquedstoolpigeon." Every day we did the Word Jumble in the newspaper. Puns littered our idle chatter. Paul never spoke my given name. Instead, he made up pet names for me, which evolved. "Pi" became "pilot" became "pilotpoet." The full menagerie of our animal love included kissel panther and lion, camel and bewilderbeast, roseate spoonbill and bush-kitten, bunny and swan, among many other passionate critters.

A lifelong aficionado of classical music, Paul had the habit of extemporizing operettas about me throughout the day, singing in his rich baritone such ad hoc ditties as: "She has a lovely little smile, / dark brown eyes like chocolate drops, / into which I *plunnnge*, and Cliffs of Dover whiteness to her teeth, / above and *beneeeeath*." I'd be washing the dishes, Paul would be on his way to the garage, and he'd idly start singing—barely loud enough for me to hear—"She washes the dishes, / rub-a-dub-dub, / soaps up the pots, / la, la-la, la, la . . ." launching into an improvisatory song about the glories of sudsy domesticity. One spring day, when we were going out and I decided I didn't need a sweater after all, he trilled:

Please leave your sweaters at home,
if you are driven to roam.
You can wear a bikini
and eat some linguini,
but please leave your sweaters at home!

Well, that was all the invitation I needed, and as we drove down the little asphalt road to the farm store, we piled on more lunatic verses involving kimonos, tuxedos, and flamingos.

Writing mainly in different genres, we thought it best to have separate agents and publishers, and our books rarely appeared at the same time. In our household, whenever possible, we didn't allow the other to read reviews that were hatchet jobs or poisonously ad hominem. We had both received both and knew it was easy enough to inadvertently push someone's button and be bombed to smithereens.

On those blessedly rare occasions, we offered comfort and hope from someone who had walked a mile in his shoes and fully understood the other's hurt. Reading each other's manuscripts first and last, we served an important role as ally, editor, critic, and advisor. I tended to be kind to a fault; Paul had a mercurial temper and didn't suffer fools.

Once, in a writing seminar, when a student kept defending an abysmally written story with a self-flattery that finally strained the class's goodwill, Paul lost his cool and declared sharply: "Listen, I'd rather lie naked in a plowed field under an incontinent horse for a week than have to read that paragraph again!"

For thirty years, he had taught graduate fiction writing, and also contemporary European and Latin American literature at Penn

State. He was infamous for making his students' brains hurt from the strain of learning how to juggle complex ideas. One day I passed a student of his in the hallway holding his head under the gush of a drinking fountain, trying to cool his mind after grappling with some of Samuel Beckett's hilariously thorny fiction in Paul's class.

In addition to being a collegiate and county cricket player in his youth, and an RAF officer who lectured on giving good lectures, he garnered several degrees, including a coveted First from Oxford, one of only four given in literature that year. I don't know how Oxford may have changed since those post–World War II days, but at the time there were only two ways to earn a First—the rough equivalent of an A+ and a guarantee of a sterling job—by breathtaking feats of scholarship or by sheer dazzle. A working-class boy on a scholarship to Oxford, he managed to do both. The dazzle came easy because Paul had a draper's touch for the unfolding fabric of a sentence, and he collected words like rare buttons.

CHAPTER 3

THE TESTS REVEALED THAT PAUL HAD A MASSIVE STROKE, one tailored to his own private hell. In the cruelest of ironies for a man whose life revolved around words, with one of the largest working English vocabularies on earth, he had suffered immense damage to the key language areas of his brain and could no longer process language in any form. Though not visible in the CAT scan's chiaroscuro world, other vital language areas had also wilted, leaving a labyrinth of fragile liaisons hushed. *Global aphasia*, it's called. Paul's aphasia was indeed global, round as his head, a grief encompassing our whole world. I'd never heard the expression before, and didn't want to think about the full cartography of loss. Yet I had no choice because someone had to make decisions about his care—informed, clear-headed decisions.

Where was the tutelary angel who should descend at such times and restore the everydayness of things? I felt acutely unqualified. I hadn't volunteered for this job, and never would have, given how much was at stake. I didn't want to be responsible for my loved one's life. Sitting in his hospital room while he was enduring more tests floors below, I could picture him in my mind's eye, glowing red with warmth as he was wheeled through the chilly haunts of the hospital, could track his travels as if I were a pit viper sensing his heat through tunnels underground. I felt very much alone, scalded by my own ineptitude, and thought: *Forget angels. Where are all the grown-ups when one really needs one?*

I knew his plight wasn't unique. Browsing the pamphlets I'd picked up in the waiting room, I discovered that stroke is the number one cause of long-term adult disability in the United States. Paul was now among the 5 to 6 million American stroke survivors, and of those he'd joined the ranks of over 1 million Americans living with aphasia—a void of language, a frustrating perpetual tip-of-the-tongue memory loss, a mute torturer of words, a jumbler of lives. Aphasia doesn't just cripple one's use of words, but the use of any symbols, including the obvious ones: numbers, arrows, semaphore, sign language, Morse code. But also the lightning bolt that spells electrical danger, the three triangles that warn of radiation, the intersecting arcs that announce a biohazard, the cross that locates a hospital on a map, even the paper-doll man and woman on restroom doors.

In 1861, French neurosurgeon Paul Broca inspected the brain of a dead patient, known as *Tan*, who'd suffered from an unusual complaint. Although he understood language, he could neither speak nor write. All he could say was the one syllable—*Tan*. Broca discovered a large lesion in the lower left front of Tan's brain, and when he autopsied the brains of other patients in similar straits and found matching wounds, he declared the peanut-sized area the home of language. That was the first patch of the brain pegged to a specific function, and it still bears Broca's name. Ten years later, German neurologist Carl Wernicke realized that patients with a lesion in the left rear of the brain often spoke incoherently, and he flagged this second area as key to comprehending language.

For the longest time, people believed that the neural pathways of language curved along a Silk Road, journeying from Wernicke's area to Broca's, and when Paul had his stroke, that's what all the textbooks taught and I accepted. But recent strides in brain imaging now suggest that word signals spread widely, detour through mazy souks in the temporal lobe, and strike Wernicke's and Broca's almost in parallel. It seems those two classic word-mills don't so much specialize as conspire to fabricate language, and other artisans contribute to the neural weave.

When we hear a noise, the brain analyzes the incoming stimuli, asking itself: *Is that weird yammering human? Is it a syllable, a real word, just nonsense sounds?* If it resembles speech, the brain conjures up the memory of how certain words sound, associates them with meaning, and furnishes instructions on how to use the muscles of the tongue, throat, lips, and mouth to dispatch a reply.

In so-called *convergence zones*, cargo from the senses combines with emotions, resemblances, a tangle of memories, and other mental spices. As neural traders hobnob (wiring and firing together), they grow stronger ties in the process, establishing a quick route for future trade. The brain relies on such guilds of neurons firing in synchrony, but they don't have to be neighbors. They don't even have to share the same hemisphere. Still, they forge vast assemblies of cells. One such convergence zone in the parietal lobe, gravely damaged during Paul's stroke, is associated with drawing meaning and emotion from language, with providing music's rhythmic enchantment, numbers' clout, writing's constellations, telling left from right, directing thoughts outward to the bright spangled world, and deflecting thoughts inward to judge a feeling or hatch a plan. Adding to the carnage, adjacent cells that spur movement can be injured, too. It's the equivalent of knocking out a state's electrical grids. After that comes a cascade of silently detonating disabilities.

My mind raced. In an instant, Paul had moved to a land of foreigners, whose language he didn't speak and who couldn't understand him. He'd become the unspoken, the unspeakable. In our most talkative of worlds, where lovers coo and confide, friends and family chatter, employers dictate, stores pitch, and all the ready forms of entertainment for the sedentary or sick (TV, books, doctor's office magazines, newspaper, movies) babble language. Suddenly he could not comment, share thoughts, voice feelings, describe hurts or desires, ask for help.

Over the next day, Paul slept a lot, thank heavens, and, in a stupor, I dragged home to shower and nap, and also cancel upcoming book tour events. I needed to let the venues know so that, with any luck, people might see the last-minute "canceled because of family illness" postings. But I still felt guilty imagining them arriving at events only to find a cryptic sign awaiting them. I emailed editors who expected work to be turned in, and canceled all assignments. My project lay in a narrow bed across the lake.

ON DAY TWO, I swooped up the highway edging Lake Cayuga, a cavernous lake too murky for scuba diving, with a rumored underground passage connecting it to Lake Seneca, and a legend of long-necked monsters. Small white sails battled chop on the steel-blue water. I'd admired the lake thousands of times, and glimpsed it while driving thousands more. It always looked different, depending on its mood, and mine. As I drove, it stabbed at the corner of one eye, shining dimly, not glacial at all, but like some impure metal, with slaggy brown inlets, and at times a glaring surface tense as aluminum. Every landmark I passed held spring-loaded memories.

The hospital is located on a hill overlooking the lake, and just past the Finger Lakes Massage School, Paleontological Research Institute, and Museum of the Earth, which houses over 2 million species of fossils. Paul used to chuckle about the road being an avenue not of pines but of spines, traveling from spiny trilobites to spinal taps, and enjoyed the jazzy rhythm of the fossil syllables: "Cenozoic benthic foraminifera." Whenever we drove past it, he'd pronounce "mollusk" very slowly and roundly, just for the mouth-feel.

Near the hospital intersection, a roadwork sign warned: BE PREPARED TO STOP AT ANY MOMENT. I felt my jaw dropping. It sounded like a warning, and also a reminder, as if I needed one, that most likely I wouldn't be hearing Paul say "Cenozoic benthic foraminifera" anytime soon. Or playfully rounding out "mollusk," either. Would we ever laugh together again? Glancing down to find myself grinding one fist on the steering wheel, I wondered, *How long have I been doing that?* but kept right on doing it. Parking, then a space walk into the hospital.

When at last I braced myself and entered Paul's room, I crossed the threshhold into a world that was unfamiliar, with an unfamiliar man lying in it. Although he looked like Paul, he wore a distorted scowl, and seemed to unhinge his whole body in a vain attempt to speak, reeling upright, flexing his shoulders at odd angles and flailing his arms against the bed. Then he switched to just a facial tantrum—cheeks, eyelashes, jowls, and nose writhing as he desperately fought to communicate *something*. His mouth slouched to the right, his lip curled, and for a moment all I could see was a glint of drool at the corner of his mouth, a thin shiny trail like the rune left by a slug.

"Hi, honey," I said, trying to rally a small smile from somewhere in the coal-pits of my belly.

He stared at me, his eyes declaring: *What on earth are you driving at?*

Then he fidgeted about in a vain attempt to muster all the aggregate parts of his being, but only finding a blurred view of what had once moved in unison, he spluttered: "Mem." When I didn't respond, bringing down his clenched fist on the bed railing, he repeated it in loud italics: "*MEM, MEM, MEM!*"

"Easy now, easy, quiet down, it's okay," I said in what I hoped was a calming tone, the same one I'd used as a coed to quiet headstrong riding-school horses when I was afraid one might gallop into a tree. But his flare up shook me so much that I had trouble steadying my voice.

Paul would tell me later that he felt different than before, newly embedded in himself, as if trapped in statuary. His room seemed to be full of Hopi dancers and dazzling as Mardi Gras. Almost festive. He felt his teeth blink. Something pagan was going on, with a mad ring to it, like a disturbed vibraphone. People were speaking a foreign language. Maybe Senegalese or Quechua. And they didn't seem aware of the pandemonium light show and cacophony he was enduring.

When I tried to wrap an arm around him, he threw it off.

"How are you?" I persisted.

He struggled to respond, then he spat a little sound—*whgggggggg*—as if he were blowing at a candle, followed by a sibilant parade of *s*'s. On he wrestled, and the more words eluded him, the more frustrated he became, until his temper boiled, his face flushed, his jaw opened and closed in silent damnation, and his eyes darted around the room. At last, he glared at me with pupils tiny and hard as BBs. Suddenly he clenched his fists and thrashed his arms as he shouted: "MEM-MEM-MEM-MEM-MEM!"

I flinched, and seeing that he'd scared me, he quieted down.

"I wish I could understand you," I said, more to myself than to Paul.

When I reached for his trembling hand, he yanked it away. Thus far, his tantrum hadn't invaded his legs and feet, which seemed somehow immune to all the turmoil. How strange—his temper stalked only his face and torso, while his lower body stayed calm, free from his rage. I'd once heard that Inuit dancers, to conserve their body heat, danced while seated on fur rugs, using only their upper bodies. Was his brain playing favorites and saving energy in a similar way?

It was an exhausting one-way conversation. I repeated: "How are you?" Not meaning anything by the question except *I'm here, I'm sharing your suffering, I wish I could help you.*

Paul looked at me with controlled exasperation. All that came back from him was a yawning croak twice, a silent cough three times, and "MEM" barked seven times, and finally murmured almost inaudibly, like the last word from a dying man, as if this syllable alone formed the basis of some life to come. He later told me that he already hated that willful word that sprang loose and clogged his mouth, over and over, no matter what he longed to say. In his mind's eye, he saw the syllable compulsively scurrying, like a rat in pursuit of a sandwich. *If only the right word would present itself,* his eyes said, *I could still be saved.*

"Mem, mem, mem," I repeated quietly.

"Mem, mem, mem," he echoed back with a desolation that broke my heart.

Paul fell silent. But the rest of our new habitat was noisy. Remote voices sounded like cats scratching on wood, or monastic prayers, and grew louder as they approached our room, striking a distinct sentence or two as they passed—"*Wouldn't you think?*" "*I dunno*"— before dwindling to sound scraps once more, recognizable only as the distant lilt of human pipes. Low-heeled shoes shuffled past on the linoleum floors. Anonymous skirts and jackets swished like the breath sounds of small whales. Unseen trays and trolleys clanked and clattered through the hallway. Inside the room, the *wild tone*— that barely-audible background stir we perceive as *silence*—included purring machines, syncopated pings, the wind *shushing* behind but-toned-up windows, and faintly humming walls.

"Hawk! Hawk! Hawk! Hawk! Hawk! Hawk!" several crows warned one another so loudly that Paul and I both swooped our eyes toward the windows, searching instinctively for the *danger from above* of their alarm call, a strident clamor we'd heard often enough in our own backyard. I half expected to see the speckled bloomers of a red-tail perching on the window ledge.

"Must be a hawk around," I said, mustering a little chat to fill the silence, to help keep up morale.

Paul settled back rigidly on the bed, looking like a sad fallen old idol. *Even the crows can communicate*, his eyes seemed to say.

WAS I GETTING used to his not speaking? Maybe so, because the next day I began noticing other changes, like his weak, claw-bent hand trying to grip the hospital blanket and tug it up tighter as he settled into a comfortable position. During the stroke, his misfiring brain had told two fingers that something was terribly wrong and to protect themselves by tightening. But the muscles that bend joints are bigger and stronger than those that extend joints, and they always win. *Ah, those scrambled nerve signals*, I thought, *they're forcing his pinkie and ring finger to contract and stay clenched like this. Poor guy.*

Too easily, without warning, my mind kept switching between attention and sensation: the autopilot a parent flies when tending a sick child, and a bedeviled swirling. At home, I thought I heard a unique sound of summer nights in the country: the occasional small sneezes of skunks and raccoons clearing dust from their noses as they snuffle in the dirt and forage through garbage. How we'd loved that sultry July evening when a mother skunk had marched her four kits past the screen door and across the patio. Striped from birth, the young are born blind, deaf, and furry, so we'd assumed they were on one of their first patrols and that mom kept a well-clawed burrow somewhere in the yard.

"They don't look real, do they?" Paul, tickled with wonder.

I'd tugged at his sleeve in *Look, look!* excitement. "Each one with a little white cap—*perfect!*—and an exclamation point down its nose! *Sweet.*"

"I could use the tails as paintbrushes. . . . Want one as a pet?" He'd sounded half serious.

I'd smacked his hand lightly. "No, no, wild animals stay where they belong."

"Do we belong *indoors*?"

"Point taken."

He'd curled an arm around my shoulder. "Anywhere with you, my lamb."

I'd *baah*ed quietly. Night was falling then, and humans belonged undercover at least.

Not in the belly of a hospital for any length of time. Lifting his hand now as if it were a large, delicate seashell, I pried open the fingers and wrapped them around a Styrofoam cone lying on the bed for that purpose. This was like a trick I'd used at home with tight knee-high socks, fresh from the wash, forcing their fibers to stretch by wrapping them around flexible plastic hoops. Did it really work on the textiles of flesh and bone? At least it prevented his fingernails from gouging his palm, but the cone kept slipping free, since Styrofoam is slick and his hand, swollen from lack of use, had already grown stiff and inflexible. Again I lifted what had been a beefy, reassuring paw, which didn't *feel* like Paul's hand any longer, but bloated and cool. More like the hand of a drowned sailor, washed ashore on the pebbled beach of the cold lake. The thought gave me goose bumps.

"The nurse said to elevate your hand to ease the swelling," I murmured as I propped it up on a pillow. Paul looked at me blankly, making it clear that he hadn't a clue what I was saying, but would peacefully surrender a body part there was no use in fighting over.

A young aide appeared and guided him into the bathroom, and to my horror I watched a strange drama unfolding as Paul tried to groom himself.

"Here you go, Mr. West," she said, handing him a black plastic comb. "Would you like to comb your hair?"

There was a time, long ago, when raking his thick hair with such small tines would have left the comb gap-toothed. Using both hands, he now held the comb for a moment and considered it as if it were an object from deep space. Then he struggled to wrap his puffy fingers around it, and dragged the comb along the side of his head, smoothing his hair, not combing it, as if he'd forgotten how a comb worked, but remembered where it went and the general motion. Was combing your hair difficult? I tried to remember when I first learned how to hold a comb, and what movements guided what mirror images, which motions led to which results. But I couldn't travel that far back into the electric mists of my childhood.

The aide repositioned the comb, holding Paul's burly hand in her small one, steering it gently. I struggled to keep my hopes from plummeting. How much of his difficulty came from sheer bewilderment, I wondered, how much from lack of coordination? The end result was the same either way, and not just with combing. Ham-fisted fumbling when he tried to open the water taps at the sink, which he couldn't manage without assistance. Confusion about how to lower himself safely onto the low toilet, and after that a look of humble desperation as he gripped a wad of toilet paper in one hand, not knowing how to use it, his eyes silently pleading for my help.

"Here you go. Take it slowly. You'll be all right." I could only babble reassuringly, though I doubted he understood, and I hadn't a clue what his future might hold. No one did. *Your poor battered brain*, I thought, trying to peer through bone on the left side of his head, to where the brain stores the memories of how things are done, how to perform simple tasks. His stroke somewhere in that region had clearly unskilled him. Now his years had come unglued.

Walking back to bed, he veered and tottered, hands jutting out from his sides and then reaching in front of him, as if he were navigating through a dimly lit house. He could see well enough for the short journey, but all of his senses had been rattled by the stroke, it was as if (he later said) someone had reached a hand inside his head and turned the dials up high—everything was too loud, too bright, too fast—and he could no longer trust his eyes. He wasn't walking the way most adults do, with only one foot on the ground at a time and the legs swinging as a double pendulum. More like stepping over rock fragments at the bottom of a cliff: lifting one foot, putting it back down without moving forward, lifting the other foot, taking a step. And sleepwalker's hands. It was nothing I had seen before. He didn't walk like a one-year-old, discovering how. He walked as if he were inventing walking for the first time. Not the breezy strides of a professor across a dappled quad, not the spry shuffle of playing croquet on the lawn, not the march down the driveway to collect the mail.

The bed might just as well have been a rowboat lashed to a dock in a hurricane. Pressing a button, the aide lowered it as far as possible, and turned Paul sideways, planting his weak right hand on the bed rail. But Paul didn't seem to understand that he needed to lift one leg up while leaning forward in a controlled fall, while simultaneously swiveling onto his side. It wasn't one motion at all, but three contrary moves. I hadn't thought about the complexity of climbing into bed before. *How can the body forget that?* I rushed with tenderness as I watched him struggling with a skill he'd practiced at least thirty thousand times in his seventy-five years. With a half-jump from Paul, a heave from the aide, and a tug from me, he

finally landed in bed, on his back, out of puff, and the aide raised
the bed once more.

All I'd done was stand nearby, and tug when needed, walk
nowhere, say little, lift nothing—and yet I felt winded and tired.

At breakfast, a cheery young man delivered the local newspaper,
which Paul had idly perused during his pre-stroke weeks in the
hospital, when, exiled across town from his house and haunts, he
was desperately in need of distractions. He'd enjoyed its small-
town flavor—diner closing for health reasons, hospital planning a
new wing, bloody shoes found in a murder trial, zebra mussels
invading the inlet, historic building preservations, a man cleared of
shooting his mother-in-law with a shotgun on the grounds that he
mistook her for a raccoon, citizens sharing pothole alerts. Now the
paper lay untouched, and after a while I handed it to him, thinking
that, even if he couldn't speak, maybe, just maybe, he could read a
headline or two, or at least look at the photographs?

Paul dutifully accepted the newspaper, and opened it with a
crackling flourish, holding it like an oversized storybook or menu.
He stared vaguely at the pages, one after another, until his brow
began puckering and he grew bewildered. He knew he should be
doing *something* with the newspaper. But whatever the *something*
was, it wasn't happening. The mossy-smelling, freshly inked letters
were just two-dimensional daubs, arranged tidily, but completely
without meaning. Paul cocked his head and squinted as he tried to
decipher the arcane symbols, flustered, but also a little embarrassed.
At last he set the paper down, glanced at me hard as if I'd ambushed
him, glanced away.

Oh my god, he really can't read! I realized, as the enormity of his
affliction began seeping even deeper into my ken. *Not the signs in
the hall—Entrance, Lavatory, Danger—not street signs. Not the thousands of books in our library at home that we've painstakingly, joyously
collected over the years. Not Shakespeare, Rilke, or Beckett. Not his
own work.*

On the wall, an oversized clock ticked away the hours, though
he couldn't pronounce the numbers, couldn't do numbers period.

His parietal lobe had been crippled, and in it somewhere, all the accountants had died.

"Do you know what time it is?" I asked, still grasping for the miracle of a right answer, any sign at all of improvement. His gaze followed mine to the clock, and he knew that *time* had something to do with the moon-faced white object on the wall decorated with cryptic symbols. I later learned that they reminded him of markings on the debris supposedly left by a UFO at Area 51.

Beneath the clock, glaring at him like some Kafkaesque depravity, hung a white wipe-board on which aides wrote each day's schedule in large block letters. All day long, he faced that roll call of the nurses on duty and the rendezvous with physical and speech therapists that awaited him. Unable to glean even the slightest shred of meaning from the schedule, he floated anxiously, with nerves frayed and scrambled, through blurred time, not knowing who or what would come next.

"But such sensations and noises belonged presumably to no one else," he would tell me later, *"and I took pride in that, while yearning for the quiet I once knew. I, who had been a little slothful, now felt constantly agitated. Yes, it was all a matter of what came next. Life had seemed to me a toss-up between not knowing what came next and a bright insistent message that everything was all right. I had no idea what or who or when. Only where, only here, and even that was hazy.*

"I was a case of a man who had come round from delirium to find a cascade of minute changes in his world, which couldn't be ignored as the big bustle of everyday living took charge. I sensed in the complex fabric of my being that I had been remarkably altered. Changes irrevocable and final. I accepted these hammer blows from creation as overdue, as part of the mystery that people simply have to be dispatched for other people to replace them."

My own mind returned to the chilling road sign: BE PREPARED TO STOP AT ANY MOMENT. Then, instead of a void or a blockade, I remembered a day I happened upon Paul in our library, humming happily as he rummaged through his treasures. He collected spotters' guides to world aircraft; lavishly illustrated views of astronomy and the oceans; airplane magazines; British schoolboys' adventures; accounts of WWII; movie guides; and biographies of composers, boxers, cricket players, gunmen of the Old West, and UFO abductees. On this occasion he was searching through his old railway timetables from countries he'd never visited (just because he enjoyed imagining the trains chugging through the landscapes) for a nineteenth-century schedule of tea trains in Ceylon. Not even for research. He just wanted to thumb through it in the sun and imagine catching a ride.

"I see you're up to your old tricks," was all I'd needed to say.

"It's that, or pack a duffel bag for India . . . ah-hah!" He pulled a moth-eaten pocket-size booklet from a shelf. "This is cheaper."

What would he thumb through now? Maybe photography books . . .

A green-garbed cafeteria worker swooshed in bearing a tray, plunked it down heavily on a side table, and I helped swivel it into position over Paul's bed. Hovering, I supported his back with extra pillows so that he could sit up straight, as we'd been soberly instructed to do since Paul was having difficulty swallowing and he'd be less likely to choke if sitting upright. Then I coaxed him to lean forward as he ate, and urged him to take very small bites. Meal trays offered soft food and stiff trials.

"Here's your spoon, honey." I handed him the normal cafeteria spoon, which twiddled right out of his fingers and rang as it hit the floor. Next he tried a spoon with a fat handle—more like the Styrofoam cone—better for grasping. I placed it slowly in his hand and locked the fingers around it. He moved it like a snow shovel, plowing at the scrambled eggs until some ridged onto the spoon, then spilling most of it down his gown before it reached his mouth. He closed his eyes in disgust and waited while I laid a towel over his chest to catch further spills. Instead of saying "Mem, mem, mem," he tried to pronounce something alien and profound, which came out as "Mem, mem, mem, mem," nonetheless. He meant: *What's wrong with me that a jam-butty can't fix?* Jam-butty: the strawberry-jam-and-butter slabs of bread that highlighted his childhood. If the jam made it to his mouth, that is, without plummeting down his chest.

"That's okay. Your coordination is a little off. Try again."

Wrapping his fingers around the log-like handle, I helped him scoop up eggs and aim for his mouth, which he opened much wider than he needed to, offering a gaping target, and I thought he smiled a little as the eggs fell in. But with a rubbery, uncoordinated jaw, his mouth couldn't trap the food, a dash of which seeped from one corner and onto the towel, creating a lumpy yellow tie. Quickly he wiped his chin with the towel, smeared it really. Paul looked horrified by the mess he had become. Yet he insisted on trying to feed himself again. Up came another spoonful, but soon after liftoff his spoon tilted sideways, spilling the yellow curds onto the lip of his plate. Still holding the spoon aloft, swinging it sideways like a construction crane, he began searching his tray for the fallen egg, unable to find it.

"It's right here." I collected the morsels with a cafeteria spoon and fed him by hand, as if feeding a baby, stunned by the new routine. One minute I was crying at home, the next spoon feeding my husband.

It was becoming painfully clear that he would need lots of rehabilitation to be able to return home—if living at home was even possible. If not, I would need to consider the unthinkable, the unspeakable, something so mind-blowing I didn't dare give it words lest they act as a jinx, something that felt too old, too wrong. *A nursing home.* How could this be? Was life really so different than it had been only days ago?

Wistfully, I replayed a phone conversation we'd had just a few weeks before. I was on the West Coast, and we'd talked for half an hour or so, about nothing, about everything, including a painful predicament I'd found myself in with a good friend.

"Some mess, huh?" I'd simmered into the mouthpiece of the telephone. "How can anyone not love life, when given enough time it will exercise absolutely *all* the tender little muscles of one's heart?"

"You *are* an earth ecstatic," I'd heard Paul sigh.

"Was there any doubt?"

"Just don't get too nutsy about looking for answers," he'd

advised, half seriously. "As Confucius said, enjoy the heist. Don't buck the current. Try to keep on top of the dung heap. Maybe you'll find the open-sesame of matter after all."

I'd laughed and parried: "If I were Herod in the middle of the Massacre of the Innocents, I would *pause* just to marvel at the confusion of that image!"

"Listen, puddin' cheeks . . ."

"*Puddin' cheeks?*" My eyebrows had leapt up.

"It's part of my British ethnic revival. I've got to get back to work before the secretary blows the whistle on me."

"Blows your what? Sure you wouldn't like to step into the darkroom with me and see what develops?" I'd said this in my best Mae West voice.

"Ha-ha . . . something just occurred to me."

"What's that?"

"We *can* go on meeting like this," he'd said tenderly. "Over and over and over."

"Thank God."

Then semi-jokingly: ". . . You know, your agnosticism is much too vocative to take seriously . . ."

"Hey, I thought we just finished that part of the conversation. This is the part of the conversation where we make nice-nice and hang up."

I tried to push the memory away, but it floated like an iceberg, glassy, blue-streaked, riddled with air bubbles from an earlier age. Was that flavorful part of my life really over?

As the hours splintered and Paul underwent another barrage of tests, my hope died a little with each one. His brain was woefully scrambled by the stroke, and, worst of all, he kept throwing childlike tantrums.

"What shall we do?" I asked Dr. Ann, my voice flattened by despair. "Maybe I should take him to a rehab center somewhere? I looked up some on the Internet, and there's one at the University of Michigan that sounds like it might be good. . . . I can't believe I have to think about this. I don't even know how to. The choices are overwhelming."

"I'll help you," Ann said, wrapping a strong arm around me, a swimmer's arm. "We'll figure this out together."

We were standing at the nurses' station, out of Paul's hearing, huddled at a counter in a wash of stark light, as if inside one of Edward Hopper's lonely paintings. I had little family left, Paul was almost all of it, but, like family, Ann knew our joys and sorrows. Together we mulled over several large urban hospitals offering intensive stroke rehabilitation programs.

"I could contact a friend at Hopkins," she offered somberly.

"But, at seventy-four," I thought out loud, "with his heart trouble and diabetes, could he even handle the upheaval of the trip, and cope with living in a hotel, let alone a strange city, all the new faces—*he's so confused!*—and completely unfamiliar doctors and therapists? Could his heart take the upheaval?"

"I don't know," she said truthfully. "And, you know, he may have to wait a week or two for an opening . . . then we can arrange to have him transferred. . . . Or he could stay here, and maybe go into the Rehab Unit downstairs—maybe even tomorrow, if they have a free bed."

"There's a rehab unit downstairs?"

That was a land I didn't know about and had never visited. In my imagination, it existed as the Land That Time Forgot, a preserve of dinosaur-like patients lumbering over linoleum floors. *Or will it be brisker and brighter than that,* I hoped, *more of a workshop for broken racing yachts?*

Over the years, while he coped with diabetes and a pacemaker, the hospital had already become a too-frequent port for Paul. Now it would be a salvage yard, for how long I didn't know—surely a few weeks. But that made the most sense, at least for now. I returned to Paul's room.

"MEM, MEM, MEM, MEM?!" he demanded hoarsely, which I took to mean, *Where did you go! Don't leave me!*

"I was nearby, at the nurses' station, talking with Dr. Ann." Bedbound as he was, I might just as well have been in China.

In a fog, without sleep, I tried to explain to Paul what was happening and discuss where he would be going—instead of home. He understood just a fraction. "Mem," he uttered first pleadingly, then angrily, over and over.

CHAPTER 4

A S I WOKE, THE SUNLIGHT, FILTERING IN THROUGH THE bedroom window, shimmered across the floral quilt and hit my eyes. I raised myself languidly onto my elbows. Distant gagging and ripping sounds trickled through the windows. But that was only the raving of crows and the downshift arpeggios of trucks, scattered voices of summer. I dropped back onto the bed with a groan. I used to feel a sensuous joy in waking up, sometimes slithering around in bed for a few moments, just taking pleasure in having limbs that glide in different directions, and enjoying the feel of the soft warm sheet under my shoulders, before padding across the ridged carpet in bare feet to a skylit bathroom, where I was greeted by teal and lavender tiles and a wallpaper motif of peacocks and trees of life.

Now I woke in a state of anxious hurry, rushing to wash and dress, while worrying about how Paul might have passed the night and what momentum, if any, his brain might have gained. The idea of breakfast simply didn't occur. Driving to the hospital with a dry metallic taste in my mouth, I felt as if the minerals were leaching out of my bones. I wanted somehow, miraculously, to right the wrongs in Paul's head. But, at the same time, I didn't want ever to arrive and face the helplessness and emotional turmoil that awaited me. Between those two fates, the miles evaporated and I found myself turning into a woodsy parking lot, forgetting to lock my car door, lumbering into the building without a sense of walking.

At first it was easy to get lost in the hospital's maze of shiny hallways linking whole neighborhoods of rooms and winding past departments called Emergency, Imaging, Intensive Care, that appeared out of the fluorescent dusk like brightly lit upstate towns. Hadn't I just passed the cafeteria and kitchen? Where was the Rehab Unit? I pressed on, entering hallways that narrowed and widened and narrowed again, branching like a well-lit circulatory system.

Quietly, sometimes unawares, I found myself slipping into my naturalist's way of knowing, coping by detaching myself enough to appreciate the ecology of the medical world I was traveling through, rather than being totally overwhelmed by it and drowned. No, this other sense of *lost* was what I needed. How coolly the brain obliges, and isolates, compartmentalizes, shifting its gaze from one hub of action to another, composing the tone poem of a different mood, when need be, or running a bold new face up the flagpole.

Disassociating, mindfulness, transcendence—whatever the label—it's a sort of loophole in our contract with reality, a form of self-rescue. Linked neurons, firing like sparklers, make the sudden change feel seamless, and seemless. One network dims as another wakes to high noon. Both stay wired and ready to serve, like unheated spare rooms in a large old Victorian mansion. Why expose them all to scrutiny? Be rational about religion? Too scary; hide religion from critical thought. Apply human codes of ethics to how we treat animals? A slippery slope; don't stroll there. Agonize nonstop about Paul's stroke? It would fry the wiring; transcend if possible. Lose yourself in nature's dens and crevasses, and turn the key on heartache. When you can't, toss drop cloths over everything, lower the heat to save energy, and allow a sedated overseer to take charge. Drift on autopilot. Just go through the motions.

As I continued down unfamiliar corridors, white-robed people, green people in green mushroom-shaped hats, and people pushing patients on beds all passed in slow motion. But in the firmament of fluorescent lights overhead, excited atoms were shooting electrons into higher orbits far from their home, where they paused for a tiny fraction of a second too quick to imagine, almost immediately tugged back down again. Falling toward their hub, the electrons released extra energy as photons of light. Walking down an endless hallway, I smiled glumly, feeling far from my own center.

Everything about this Oz took getting used to: the uniforms, dialect, climate, food, geography, machinery, protocols, hierarchies, and low ambient sounds of whirring, squealing, gnashing, and incessant beeping. Stricken families were duty-bound to learn enough of its culture to speak with the natives and help a loved one survive. So it felt right that I needed to cross a bridge en route to the hospital, and another bridge walking from the parking lot to a set of space-age doors that saw me coming and sprang open, let me pause a moment inside a toasty vestibule, before the inner doors glided open, ushering me into a world apart, one with chilly corridors and overexcited atoms.

A FEW DAYS post-stroke, Paul now seemed to recognize a spattering of words, yet he was still woefully confused. I kept waiting for him to rebound, but the signs were ominous as I played them over in my mind. He couldn't read the newspaper or tell time by the large clock on the wall. He couldn't drink without choking. He couldn't do basic addition. When he tried to stand, he surprised himself by how wobbly he was. He needed to be retaught how to sit in a chair, use the toilet, work the taps in the bathroom, shave, walk without weaving or falling. The fourth and fifth fingers on his right hand had curled into a claw. But most of all, there was the aphasia. Although he was able to make some of his feelings known through facial expressions and gestures, he was frustrated and furious that no one could understand his gibberish when it clearly made sense to *him*. He didn't know his own name or mine, and kept gesturing wildly that he wanted to go home.

While I watched, Kelly, a petite and cheerful blond speech therapist, stood beside his bed and calmly tested his mouth and throat
muscles, showing him by example how she wanted him to move
his jaw, tongue, lips. The right side of his face still drooped, but he
could stick out his tongue and push it around his mouth like a wayward eel. If she scrunched up his lips he held a pucker, but he
couldn't pucker his lips by himself.

On her chart, Kelly noted that Paul answered simple yes/no
questions—"Are you in bed? Is this a hospital?"—by nodding,
with 80 percent accuracy. But his responses were accurate less than
25 percent of the time when she asked him to do simple things.
When he was shown two objects and asked to point to one of
them, he always pointed to the object on his left. If she asked him
to say "Aah," he followed the command only 30 percent of the
time. She jotted down:

> Unable to repeat single syllable words.
> Did not name common objects.
> No functional verbal communication.
> When asked to sing/count along with me, opened mouth very
> wide, intermittent voicing, but no articulation despite some
> movement of the lips.

His inability to respond seemed unreal, and though I wanted to
cry, I forced myself to watch. She handed him an 8-by-10-inch
communication board, covered with drawings of common items
or actions, and asked him to point to the objects she named—a key,
a clock, a child—but he was unable to. She showed him an alphabet board and asked him to spell his name. Mutely observing his
struggle, I felt my hope dissolving, as if touched by acid. His Oxford
First and fifty-one published books meant nothing now. He
couldn't spell his own name. When she wrote down *Raise your
hand*, he opened his mouth wide and made a strange low murmuring as if trying to read out loud. Most poignant of all, when she
handed him a pen, the tool he'd wielded with mastery throughout

his career, one I'd associated with him the way one links seahorses with ocean, he tried to hold it in his weak right hand and it slipped from his grip. Kelly suggested his left hand, but he didn't try. She offered him a thick crayon and blank sheet of paper.

"Can you *write* your name?"

With difficulty, starting and stopping several times, Paul scrawled *P-O-O-P.*

Somehow managing to look both nonplussed and mystified, Kelly asked: "Do you need to use the toilet?"

He tilted his head blankly, the way animals sometimes do when they're puzzled. So I pointed to the bathroom and asked slowly, "Toilet?"

Surprised, he shook his head no.

Her evaluation read:

Oral apraxia. Severe apraxia of speech.
Expressive and receptive aphasia.
Dysphagia with risk of aspiration.

Translated, it meant: my Paul couldn't coordinate the movements of his jaw, tongue, and lips (*apraxia*). He had the worst degree of trouble saying what he wanted to, or understanding what people said to him (*expressive and receptive aphasia*). And a swallowing problem put him at risk of aspiration (*dysphagia*). Soon after his stroke, an X-ray video evaluation of Paul swallowing barium-coated fruit, crackers, and apple sauce had shown that he was silently inhaling particles into his lungs. When asked to cough, he couldn't flex his throat muscles enough to cough the particles out. *Silently* aspirating. Sowing the seeds of possibly deadly pneumonia without any feeling that food had gone down the wrong pipe.

Kelly explained he could rule the liquid only when it was in his mouth. After that pure reflex is supposed to take over. When we swallow normally, a valve opens, allowing food to enter the esophagus, while closing the windpipe to prevent food from blocking the airway. This reflexive combo happens in less than half a second. But a stroke, especially one that produces slurred speech, can weaken the throat's muscles. Thicker fluids or solid food flow lava-slowly and are easier to guide with drab muscles and dulled reflexes, lessening the chance of dripping fluid into the wrong tube. The hospital's levels of thickened liquids were termed: *nectar, honey, pudding.*

"Pudding-thick only," Kelly decreed. For a while at least, all liquids would be mixed with a powder called Thick-It, that smelled like a dry cast-off chrysalis and tasted gray, added until a spoon could stand up in the liquid. For Paul, clear water only if thickened to sludge. No milk, his favorite drink. No refreshment from a sparkling fizzy sip of Dr. Brown's Diet Cream Soda. Nothing thin enough to quench a thirst.

You'd think *choking* would have stood out as the scariest assessment, but what shattered me was the note: "No functional verbal communication." The stroke had done far more than damage his ability to read, write, or talk—his brain no longer wanted to process language at all. Yet I hoped to take him home sometime soon.

What on earth will going home be like? The thought pinwheeled through my head. *Sad ghosts? A shrivel of silence in his study? Not even the clacking of typewriter keys? Or will I hear a plaintive stream of "mem, mem, mem"? How will I be able to look after him at home?* I'd grown used to our household of two adults. What would life be like having him at home and handicapped, in need of supervision, unable to communicate his desires in words, and full of tantrums as a result?

Kelly and I left Paul to rest and we sat on chairs in the hallway to confer. She recommended further swallowing studies to monitor for signs of improvement, and also speech therapy five days a week.

"In terms of language," I asked tentatively, "what do you think?"

She paused a moment to frame her thoughts, as fluorescent light showered down on us like silently accumulating snowfall.

"Long-term, I hope he'll be able to communicate his basic wants and needs," she said slowly, allowing time for the words to sink in, "verbally or in gestures or maybe using a communication board, with about 80 percent accuracy."

Basic wants and needs, I heard her say. *Basic wants and needs.* The phrase spun in my mind. As if that could ever be enough for normal people, let alone word-besotted creatures like us. Life lives in nuances and innuendos. How could Paul's immense cosmos of words shrink to the size of a communication board overnight? How could *ours*?

"Short-term," she continued with maddening practicality, "we'll be striving for about 50 percent accuracy in naming common objects. I'd like him to be able to choose between two items, when you name them, about 80 percent of the time, and follow simple commands with 80 percent accuracy."

Would you like the "pants" or the "shorts," the "pillow" or the "blanket"? That would be life from now on? My thoughts spiraled, and I felt not just psychic pain, but a specific ache I could locate in several muscles between my ribs. *Global* aphasia. Woundingly right. Our couple, *DianeandPaul*, had been a ghostly continent of two countries. What would become of it? Would a boundary of silence fall between us? No more Paul touching voices by telephone many times a day when I traveled? No more Paul calling to me across the hallway, "Poet, what's a word for . . . ?" No more Paul tucking me in at night and leaving refrigerator notes in the morning? No more confiding, whispering intimacies, playing with words, *sharing* the world? *It's beastly*, I thought, *completely unthinkable.* And if he couldn't read or work, what would he do all day? Probably want me to keep him company—and that was understandable—though devastating to my work, my freedom. I would need to be able to write for my own joy and sanity, but also now to support the household and help pay for Paul's care. Still, I felt deeply ashamed to be indulging in such self-centered worries.

When Kelly left, I went to a windowed alcove just beyond the Rehab Unit doors and wept. Out of shame that I couldn't fix things, and out of grief. I'd never before had to mourn for someone who was still alive. I mourned for Paul, and I also mourned for myself, and for the loss of the word-drenched companionship we'd created, due to a tiny land mine traveling through his blood vessels. Beneath our civilized hair and hide, and beneath awareness even, we easily destroy ourselves. To be so godlike, and yet so fragile. But it didn't help to lump him with the rest of humanity. The loss was too intimate. It had settled in like a lonely lodger with a scrapbook of memories.

For example, this was Sunday, a day when, before the stroke, Paul usually viewed one, sometimes two, English premier-league soccer matches on television. I remembered a conversation we'd had ages before, when I was hanging out at Giants Stadium, home of the New York Cosmos soccer team, which had collected a peerless array of international players. I'd agreed to write several articles, and was deeply embedded in the soccer world, absorbing atmosphere for a novel. In the press box during halftime, I'd phoned Paul and found him in a sort of halftime, too, in his office between seminars, eating a can of smoked kippers.

"What's up?"

"Oh, nothing much," he'd answered without missing a beat. "The usual struggle for survival with its attendant erosion of moral standards and so on." A mouthful of fish and hungry chewing. "What's new with you, doll?"

"I'm going to Bakewell to interview the tarts," I'd teased. "Actually, I thought I'd go to the Cosmos' training camp in the Bahamas and interview Beckenbauer."

Franz Beckenbauer, the smart, elegantly sexy player who somehow managed to combine grace, precision, and power. Whenever I watched him gather the urgent rhythms of a game, a mental depth charge went off inside me.

At this, Paul had laughed so loud that I worried he'd drop the phone.

"Strictly business," I'd insisted. "I want to ask him about the ceremonial violence of the game. I know he's a big opera fan—maybe the two connect for him. You know, what he hears and sees while he's playing. Stuff like that."

"It's bad enough you want me to believe you're being honest with me," Paul had said with an edgy twinkle in his voice, "I'm also supposed not to notice when you're not telling me the truth."

"If you *always* tell the truth, you never get into trouble," I'd replied with as much innocence as I could muster.

"Or if you always lie," he'd countered.

"Okay, so I'll be having some fun, too. What can I tell you, I'm in love."

"With him?"

"With the game, silly."

"Which game?"

"Soccer!"

"What does soccer have to do with the *game*?"

"Where did I take the off-ramp from this conversation? Which game are you talking about?"

"Which game are *you* talking about?"

"Ahh," I'd said slowly, "I see. Well, I'm not sure."

"Don't let me know when you find out; I love you as unfathomable as you are." The sound of ice tinkling in a glass, as he drank the evening's first scotch.

"Not even a telegram from the Bahamas?"

"What could it say in under fifteen words?"

". . . How about *habeas porpoise*?"

What a crazy season that had been, splitting my focus between teaching rarefied graduate poets and following the exploits of men whose genius was physical. I never did go to training camp in the Bahamas, never did finish the soccer novel. But Paul shared my enthusiasm for soccer, and we often watched games together on television, sometimes spreading a blanket on the floor and eating a store-bought rotisserie chicken with yellow mustard and canned asparagus, our "soccer picnic."

With a tender smile, I eased the memory from the heavy slate of my mind.

In the hallway, a table passed on which metal instruments inside a gleaming bowl rattled with a sound like machine-gun fire. Somehow its bleakness shook me out of my mournful trance. At least I could still give comfort and affection, that part remained. But was there any hope he might recover?

I knew from my studies that what we used to think about the brain—that it's immutable and we're born with all the brain cells we'll ever have—was wrong. Brains are surprisingly resourceful, they can adapt and grow, forge new neural pathways, redirect signals, and sometimes even mint a handful of fresh neurons. Unless damaged beyond growth or repair. Could anything be done? Clots had stopped oxygen from reaching the deep, central language areas of Paul's brain—cells had suffocated and died. "Time is brain," the medical adage goes. During every minute without oxygen, a plot of brain loses 1.9 million neurons, 14 billion synapses, 7.5 miles of protective fibers. After only twelve minutes without oxygen, a pea-sized chapter of brain dies. His body was still alive, but his mind was a specter of itself. Yet these were early days, his brain was still swollen and inflamed from the stroke. As the neurons cooled, survivors might stir among the wreckage.

To keep my spirits up, I often reminded myself of the brain's plasticity, how it can modify itself, effloresce, revise its habits, unearth new skills. Throughout our lives, whenever we learn something, the brain creates connections or revives old pathways, neurons grow new twigs along their branches and some of the branches themselves become stronger. A brain *can* rewire itself. We do it all the time when we become doctors, master the bicycle, or learn to use an iPod. Expert violinists develop more motor cortex for the busy left hand than for the right. London taxi drivers increase the size of their hippocampus from memorizing thousands of routes around the city. But how often does a violinist have to perform a tricky movement's many parts before really nailing it? Probably hundreds of thousands of times. After all, they practice for several hours every day for years. Learning how to ride a bike or drive a car or even pilot a space shuttle doesn't require as much rehearsal.

Learning most things by rote, the brain keeps digging at something until it creates a channel along which messages can flow. How spiritless and stale that can be, how wearisome and boring. Or how seductively exciting, if it's something you love. A born acrobat, the brain schools itself, becomes its own taskmaster. That takes focus, industry, and muscle. Not everyone can be bothered. Others haven't the zest to try. A college athlete, Paul grasped the piety of training day in and out. And as someone who halfheartedly practiced violin when I was a girl (and never got past the stage of sounding like I was torturing small creatures), I knew the diligent rigor every victory would take. As if it were an ancient Greek god, I begged the spirit of Plasticity, the brain's knack of changing as it learns, to rewire itself based on all of Paul's efforts. Press a hand into clay and the clay changes to record the shape of the hand. Photograph a hand and the film changes to retain the image of the hand. From daily pressure and exposure, Paul's brain might change itself, probably by reassigning some lost language skills to surviving neurons. How long would that continue, I wondered, and, more importantly, how much ground could he regain?

For now, the only remnant of language he had was the one solitary syllable: "Mem, mem, mem." He groaned it, he whispered it, he uttered it civilly as a greeting, he barked it in anger, he solicited help with it, and finally in frustration, when none of that worked, he sat upright in bed and spat it out as a curse.

CHAPTER 5

RAIN STREAKED THROUGH THE AIR. CAR WINDSHIELD wipers ticked like out-of-sync metronomes. In the hospital parking lot, blue-faced people, squinting with eyes thin as razor blades, ran toward the building. Others death-gripped umbrellas, and some jogged with a newspaper or magazine held flat overhead, as if waiting for an updraft. I felt the peal of water on my hair, trickling to my scalp, then spilling over my forehead, through my lashes, around the ridge of my nose, in rivulets from my chin. In the front vestibule, I shook the water off and headed for Paul's room.

He was standing at the window.

"Nice day for ducks," I said gently.

Paul stared into the rain without answering, his face bold, bluff, and nearly perpendicular, like some coastlines. He was trying to remember something that had almost faded. With great effort, he could remember a little of how he used to see and feel the world, but not easily. He'd lost track of his body's edges, and yet his life felt completely internal. A loud grating background noise drowned out everything; he was even aware of it while he slept. Raindrops sounded like they were being fired by nail guns.

This sensory warping was not unusual. Even a migraine is

enough to overstimulate the brain, causing changes in nerve firings, and in the ebb and flow of blood vessels. As a lifelong migraine sufferer, Paul knew that caterwauling, when the neurons don't respond right to anything. I knew it, too. Artists often are migraineurs, who report greater light, sound, smell, touch, taste sensitivity. His migraines had been worse and more frequent than mine; but we'd both experienced them with turrets of flashing light. A stroke whips up nerve and blood flow changes on a tempestuous scale. I didn't envy him the sensory drubbing.

"Hey there," I tried once more, this time taking him by the arm. He let me guide him back unsteadily to bed, tuck him in, and talk idly, just for the sake of talking, hoping my voice might soothe us both. Then silence thickened, until the air felt caked with it, as we sat absorbing the sights and sounds of our strange new habitat.

The Rehab Unit's rhythms and the hospital's had begun to envelop me. For three weeks, during Paul's kidney infection, I'd spent a lot of time at the hospital, but it was really only in this fourth week, when I wasn't so much visiting the hospital as living in it, that I became aware of its subtle effects on a patient's (and visitor's) psyche and nervous system. Enter most public buildings and it's bound to feel unnatural. Nature loves a curve or a spiral. We humans, on the other hand, seem to worship sharp edges. We build our sermons in steel and glass. Sunlight slanting through the hospital windows bounced off the white tiles and miles of linoleum floor. Long stray shafts of light struck the conjoined cubes, mesas, and countertops coated in fake veneer. Sometimes a spike of sun flashed off stainless steel pan, instruments, wheeled table, or tall IV pole sprouting a medusa of tubes.

Outside, the sun's light fell into shadows as flighty blues that deepened or flickered with the changing hour. Inside the hospital, cast mainly by overhead bulbs, flat shadows stayed put, signaling the brain that the sun was always at noon. And only one season existed: an austere, bedridden, air-conditioned winter.

Although the summer sun was a mirrored disco ball, whose heat was quickly ripening the local grapes, we couldn't feel a lick of it because the windows didn't open, despite the folk wisdom of fresh air being good for the sick. A quarter of an inch of glass was all it took to separate a patient from nature, just when he felt derelict and adrift anyway, and scared out of his senses. Small wonder that in city hospitals patients with a view of trees heal faster than those forced to stare at buildings.

Nothing starches the mind quite like the hospital's array of anti-septic smells and colors. The visually stark, sharp, false, and sanitary greeted us everywhere. Most of the interior landscape was frosty white: sheets, pillows, curtains, coats, shoes, porcelain sinks, toilets, and a "whiteboard" on the wall where nurses sign their names when shifts change. I don't know why we classify white as a clean color, healthy, hygienic, wholesome, and even innocent, epitomized by a bride's white dress. To the people of China, Japan, Vietnam, and Korea, white is the color of mourning and death. But for us it communicates all that is sterile. Stiff white blankets, liners, pads, pillows, and linens cocooned Paul's hospital bed. I sometimes saw the draped sheets as white flags of surrender. But I didn't have Paul's happy memories of cricket "whites." Since cricket was a summer game, players wore white to stay cool in the afternoon sun. Long ago, his mother had knitted him a white cricket sweater, laddered with white cables, to protect her boy from the chill of early morning or evening play.

We existed among a host of pervasive *clean* smells: stale disinfec-tant, and heated bleach from the small armada of washing machines and dryers in the basement. Sometimes these were joined by the sweetness of infection; the cheesy smell of men's sweat, the oniony smell of women's; or sickbed urine that smelled of must, maple syrup, or rancid bacon. None of these oddities really mattered in the grand scheme of health vs. disease, but they jangled the senses, they didn't inspire calm.

Strangers in a strange land, we slumbered among unfamiliar constellations. At night, too jittery to sleep but too tired to drive home, I sometimes roamed the empty hallways. Lightning-bug lights flashed from nearly invisible machines, green auroras swirled in the imaging rooms, dull light poured from the sconces of office windows, and in the larger wards, the nursing stations flickered with the St. Elmo's fire of computer screens, on which I glimpsed parts of bodies parading: a CT scan of the abdomen, an MRI of the brain. I marveled at how computers can be trained to display the body three-dimensionally.

Then, returning to Paul's room, I'd startle at every noise while I half slept in a reclining chair by his side, on the alert in case he needed help, in a room never quite dark enough to resemble night, with a gust of light from the hallway shining in like a low unmoving moon. Yellow, white, and red eyes blinked among the hanging vines of wires and tubes.

Phantom hospital staff entered the room throughout the night, in what sometimes looked like an alien abduction scene—Paul in bed, being probed by shadowy creatures inordinately interested in body fluids. I chuckled with a wave of black humor. He'd been fascinated by the possibility of extraterrestrial visitors ever since the summer day years ago when he swore he saw a cigar-shaped UFO hovering above him in the swimming pool, hugely present 1,000 feet above. He'd insisted that, with strips of windows visible, it looked nothing like a mirage or apparition, but floated tangible and still for several minutes, then streaked away at an unearthly speed. When he told me later about the sighting, I assumed it was military, experimental. Not he. And now here he was, brain-rattled, and peered at by creatures dressed all in green or white, some wearing oddly shaped hats or coats, inspected in darkness by alien hands.

Each morning, Paul woke up confused, his sense of time and place utterly muddled. Strangers spiraled around him like flies pestering a wound, the standard hospital routine of people barging into a patient's room at odd hours to check vital signs and inject or remove fluids. They came from everywhere, unannounced, this remedy of aides and nurses, sometimes with a nursing student in tow. As shifts changed, each new nurse breezed in with stethoscope and blood pressure cuff to do a physical exam, take tempera-

ture, listen to lungs and heart, attach a snakehead-shaped clamp to
one finger to test oxygen level, and prick another finger to test
blood sugar. Later to reappear with a syringe to give a jab of insulin. Doctors swept in for consultation, and I was afraid to leave the
room for fear of missing them. At least once, a social worker glided
in with notebook and questions: "How would you describe your
support group?" "How many stairs do you need to climb to get
into your house?" "Do you have a house with one or multiple
floors?"

At times they seemed to arrive like a long line of leaf-cutter ants,
carrying not clipboards but kite-like bits of leaves to use as compost in their fungus gardens. A cacophony of caregivers. Speech
therapists. Physical therapists. A dietary specialist brought menus to
be filled out, even if the patient couldn't speak, write, or read.
Food service delivered plastic trays, returning later to collect them.
A brawny man or woman pushing a wheelchair, to escort Paul to
the imaging department for an X-ray, CAT scan, or echocardio-
gram. A technician with an ultrasound machine and cold jelly to
smear on his chest, before peering at his heart through a cloudy
window of flesh. People scrupulously measured everything entering or leaving his body, all food and liquids, urine and bowel
movements.

I could tell the randomly arriving citizenry annoyed Paul. He
was always a bit of a hermit, who found dinner parties particularly
unnerving. "You never know whom you'll get trapped next to!"
he'd protest. Paul enjoyed his students, and whenever he did socialize, he spoke amiably and well with people. He always looked forward to chatting with the handyman, a salty ex-sailor who'd served
in Korea and fathered eight children. Some dinner parties he welcomed, like Carl Sagan's fiftieth birthday party, where we sat across
the table from Hans Bethe (pronounced BAY-ta), the physicist
who had figured out how the sun shines. Paul delighted in the
revelations of science, but novelists have their own brand of physics, in which they re-create the process of life through a whole
register of intricate, almost-touchable images and events.

"What are you writing?" Bethe had asked him.

"A novel. At the moment, the main character is constructing a Milky Way in his basement."

Much to Paul's amusement, Bethe had mischievously replied, "A working model?"

I still relish the day, at the local airport years later, when Paul and I happened to be in line behind nonagenarian Bethe at the ticket counter, and overheard the clerk say to him, slowly and in a louder voice than needed, as if he were carrying an invisible ear trumpet and must, at his age, be lost in senility:

"Now, Mr. *Beth-ee*, you'll be arriving at Gate 21 in Pittsburgh and going to Gate number 27. That's *six* gates away."

A small bemused smile had flitted across Bethe's creased and age-freckled face. "Oh, I think I can do the math," he'd said.

Such events seemed eons in the past. Post-stroke, Paul didn't want to see anyone but me. Being swarmed over in the hospital was a recipe for exhaustion in a person who was feeling well, let alone someone speechless, anxious, and baffled. And there was no relief outside his room, either in the hallways or in group therapy, where, against his will, he was asked to mix with other rehab patients, whose afflictions reminded him of his own.

Just as big cities can deplete you with their noise and crowds and sheer sensory overload, a hospital can exhaust you, as its changing faces and personalities blur and strangers wake you repeatedly. Like all post-stroke patients, Paul really needed rest to recover from the massive injury to his brain. But he also needed to start flexing his mind as soon as possible. So, should he rest his brain or exercise it after the stroke? Both, I figured.

It's like a knee replacement patient being encouraged to climb out of bed and churn his leg around the day after surgery. Cycling the post-op knee hurts and is fatiguing, as is pushing an inflamed brain. Even a healthy brain is constantly balancing between arousal and rest. If life is too stimulating, it seeks relaxation, if it's too boring it craves stimuli (skating on a blade-edge between too much excitement and too little). A perfect balance is possible to imagine, but impossible to reach, so one is always trembling along an arc from too excited to too bored and back again. Everything we love most—be it sweetheart or flower—looks majestic because it seems to be trembling out of balance.

While Paul napped, I wandered through the Rehab Unit, which lay on the second floor in the east wing of the hospital. Beyond a head nurse's office and supply room, an open bay gave nurses and doctors a good overview of the floor and a convenient depot to write orders, gather medications, eye monitors, and await the urgent pinging of bells. All of the patients' rooms were arranged side by side across a narrow corridor. Walking past open doors, I glimpsed snapshots of humanity *in extremis*, a surprising range of young and old men and women from many walks of life, all assigned to Rehab's ill-fated club. During Paul's physical therapy or in the halls, I sometimes fraternized with fellow residents and their families, learning a little of their stories.

In one room with the door propped open, the sun cast dark shadows against the pale walls, and for a moment a crowd seemed to be excavating something. As the light shifted, I recognized two nurses helping an obese woman back into bed, struggling to lift her huge swollen leg, where at least 100 pounds of fluid pooled. Her lymph system had gone awry, creating floods and blockages, until it took a draft of people to move her. She once told me she was married but her husband rarely visited, and that she preferred life in the unit, where the nurses looked after her, even filing her nails and washing her hair.

Down the hall, a young woman, who had suffered a stroke, dragged her left leg and arm, holding the wall while shuffling with the aid of a physical therapist, who was helping her relearn how to walk. She looked up at me with sunken eyes, chin slanted to one side, her face engraved with sorrow. She spoke rarely, in a thin voice that lisped at a whisper. She reminded me of my next-door neighbor many years ago, a healthy realtor in her thirties, who had suffered a stroke that changed her life forever. Her husband had had a swimming pool installed for her to do therapy in, thus beginning the fashion of pools in the neighborhood. An old backyard pool came with my own small house, and Paul adored swimming, but I never dreamed he would be using it for physical therapy one day as well.

Another resident of Rehab was a young African-American man with shoulder-length dreadlocks. Because of chronic infection exacerbated by his diabetes, one leg had been amputated below the knee. In a flat voice, he told me how nurses cleaned the sutures (staples) with soap and water, then applied the acrid, red-ochre antiseptic, Betadine, which smelled like his mother's nail-polish remover, and pulled a bandage tightly around the stump, to shrink and mold it for an eventual prosthesis. Most of the time he sat listlessly in a chair, and I heard nurses chiding him for neglecting an ulcer on his remaining foot. I never saw anyone visit him, not family or friends.

Two doors down lived a slender middle-aged woman, who had had a stroke resulting in a devastatingly enfeebled left arm and leg, but her mind seemed untouched, and while I pitied her fate, I admired her resolve. For although her lax limbs made it arduous, she was learning to use a walker without falling, and I sometimes saw her in physical therapy, patiently aided by a therapist, lifting the aluminum frame and inching it forward, step-sliding into the cage with both feet, then inching forward again, all with a deliberate, unhurried slowness, her height rising and falling at each effort. A professor at one of the local colleges, she was often visited by young women, not a family in the traditional sense but a loyal network of friends and students. She told me she spritzed her pillow several times a day with clary sage, to help her relax and keep up her spirits. Passing her room, I'd catch the piquant scent of desert creosote bushes wafting gently through her open door.

A college hockey player occupied another room. His bandaged face fixed in a slight curl, he always looked sickened by a bad smell. His was a particularly sad case, but a terribly common story. One night, after he and some frat mates had been drinking, he had crashed his car on the long, unevenly lit highway edging town. His

head stove into the windshield, and soon afterward he arrived at
the hospital with multiple injuries and disabilities, including loss of
high-level brain function. All the so-called *executive functions* were
permanently impaired, and executives are a busy tribe—oversee-
ing the workers and machinery, setting goals, brokering deals,
assigning duties, doling out resources, liaising with others. Never
again would he find it easy to learn or remember. His attentive
parents arrived every day, and he seemed elated to see them, but
the tragedy on their faces spiraled right into me. *Is this the desert of
hope I have in store for me? Paul no longer able to learn and grow? What
if he can't even remember what I say from day to day, or what he's already
said? What a wasteland that would be.* Silently saying the word *wasteland*, my memory bounced into action and tagged T. S. Eliot's *The
Waste Land*, a poem of disillusionment which I first read in college
when I was this boy's age. He probably did, too. But what would
he remember of anything he'd learned? Or hoped to learn? Which
is crueler, an old man's lost memories of a life lived, or a young
man's lost memories of the life he meant to live?

Another of Paul's companions was a slim woman in her sixties,
newly retired, admitted for routine surgery, after which a large clot
broke loose, sparking a massive stroke. She was the unlikely statis-
tic, the 1 in about 10,000 who had suffered stroke as a complication
of a simple procedure. Unable to walk, she was confined to a
wheelchair, body atrophying but mind and speech intact. She told
me she had been planning a tour to the national parks with her
husband, whom I saw visiting her every day, always wearing a
checked long-sleeved shirt and looking perpetually adrift. I imagined the psychic whiplash they felt from this sudden change in life's
trajectory. She'd gone from self-reliance to hospital idleness; and he
found himself looking after a completely dependent wife. Was *this*
what awaited me?

The last complement to the ward was a deeply tanned man in his
mid-seventies, who had been admitted to the hospital with a kidney stone obstructing the right ureter and a somewhat routine uri-
nary tract infection, but suffered a stroke with aphasia while at the

hospital. A pacemaker aided his irregular heart. His wife, a woman in her mid-fifties with a pile of black hair, usually arrived wearing T-shirt dresses, leggings, and tennis shoes, stayed with him all day, and sometimes slept in an armchair at his bedside. Paul was this last among a propinquity of souls, and I the wife who always looked so distraught and exhausted.

WHEN I ARRIVED one morning, Paul sat scowling and grumbled grouchily: "Mem, mem, mem!!" He held up five fingers twice, as if he were pushing a palm-sized button, and gestured toward the nurses' station.

"Lots of nurses have been in . . . and they're not being nice to you?"

He nodded curtly with a stormy black look.

Swinging into gear, I started going down a mental checklist of things they could have forgotten:

"Are they forgetting your medication?"

No response.

He dropped back into his bed, his eyes full of contempt.

"Are they forgetting your meals?"

No response. I rested my hand on his arm only to have him brush it away.

"Are they not helping you to the bathroom?" I tried, bending to keep eye contact as he turned away from me yet again, revealing the back of his head—unwashed, matted fleece. *Your hair is like a flock of goats*, I thought.

Finally, it dawned on me to ask: "Are they treating you like you're a child?"

He knotted his face angrily and blurted out a long smudge of syllables "Rhey wickyderm stumpf yagtarggritty andortmfgv-pfl!!!!!" and I sensed he was saying something like, *I'm a grown man—I know how to do this stuff! And they're treating me like I don't know how to stand up!*

He pointed to the whiteboard which showed his schedule for the day—a busy one full of speech and physical therapy—and made one of those universal gestures that means, *Screw them all! I'm not going to do it, forget about it, it's out of the question, no one is going to tell me what to do!* That much I got. His anger burned like lava, and filled the room with a dark presence that made me feel physically smaller. Still, I half convinced myself it was good that he was trying to talk at all, so I didn't discourage him. But interpreting was grueling, and he grew madder and madder at me for not understanding, until the room finally became too hot and I started to hyperventilate.

"I've got to go," I sighed, exhausted.

Perfectly legible, his face yelled: *Why?!*

Several days later, as his besieged brain began to quiet down, Paul said his first intelligible words, uttered in frustration while yet again struggling to make himself understood. He wanted me to do something, something urgently important, something involving small square things (which he outlined in space), something located at home.

"Stir the nevis! Stir the nevis! Mem, mem, mem!" he kept insisting. "You gad clottal to stir the nevis!!!" He chopped the air with both hands, as if he were a martial artist breaking wooden boards.

The only *nevis* I knew of was an island in the West Indies.

"It's related to an island, to the West Indies? It's shaped like the island?" Thumbs touching, then fingertips, I made an outline of the lush, round, rain-forested island.

Words seemed to be tweaking the edges of his mind. "No!" he finally roared in frustration. "It's simple!!!" He fell back in disappointment, his face askew from the effort of producing that small collection of sounds.

He's speaking! I realized in shock. *Thank heavens! He just made sense! But what on earth does he mean?* Collecting my wits about me, I said as calmly as I could: "I'm sorry, but I don't know what you're saying. I *am* trying to understand. I know this is hard but it's *not* easy for me either. Can we please take a rest and try again later?"

An hour later, he insisted once more that I do something with or about or on the island of Nevis. Unless the word was *nevus,* but why would Paul be struggling so hard to communicate something about a mole? As an Interplast volunteer, I'd watched doctors remove a large hairy nevus from the cheek of a boy in Honduras, in an old operating room with an opaque wall of glass bricks. When electricity failed one evening, a doctor had parked his car beside the wall and turned on the headlamps, so that surgeons could finish their operations.

"You don't mean a *nevus*, like a mole?"

"No!" he moaned.

It took several days, and Paul flicking the light switch on and off repeatedly, while pointing at me with his free hand, to figure out that what he wanted me to do was pay the electric bill.

A few other words returned to Paul helter-skelter, including one usually slurred as a plea and often as a demand: "Home!" For Paul, *true home* (like true north) existed as his childhood village, where almost everything was taller than he was, and where he could be shielded by his mother Mildred's benevolent arms. Home was where he directed miniature armies, and where he hid from terrifying dangers he couldn't picture or name. I understood his fervor. For me, home was a small suburb of Chicago, in a house with carpeted stairs I bumped down on my bum; pet turtles; and a dancing-partner doll, with yellow pigtails and elastic feet, who stood as tall as I did and clung as we waltzed around the kitchen.

"I'm very sorry, honey, but you just can't go home yet. You've had a bad stroke," I slowly reminded him yet again, allowing time for him to absorb each word. "Do you think you're going to recover and get your speech back on your own?"

He seemed to understand—or he just knew that I was asking a yes/no question—and he nodded a vehement *yes.*

"I'm so sorry, but it's not going to happen like that. You'll improve, I know you will, but even at home you will need help. And a speech therapist."

Was it true? Did he understand anything I was saying? Could he talk to himself about it—did he still have an inner dialogue? I wasn't sure.

The brain usually toils seamlessly, above and below the pond scum of awareness, integrating millions of messages, calculations, appraisals, and updates. To its named owner, it speaks in streams of consciousness, image and back talk, a conversation that runs from birth to death, a voice that wells within us, as if a tailor-made talk show host took the stage each day and spoke only to us. That inner voice feels like an *I*, but also like an *other*, an observer. When they think no one is listening, people often narrate their doings in the third person, usually in the idiom of a sportscaster or TV interviewer. While *The Tonight Show Starring Johnny Carson* reigned, many people admitted to secretly fantasizing about being a guest on the show, silently staging the questions Johnny would ask them and their clever replies.

And if the brain is scrambled like Paul's, its bridges burned, its wires crossed, leaving decimated hillocks and gullies? How does a self reassemble itself from the rubble? Does it have to reconstitute its "inner voice"? How does it do that? By digging through the scorched earth for remembered voices? Maybe so, maybe in time they merge.

With both Broca's and Wernicke's aphasia, he had little chance of following everything people said to him. People with Wernicke's aphasia typically speak in long rambling sentences, or find their normal sentences invaded by lots of extra words, or mint neologisms, or utter gibberish. An example of this was Paul's saying "You gad clottal to stir the nevis!!!" when he meant: "You've got to pay the electric bill." They don't understand simple instructions, yet their language may be grammatical, and *fluent*—strikingly natural in rhythm and tone—but jammed with jargon and gibberish.

It made sense that Paul had abbreviated what he was feeling to "go home." People with Broca's aphasia tend to speak telegraphically in short halting phrases that may make sense but are staged with enormous effort because neurons in the Broca's region of the brain are important in coordinating the muscles that move the lips, palate, tongue, and vocal cords. And Broca's aphasia often leads to the frustration of knowing what you want to say without being able to say it. In Wernicke's, the words tumble out in fits and starts, and sufferers often omit the small linking words "as," "and," or "the"; they may also omit parts of verbs. So when Paul said, "Go home," he meant: "I want to go home." He might also have meant: "I want you to go home," or, depending on the context, "I'm losing my home." If he were only suffering from Broca's aphasia, he'd understand some of what people were saying to him—enough to know he had a speech problem and to feel horribly frustrated by it. In a way, Wernicke's is more insidious; you don't know you're speaking gibberish.

People like Paul, doubly stricken with global aphasia, have extensive damage to their language areas, and lose most of their ability to speak *and* understand language. So this meant that when I, the nurses, or the doctors talked, Paul had two problems: he couldn't necessarily comprehend what we were saying, and he was unable to find words to respond. For people with such severe aphasia, everything verbal may suddenly vanish from their lives, leaving them only with gestures and facial expressions when they try to communicate. Paralysis of the right face and arm usually accompanies Broca's aphasia (because the frontal lobe is also important for movement). So Paul's numb hand, drooping face, and swollen arm were to be expected. And since the left hemisphere stores memories of how to perform skilled acts, I shouldn't be surprised that he couldn't remember how to comb his hair. Despite the brain's plasticity, global aphasia isn't something that disappears; Paul's brain was extensively scarred. Making any improvement, even the smallest, would take him a devilish amount of work.

He *was* speaking, but most of what he said was a stream of nonsense words.

"Would you like anything from home?" I asked casually, more as an aired thought than a real question.

Nonetheless, he humored me with a run at an answer: "Hrfg! Memememememememem. Bbbnto."

"*Bbbnto*" I repeated. "Does a bento box have something to do with it? It's divided into little rooms?"

He looked at me as if I'd just recited the Kaballah in Japanese, and shouted this time: "MEM, MEM, MEM!"

Startled, I backed up, and he fell silent again.

In the confines of his small hospital room, hour after hour, he struggled to talk and understand, which was arduous if good practice for him, and bone-wearying for me, a frantic game of "Twenty Questions" played with nothing but enigmas. Strangest of all, he seemed convinced that he was making perfect sense and everyone else should understand him, but for some stubborn, spiteful, villainous reason, we were all pretending to be clueless.

CHAPTER 6

A S I PREPARED TO LEAVE FOR THE NIGHT, PAUL WORE AN expression of fear, bewilderment, impending doom.

"*Noooo,*" he said, first imploringly, then urgently, then willfully, then angrily, and finally, his eyes metallic with hurt, he turned from me in a bitter sulk. When I tried to hug him, he pushed me away.

"*Nooo!*" he hissed again, this time with a visibly damp forehead. He clung to the bed rail as if to gain time on the eve of a great abandonment, stampeded by panic but with nowhere to run.

"I'm sorry, honey, but I swear I'll be back tomorrow morning," I tried to reassure him. "You'll be all right. You'll sleep. The nurses will look after you. You'll be all right. I'll be back soon."

But he didn't believe me. His face bunched up tight, as if soured by lemons.

Loss, confusion, powerlessness, plus not being able to communicate: that bolus of misery led to frustration so visceral it often triggered angry outbursts. But a stroke can also injure a part of the brain that *controls* angry emotions. Usually the reasonable prefrontal cortex reins in the boisterous, impetuous limbic system by putting things in perspective, judging the danger, advising compromise or restraint as need be. The feel of that balance is what we call *well-*

being. Paul's stroke had damaged his prefrontal cortex. No wonder his emotions were skidding out of control.

Paul's continual indignation—which he expressed with fierce glares and snarling, loud, mainly unintelligible recriminations—began to unsettle me. I already felt frayed to exhaustion from conferring with doctors and making decisions about his daily life, safety, progress, and comfort. Taxing enough if I felt he appreciated my efforts. An irate, helpless, demanding spouse at times filled *me* with anger. In such moments, I might silently fume: *What an ingrate! What do I need this for? I'm not your spinster daughter!* And I could see why stroke victims were often entrusted to nursing homes; it was like a divorce from someone you nonetheless loved, wanted to help, and were fated to look after.

Paul begged me to stay with him twenty-four hours a day, a panic I could understand, since I was the only continuity in his chaos. As children we often find the world littered with baffling frights, which only a parent's soothing can calm. I remembered hiding behind my mother's skirts at such moments when I was a girl. All I had to do was stretch up my arms and look scared, and my father would lift me onto his solid shoulders, away from the hurly-burly of a crowded street or beach. Paul had only me.

Furious as Paul was about my leaving at night, he was doubly enraged that I wouldn't take him home. Summer bloomed beyond the windows. A lifelong sun-worshipper, Paul used to tan until he looked like furniture—a rich mahogany burnish he had kept well into the winter—and he obsessed about swimming. *Pool* was one of the few words he could reliably summon from his battered attic.

"Pool!" Paul would demand, his eyes threatening and hard.

"Pool," he would moan in barely audible yearning.

"Pool," he would tell doctors when they inquired how he was feeling. They understood: He wanted to go home and enjoy the long-awaited fruits of summer. A normal desire. But I doubt they grasped that, in his picturesque brain, *pool* had become the symbol for everything un-hospital, life before the stroke, typified by hours

afloat in the sun. Like a child, Paul was using his first words to
evoke whole situations, not just specific things. Pool time often had
included my climbing, half floating and nearly weightless, into his
arms, wrapping my legs around his waist, and laying my head on
his shoulder, while he carried me through the shimmering blue,
my face in shade, his catching the rays, like a knot of frogs basking
in the sun. Ever since his retirement a decade earlier, he'd luxuri-
ated in the water for hours each summer day. Rain or shine. If it
was chilly Paul had worn long thermal underwear that we called
his "germ suit" (because he looked like a giant microbe in it), and
if it was merely raining, he'd swim naked but wear a cap, sometimes while smoking a cigar. Unable to explain all that, he encap-
sulated his yearning into the single word *pool*, a symbol he knew I
would understand. At times he said the word in a heartbreaking
whimper that roughly meant: How could I leave him *and* leave
him in exile?

But I continued to go home most nights, even though it felt at
times like fleeing the scene of a crime, and after a few days, when
he realized I would return in the morning and he'd been able to
weather the nights on his own, his anger at me subsided. At last he
let me crawl in bed with him, and we snuggled for hours. A mellow nurse, on her rounds, caught us and smiled, but didn't suggest
I get out of bed. She simply pulled the privacy curtain around us,
and then we were transported to the barely private rooms in an
ancient Japanese palace where the walls were a fabric that billowed
in the breeze. For those court ladies, being private in public had
become an art form. For us, sheer necessity.

We couldn't stay like that for long; nurses and aides needed
access to him, and I needed to try my best to rest. So when at last
Paul began breathing deeply in sleep, I'd steal away and drive down
the forested hill leading into town, cross over the inlet, then take a
curving highway uphill, with the hospital lights small lanterns
from a floating world across the lake, and a mist-shrouded summer
moon ahead.

THERE WAS A time when I could be decoyed out of bed by the simple beauty of a summer morning. Now I awoke tangled in worry. All I could do was wither and wait, breathing shallowly, as one often does when beleaguered. I needed to find some calm and continuity again, so I practiced a few minutes of *toning*, a four-teenth-century word for singing or chanting in elongated vowels. Inhaling deeply, I exhaled *ah* until my breath faded, inhaled again and exhaled a louder steadier *ou* (as in soup), whose vibrations I could feel in my cheeks and ribs, then inhaled again for a more invigorating *ee*, and finally for a rotund *oh*. I sang out the sounds again, this time louder and more richly. Echoing around the bones, the vibrations steadied my breath, focused my mind like a mantra, and relaxed my body. It helped calm me a little, just as it always had, not only by deepening my breath, but by vibrating my carti-lage, sinuses, and bones in a sort of tonal massage.

I knew I needed to ground myself, so in the early-morning light, I strolled through the neighborhood, admiring tar patches poured in random squiggles on the roads, imagining they were poems in Japanese, Chinese, or Tibetan, which I translated. Working on a haiku as I walked helped me focus my mind on something other than illness, something natural and timeless, such as: "Orange stars on stilts: / Late summer in the garden / Before the leaves fly." Returning home, I noticed a bush of yellow peonies blooming like brilliant handkerchiefs against a backdrop of multicolored tulips. Glossy, purple, spaniel-eared irises were swaying next to their wilder yellow cousins, the Siberian irises, which had traveled a long distance from their ancestors on the Siberian steppes. *We've all traveled*, I thought. *Parts of us, anyway.* Some of my traveling parts would end with me since I had no offspring. For a moment that fact saddened me. There was a time when I'd thought of my books in that way, as extensions of myself that would outlive me. I no longer did. These moments all alone before the peonies and irises

in the dappled light of a summer morning seemed enough. This
little everywhere, this nowhere else.

~~~~~~

I ARRIVED AT Paul's room with a few home comforts: favorite pillows; sugar free chocolate pudding, blueberry-orange vegan muf-
fins (comfort food for me); photographs of friends and family, to
help orient him; a book of cricket photographs to page through
when he was bored, his coziest robe; and "Bear," a plush teddy
bear we'd adopted in Florida, whom Paul had sometimes chatted
with and nestled beside for TV viewing. I really wanted to bring
him his favorite foods but wasn't allowed. So no old eccentric habits of dining on fish paste, Wasa bread, Dr. Brown's Cream Soda,
and Cheshire cheese.

"Did you sleep well?" I asked, adding a cartoonish pantomime
of someone sleeping: eyes closed, palms pressed together under a
nearly horizontal cheek.

"Nothing!" He said the word with a pronounced shiver, as if
wishing to be rid of the whole concept.

I pictured him waking worried, hungry, miserable, and alone,
still in the hospital and unnervingly tongue-tied, almost mute, to
lie in bed doing nothing, unable to read or write. He couldn't even
watch the clock and count down the minutes, since he was unable
to read the numbers. Although he returned to wearing his wristwatch each day, he'd usually put it on upside down. It made no
difference if I told him "I'll be back in one *hour*" or "in one *day*."
A day was not greater than an hour; either fetched the same vacant
stare. Breakfast wouldn't arrive for uncountable bleak hours. His
only outside visitor, I wasn't due for ages either. I knew that expanse
of empty hours poisoned him. So I arrived early each day, well
before visiting hours began, usually in time to help with breakfast,
and then persuade him to go to physical therapy, which he absolutely loathed, finding it boring beyond belief. And unnerving,
too, because he had seen many men with similar afflictions.

In post-WWI England, the walking wounded had peopled Paul's childhood and drawn sighs of pity. Beyond the estimated 10 million who died during WWI, twice as many had been wounded, many with brain injuries. No doubt there were plenty with aphasia as well, but those he never heard about. Many doctors didn't bother with formal neurological tests. They just served their patients afternoon tea and observed the balancing act of eating and drinking. Could the patient lift his dominant hand? Hold the cup and saucer without shaking? Did his spoon bang against the porcelain teacup? Did any of the fingers droop? Could he raise the cup to meet his lips? Swallow the tea without choking?

Before the war, his village's stroke patients had mainly been elderly, retired, and short-lived. But after the war, typical patients were otherwise healthy young men, longing to return to a normal life. In the first rehabilitation clinics, which sprang up in Germany, doctors based their therapy on how children learn to speak: sound by sound, then syllable by syllable, word by word, phrase by phrase. If patients couldn't make certain sounds they were told to puff out cigarette smoke and shape the motion into desired sounds. Paul would have loved the return of his cigars, which his cardiologist had banned, relegating them to dreams, old photographs, and cherished memories of curling up with a bottle of cognac.

For Paul's rehab, two physical therapists drilled patients in the humdrum skills of moving a body through daily life, motions we take for granted and barely notice because over the years they become ingrained. Skills that aren't instinctive but mastered. In some cases—such as how to hold a spoon—learned when we were in the crib. In childhood, as they were practiced, small failures could produce photo opportunities and a parent's reassuring laugh. In Rehab now they needed to be relearned, and small failures weren't cute but sad or even worrisome.

Fractious patients like Paul had to be cajoled out of their rooms, and wheelchair-bound patients slid or hoisted into a chair. Sitting in a circle in a toy-littered den, they might kick a red rubber ball back and forth to each other. Or sit at a table and slowly stack colored blocks with one unsteady hand, then the other, working both sides of the body. Paul hated these exercises, designed to improve hand-eye coordination, which he found both demeaning and very difficult. During the stroke, he'd lost a corridor of vision off to the right, a common complaint. The stroke had damaged some fibers that carry information between the eyes and the visual cortex, creating a blind spot in his right field of vision. To see the right margin of a sheet of paper, or food on the edge of his plate, he now had to remember to turn his head to the right. He couldn't grip with his dominant right hand, or discern textures with the two clenched fingers, which were numb.

In one alcove, a bare white kitchen gave patients a chance to grapple with the implements of home: slippery bowls, stemmed pots, tight jars and cans, a reluctant refrigerator door. In theory, they were taught how to cook safely and use a stove without scalding or burning themselves. Essential for people returning home and hoping to be independent. But Paul's visual gap, and also his inability to follow simple stepwise instructions, made cooking dangerous, and he rarely ventured into the empty, bright therapy kitchen.

"It was a hovel of mayhem," he told me later, *"everything leapt out at me, with sharp angles and weird shapes that dropped out of my hands. And the mirrored pots seemed to be hallucinating my face right back at me—a face that felt like the one I saw on the round metal: twisted, ghoulish, with strange white bristles jutting out here and there. No, my own face felt much more metallic by far. And the folderol of the blocks and balls—a dunce's playthings, which I couldn't stack and could barely roll."*

Negotiating the twin beds was more important. Whatever else one learned, one had to be able to get in and out of bed—a skill stored so far back in childhood memory that it seemed hereditary. And yet, strangely, it could be forgotten. The Occupational Therapy room was all about coordination, and getting yourself out of bed safely was no exception. The knack of crawling on and off a bed means balancing and rotating various parts of the body, and every body has a different center of balance. For many of the stroke

patients, an arm or a leg was dangling deadweight, and their equi-
librium had changed. It was painful to see patients, stymied by the
process, inching and dragging and sometimes losing their balance.
Watching Paul relearn how to use his limbs reminded me a little of
the summer I taught him how to float, tread water, then finally
swim. Everyone can do it, but everyone does it just a little differently, depending on the weight, angle, and flexibility of their limbs.
How strange it was to watch Paul cheered on by young physical
therapists when he successfully got out of bed. *We come to this*, I
thought mournfully, *all of us in time.*

For his next feat, Paul sat down in a chair, which he performed
as if nearly falling from a great height. A safe solid chair waited
behind and below him, but he had to trust its being there, reaching
one hand back as he descended. Rising meant shifting his weight
and launching himself up and away in a sudden lurch.

Watching the other patients, I beheld family members learning
how to use mobility aids. A flock of canes and walkers waited to be
auditioned, and Paul tried a couple and even left with a cane, which
he never used. Always too vain to wear reading glasses, he couldn't
wrap his self-image around a cane, although he would have walked
more safely with one for support. Maybe it was somehow connected to the memory of seeing his father, blinded in one eye in
WWI, a rare member of his platoon who had survived the trenches,
but not unscathed. Since those days, modern medicine has devised
clever machines for diagnosing stroke, and better therapies for
treating it, but nothing to revive the palisade of dead brain cells,
alas.

CHAPTER 7

FEELING LOST IN EVERY SENSE, IN ALL MY SENSES, I CON-
tinued to pour my efforts into supporting and encouraging
Paul. Even if he couldn't grasp what I was saying, he could watch
my face express love, sympathy, and comfort, hear my tone of voice
and inflections—all the more important now—and *sense* how I felt.
Hugs delivered voiceless words. We could still communicate
through the ancient system of *mirror neurons*, the marvelous brain
cells that allow us to watch—or even hear or read about!—what
someone else is doing, and feel as if we're doing it ourselves. Located
in the front of the brain, they helped our ancestors imitate language, skills, tool use, and society's subtle pantomimes. An author's
ally, they're why art stirs us, why we're able to outwit rivals or feel
compassion, why we can watch the Winter Olympics and half
undergo the strain and thrill of the athletes, why, if I write "I ran
through heavy rain," you can picture the scene in your mind's eye
and feel your legs in motion, the slippery street underfoot, rain
pelting your head and shoulders. All that is possible through words,
but much is still knowable without them, through facial expressions, body language, gestures, and affection. What an eerie
thought after a lifetime of words.

"Bwite," Paul suddenly rasped. "Nit sot wupid."

Awkwardly rolling and pursing his lips, curving and kiting his tongue, he continued trying to pronounce words, succeeding only half the time, and finally giving up in fatigue.

Not so different from a child, I thought, *trying to coordinate lips and mouth to speak, saying "twees" instead of "trees," "betht" instead of "best." Except that language seems to slide down a child's throat.*

A newborn's brain contains billions of neurons, many still incomplete. They bush out furiously until about the age of six, when the violent topiary work begins, and twigs are severely pruned, some strengthened, others discarded, until the brain fits both its skull and its world. Another big burst of landscaping takes place about ten years later. How does the brain decide which wiring to preserve and which to dissolve? By keeping what's useful and killing the rest, it seals its wand-like connections into place. Magic ensues. How does it guess what may be useful? Whatever it uses the most. Hence the antiquity of lessons learned by rote, the skullduggery of abuse, the longevity of bad habits. Think or act in a certain way often enough, and the brain gets really good at it. Children tend to recover much better from brain injury than adults, whose brains are already intricately thatched and patterned. And children's brains are wired quite differently from adults', with mainly shorter connections among neighboring neurons. Elaborate long-distance pathways, linking remote areas of the brain, may give adults the edge when it comes to digesting thorny information, seeing the big picture, making difficult decisions—that baggy ghost we sometimes call *wisdom*—but an adult's complex wiring is also vulnerable in many more places and easily sabotaged. Even when very young children have had the entire left hemisphere removed (to calm uncontrollable seizures), their right can run the language shop surprisingly well.

But adults? *Like cross-country skiing through crusty snow*, I thought. The first skier, plowing the path, needs muscle, but the following skier doesn't have to work quite as hard, and the next in line finds the going smoother still. Each trip packs the snow firmer, deeper, reinforcing the furrow, until it's easy to sail along with little effort.

Learning, we call it. Skiing through deep snow. The brain hurts from the effort, but the more it traces and retraces its path, the swifter the travel.

I wrapped an arm around Paul's shoulders and gave him a heartening smile. And Paul understood, despite his severe left-hemisphere injury.

The left hemisphere of the brain is like a child or a private detective; it's constantly demanding *Why? Why? Why?* Obsessed with solving riddles, it won't hesitate at making things up (a hunch, a prophecy, a superstition), because if a predator is stalking you, a wrong answer is better than no answer, and a fast half-baked guess is safer than a slow perfect answer. Neuroscientist Michael S. Gazzaniga has labeled the left brain the *interpreter*, "a device that seeks explanations for events and emotional experiences." Whatever befell our ancestors, good or bad, they needed to understand *why* so that they could predict future events and prepare for them. Mystery causes a mental itch, which the brain tries to soothe with the balm of reasonable talk. The inquisitive, meddlesome left brain, that is; the right brain prefers to stay mum.

According to Gazzaniga, it's the left hemisphere's insisting on storytelling, fiction-mongering if need be, that allows us the illusion of being rational and acting with free will. The left hemisphere's interpreter allows "self-reflection and all that goes with it . . . a running narrative of our actions, emotions, thoughts, and dreams. . . . To our bag of individual instincts, it brings theories about our life." The left brain engenders a sense of self because "these narratives of our past behavior seep into our awareness; they give us an autobiography."

Paul's left brain, his interpreter, was wounded. No wonder he labored to make sense of what was happening. He frequently lifted his open palms skyward in a *What's going on?* gesture, his brain still able to mime what he couldn't phrase. All I could do was deliberately unpleat the worry from my face, and explain slowly in a calm voice: "You've had a stroke. It has damaged the part of your brain that controls talking. You're doing okay. We'll get through this. Just rest."

How strange: Paul couldn't talk, but he hadn't lost his social sense, and he still understood the dance of etiquette. He would listen intently to the doctors, though I knew he was understanding very little and retaining less. He would greet a nurse with polite sounds, gesturing for her to enter the room or be seated, and when she offered him a small plastic cup, he took his medications gamely, with a sense of duty, as if he was once more the small son of a soldier father.

Crushed at the nurses' station, his pills became a rainbow palette of potent dust. Little more than a few grains, they packed the force of Fauvist thunderbolts. Specks of lightning in a bottle, with just as much potential for harm. *Allopurinol*, for control of kidney stones and uric acid levels, tinted the applesauce a brilliant orange; while *Coumadin*, for slowing down blood clotting, turned vanilla pudding bright blue; and *Propranolol*, for blood pressure, dyed butterscotch pudding a garish green. But other pills joined the mix and the pharmaceutical jumble smelled acrid and bitter. Paul's swollen right hand, weakened by the stroke, moved slowly, and he couldn't coordinate it well enough to take the pills himself. Instead he obediently opened his mouth to be fed like a bird.

What a different scene from the one I'd grown used to. For twenty years, he had stood at the kitchen counter each morning shaking a white plastic jar of mixed pills until the ones he wanted agitated to the top, where he could grab them. The snapping-clatter had reminded me of baseball trading cards flapping against the spokes of a bicycle wheel—a cheerful sound from my childhood. He had studied up on his medications, whose complex schedule he knew by heart. Keeping track of changing doses, he'd split tiny pills with a sharp knife and a steady hand. Cursing and growling at the labyrinth of the automated dial system, he'd phoned in refills, consulted pharmacists and cardiologists with aplomb. While I'd stayed on the sidelines, dispensing love and trying to render useful opinions, he'd steered his own medical life—not just ably but with fascination about the science. He loved knowing that he was taking blood pressure medicine derived from *bothrops*, a venomous pit viper of Central America, and that if the snake bites you it can cause a stroke, but its venom used judiciously can help prevent a stroke.

A nurse tipped in one small spoonful after another, and Paul twisted his face as each hit his taste buds and lingered in his mouth for a few seconds until he could swallow. Nonetheless, he took his pills stoically, just as he did his insulin shots, which he received in a pinch of skin on his upper back, so he wouldn't have to watch the needle enter. He'd never needed insulin before, and just in case I'd ever have to administer it at home, a nurse gave me lessons. The first time I jabbed Paul I handled the needle like a dart and he cried out in pain. His eyes snarled: *Don't THROW it!* Paul wasn't coordinated enough to inject himself, and I dreaded the thought of stabbing him every day. Not because I didn't think I'd get used to the syringes, or even the ritual of filling them, tapping away oxygen bubbles, and piercing the skin. If I misfilled a syringe and injected him with too much insulin, I could kill him. The responsibility scared me. One small slip by me could have huge consequences.

Or one big slip by him. Paul was one of the patients on the floor labeled as FALL RISK. Woefully confused, balance off-kilter, he lurched when he moved, and his vision was skewed—all of which added danger. FALL RISK earned him a notice on his door, a note in his chart, and the alarm on a string, with one end clipped to his hospital gown in a hard-to-reach spot. He was supposed to ring for an aide when he got up. But he didn't remember that instruction, and probably hadn't understood it to begin with. Moments stretched like aluminum taffy when he needed to use the toilet or wondered why he was imprisoned far from home. If he didn't wait for help, and plunged ahead on his own, an alarm would ring as he jerked the cord free. *Patient on the loose!* the bell pinged in the nurses' station. Then a nurse or aide would come running to see if he'd hurt himself or needed help with the toilet. But if no one was at the station, and I wasn't in his room, the bell might not be answered right away.

Fixated on the idea of home, Paul began trying to escape. With his hospital gown flapping open in the back, face tufted and bloody from clumsy attempts to shave, hair a short cyclone, he waited until the coast seemed clear, then took wing down the hallway, shambling and weaving at speed, subversively heading for the exit, without knowing exactly where that might be. Once, like a deluded Magellan, he circumnavigated the floor, almost making it to the elevators before a nurse and an aide captured him and led him trumpeting angrily back to bed. Several days later, despite his lack of coordination, he managed to wiggle out of his hospital gown *without setting off the alarm*, put his loafers on the wrong feet, and abscond naked down the hallway, sliding along the wall as if he were installing wallpaper.

Noncompliant was the term the nurses grumbled about Paul, the rebellious patient in Room 252, the running man. Their irritation was easy to understand. Often overworked, with a slew of demanding patients, they didn't need an errant patient who at unpredictable intervals might risk something really dangerous. Their nightmare was a rehab patient falling, breaking a hip or a wrist, hitting his head, or injuring himself in some other way while under their care. Small wonder Paul's escapes made them crabby, especially a senior nurse I'll call Martha, a brusque, stocky woman whose tone of voice drummed her rank. I had the feeling I greatly annoyed her, too, by hanging around so much and seeking a nurse's help for Paul whenever he needed it.

Trying to stay eagle-eyed, I was haunted by the memory of a close friend who had almost died in a hospital after the wrong dose of a drug was given. Fortunately, she was visited just in time by a well-wisher who happened to be a physician's assistant and acted fast when she arrived and found our friend lapsing into a coma. Slip-ups occur in hospitals far too often, and it's no wonder—shifts change, patients hate being there, difficult cases are *de rigueur*, and some doctors and nurses will be seasoned and compassionate, others less so. And Paul was *noncompliant*, which really irked Martha.

In contrast, Nurse Marty was mellow and rail-thin, a man with lanky brown hair and a genial smile, prone to discussions about old movies and philosophy of religion. Nurse Melissa, a heavyset woman in her early twenties, usually arrived grouchy, and spoke to Paul in a holler, as if his inability to comprehend speech meant that he was also hard of hearing. I've since learned how common this is for aphasics; a well-meaning friend or stranger compensating by speaking louder, as if hammering the words might somehow drive home their sense. Other nurses filtered in and out, and they soon merged into a uniform flow of uniforms. One minute the doorway to the room was empty, the next it framed a complete stranger bent on intimacies. A split second of surprise—from where had this one materialized? Then my left brain's interpreter, asking *Why?* might find a quick clue before I even knew I was curious, and feed me the most likely answer.

Liz, a senior-year nursing student interning at the hospital, first appeared as magically as everyone else did. I knew Liz was a student because she was wearing the telltale nursing-student *whites*. (Cricket players and nursing students had that in common.) And I'd seen shoals of students in the hallway with their instructors. *I'm sure she has her orders*, I thought warily, sizing up yet another new nurse, *but won't have had much experience, so I'd better monitor her.*

A tall woman of maybe thirty with short blond-streaked hair, Liz was shaped like an upside-down triangle—with muscular shoulders over slender hips and legs. We would come to know Liz very well, and in time I would learn that she'd muscled up from her part-time job, heaving bales of hay and mucking out stalls on a thoroughbred farm. Wearing no makeup, she looked cute in a healthy, outdoorsy way, and entered the room briskly, shadowed by another nurse, a slightly older woman with a stockier frame.

"I walked in hurried and rushed, as I almost always felt as a student," she would tell me later, "nursing preceptor behind me, watching to make sure I didn't flub up. Administering medication comes with piles of rules, for good reason. We were trained to start with the five R's: Right Time, Right Place—oral? subcutaneous?—IV? Right Dose, Right Drug, Right Person. Right Person means proper patient identification, which means you methodically ask the person for their name and birth date, and double-check their answer against your medication chart and their wristband.

"Which is why I recall meeting Paul so vividly. A moment of utter flummoxness when I confidently walked in with a little cup full of medications, and routinely asked Paul for his name and birth date. And he pleasantly responded with a faintly beatific smile and a bit bemused look that seemed to say something like *I'd love to help you but I really don't have any idea.* I had never met an aphasic. I stammered something to the preceptor like 'What-do-I-do-now?' I remember acutely, she answered: 'Just give him the medication. We all *know* he's Paul West.' "

From then on, Liz mainly appeared alone, and something about her manner with Paul touched me. For one thing, his plight didn't seem to disquiet or bewilder her. Had she worked with a handicapped person before? Maybe a grandparent with a stroke? She wasn't at all awkward spoon-feeding him—Did she have children? She didn't raise her voice as if he were deaf, and she spoke with him at all times like a grown-up, often smiling or joking. Her tone with Paul was strict, yet kind. When she told him it was a good idea to get out of bed and sit in the armchair for a while, just to change position, and he sulkily refused, she lifted his back up, spun his legs off the bed, shouldered his weight, and helped him into the chair—while chattering good-naturedly nonstop—before he could mobilize any sort of resistance. I laughed. He laughed. She laughed.

"Predatory nursing," she explained with an impish smile and a wink.

Then I noticed her socks. Dressed all in the mandatory white, she was sporting a pair of socks with loud orange spots. *A woman who likes cute socks,* I thought, *someone after my own heart.* It couldn't be easy to imprint one's personality on a boring uniform.

Liz told me later that when she overheard the floor nurses grumbling about Paul's flights, instead of disapproval she had felt a guilty twinge of amused respect. Paul was obviously a feisty contrarian, one wily enough to slide out of his gown when the nurses weren't looking and hightail it toward the door. She had to admit she admired that, even if, from a nursing standpoint, she also had total empathy with the lament of "He's *noncompliant!*"

I would come to learn that Liz's mom had had a stroke when Liz was young, and Liz had watched her stagger down hallways, struggle with simple tasks, and slowly relearn how to use her body, while nonetheless raising three small children. In time, her mother recovered fully, and returned to teaching kindergarten in the challenging schools of urban Washington, D.C. I think Liz had gradually absorbed her tone of determined goodwill, caring and amusing, but brooking no dispute. The "*SIT down*, we're *all* going to be reading *NOW*" tone of a teacher who finds pleasure in teaching and chasing after a posse of five-year-olds every day. Her father was a minister in a small Lake Wobegonish Midwestern town. Noticing me getting more and more bedraggled, she cautioned me about needing to "take care of the caregiver," and suggested that I go home for a hot bath and a nap.

She was right, of course, caregiving takes a colossal toll, and I was feeling its legendary strain.

CHAPTER 8

To the amazement of all, Paul began to say more words, and even string some together, but his mood was bleak.

"Finished," he muttered in a despairing tone, his face expressionless as pounded copper.

"You're *feeling* finished. Are you depressed?" I asked, feeling eroded and hollow myself, yet concerned.

Paul nodded yes, then groped for a long while. His mind seemed to bulge as a word threatened to surface. Finally, his face withered into an image of outright scorn for the thing he had to say, but getting on with it nonetheless he added: "beaten."

After thirty-five years of our living together, I could taste the acrid depths of his despair. "You're feeling finished and beaten?"

Paul's eyes welled with tears. I wrapped an arm around him and held him close. His freshly laundered gown gave off a trace of bleach. The hospital scents were starting to make his body smell unfamiliar to me.

"I understand," I said, desperately trying to reassure both of us. "It's been horrible. You've gotten a few words back. There will be others."

"Dead," he pronounced in a leaden tone.

"You're *feeling* dead?"

He stared at me hard. I sat down on the bed beside him and cradled his limp hand.

"You wish you were dead?"

He nodded yes, this time with a look so desolate raw it chilled me. I knew from my research for *An Alchemy of Mind* that gusts of sadness or bouts of anger were a familiar story with left brain injury. And I was afraid Paul was just mobile and lucid enough to find a way to kill himself. His black mood continued all day, and I hovered anxiously, not letting him out of my sight.

Sitting beside the bed while Paul slept, I agonized as I reviewed what I knew about the two sides of his brain and their contrasting outlooks on life, how they specialize in different facets of mind. The left is the chatterbox, the storyteller, the fictioneer, the con man, the liar. It's superb at list-making and alibis. It values a grid of rules (and in their absence will gladly invent some). It lines up pieces of information in logical ways, nice and tidy, before drawing conclusions. The left relishes reality, adjusts to the world it finds, and whistles a happy tune. The right, on the other hand, is Munch's terror painting *The Scream*, a cauldron of negative emotions. A wizard of insight, the right intuits an answer first, and limns the big picture, before it moves on to the details. It excels at reading facial nuances, fathoming music's spell, feeling words. It's not enough to catch the information ferried by a sentence. We also need to glean the speaker's intentions, beliefs, and emotions. The right hemisphere adds hints, leading us beyond the corridors of literal meaning into a labyrinth suffused with irony, strong emotion, metaphor, and innuendo. Pinpointing a noise in space, the right decides whether we need to respond, and if so, how intensely. Juggler, puzzle-solver, and artist, the right feels quite at home with fantasy's mirage.

Of course they're not as rigid as all that. Both halves of the brain cooperate, on math, language, music, emotion, and other curious enterprises. Most people blend left and right brain use so fluently they're not aware of the divide, or that one side toils silently while the other is questioning nonstop. Some people use both sides equally, in others one side dominates, but what we call *mind* isn't so much a duel as a collaboration, in which the brain relies on vital checks and balances. I worried that Paul's severely injured left hemisphere might be eclipsed by his right, with little to offset the glacial sadness he felt. Not just because of his new circumstances, which would be depressing enough, but simply because his brain had a crippled cheerleader.

As evening fell, sunlight flickered across the window like a rumba of snakes. For a long while, Paul and I stared at the illuminated frame.

Then, turning toward me, he pleaded, "Home."

"You can't leave yet," I insisted again. "Not until you're a little more stable. I'm sorry. . . ."

Extending both arms toward me, he drove them down sharply, as if planting something.

"H-h-here!" he said, again begging me to stay.

Pale with fatigue, I explained once more that I was bushed and had to leave for a few hours, if only to sleep a little.

"Look . . . at . . . *me!*" he whispered with a derisive laugh.

His isolation, boredom, and fear were an avalanche for him. And it was also bone-crushing, mind-crushing, soul-crushing for me.

That poor brain of yours, I thought. *Now with small graveyards of cells.* As Paul grimaced, repositioning his pillow with one hand, I wondered if he had any idea what I was thinking.

I wasn't sure what mood I'd find him in the next day, but as he yawned and finally grew heavy with sleep, I knew he'd pass the night safely.

"I'll come first thing tomorrow morning," I reassured him, too bleary to try to explain further.

Before I left I asked the nurse on duty to keep a close eye on him, and wrote a pleading note to the head of the Rehab Unit, reporting that Paul was terribly depressed and talking repeatedly about killing himself. I knew that, in Paul's eyes, in losing his words he had already died, all that remained was killing the empty husk. Even though his brain hadn't settled down yet, and we didn't know the full extent of its injury, I asked if the doctor would consider starting him on Ritalin and Zoloft immediately, two drugs sometimes prescribed after a stroke; I'd read of promising results with both.

Ritalin has been shown to stimulate the prefrontal cortex, the brain's executive suite, which plans and analyzes, and in clinical studies, patients who took Ritalin thirty minutes before language therapy sessions made faster gains. Zoloft helps with mood, but that isn't all. Typically prescribed for depression, one of Zoloft's seldom-mentioned benefits is that it spurs the growth of new brain cell connections in the hippocampus, a rich site for processing memories, including the memory of words learned. A colossal number of brain cells (hundreds to thousands) are born each day, but most die within weeks, unless the brain is forced to learn something new. Then more neurons revive and sprout connections to their brethren. The harder the task, the more survivors.

According to studies done by Tracey Shors, a neuroscientist at Rutgers University, "learning rescues these new cells from death." During a long-term depression, cell birth slows dramatically, and the hippocampus may even shrink in size. Keepsake memories vanish. Antidepressants in the class of SSRIs, such as Prozac or Zoloft, trigger the birth of new brain cells, which wire and fire with others, boosting memory while ringing the changes in mood. But, unfortunately, this wellspring usually takes four to six weeks to materialize. Now more than ever, Paul needed the ability to remember likely words, bring them into focus, and spotlight just one.

It didn't seem surprising that Ritalin, an amphetamine-like drug, was being bootlegged and sold on the streets, or that it had become hugely popular with high school and college students. Would Paul or I have taken it when we were in school? Maybe so. Or maybe the craze for it is endemic to our high-speed culture, where the merely *fast* fall behind, mail by post is for amateurs, and "one thing at a time" is *so last century*. Ritalin improves a brain's ability to focus in a sea of warring sensations, which is why it stars in the treatment of attention deficit disorder—and also in cramming for exams.

Learning something new always costs the brain a colossal amount of energy. The mind devotes countless neurons to the project, and over time recruits a web of more and more, until the effort is reinforced and the brain develops a skill. But this means paying close attention, tuning out the rowdy world while you focus on the relevant details. In Paul's brain, it was as if some filter had gone awry and too much sensory noise kept seeping in. Shutting out the background static, focusing on anything for long minutes, exhausted him. I'd read a paper by Jean-Marie Annoni, in *Neurological Sciences*, about the syndrome of "post-stroke fatigue," striking half of all stroke victims, which can last for a year or more. It's not normal tiredness, but a confused doldrums, which demands lots of sleep but isn't remedied by rest. Thoughts become hard to organize, and memory develops plugs and blockades. Yet it's not truly a memory disorder, but a rift in the brain's system for paying attention. As chaos reigns, the brain can't decipher figure from ground. Any forest becomes a smear of trees, and the exhausted brain can't focus on just one. Ritalin sharpens that focus by boosting neurotransmitters in underactive parts of the brain.

Paul spent most of each day sleeping or in therapy, but usually got a second wind after dinner, when there was little to occupy his spare hours.

In the pre-stroke years, we'd often passed the time by playing a jazzy game like the one we called Dingbats, which wasn't so much a contest as a sort of mental solitaire for two with a common object used in uncommon ways. For the last one, as I recalled, we had chosen pencils. What can you do with a pencil—other than write?

I'd begun. "Play the drums. Conduct an orchestra. Cast spells. Ball yarn. Use as a compass hand. Play pick-up sticks. Rest one eyebrow on it. Fasten a shawl. Secure hair atop the head. Use as the mast for a Lilliputian's sailboat. Play darts. Make a sundial. Spin vertically on flint to spark a fire. Combine with a thong to create a slingshot. Ignite and use as a taper. Test the depth of oil. Clean a pipe. Stir paint. Work a Ouija board. Gouge an aqueduct in the sand. Roll out dough for a pie crust. Herd balls of loose mercury. Use as the fulcrum for a spinning top. Squeegee a window. Provide a perch for your parrot . . . Passing the pencil-baton to you . . ."

"Use as a spar in a model airplane," Paul had continued. "Measure distances. Puncture a balloon. Use as a flagpole. Roll a necktie around. Tamp the gunpowder into a pint-size musket. Test bonbons for contents."

"Good one!"

"No heckling! . . . Use as a spear against hecklers. Crumble, and use the lead as a poison. Wind a kite string around. Dangle to test the direction of the wind. Pull juicy ants from a log with if you're a wild chimpanzee. Create a fan-shaped design on wet painted walls. Write your name in fresh cement . . . Let's see . . . A musketeer mouse could fence with it, or a knight could joust with it. Test for quicksand. Hold a tarantula at bay. Put up your nose. Douse for water."

And so we'd volleyed back and forth, until after a while our mental springs tired and unwound, or we just grew bored.

To pass the time now, Paul watched television, though I wasn't sure he knew what was really happening onscreen, and he had trouble working the simplified remote. The nurse's call button still confused him. Over and over I showed him how to use the two devices, but the coaching just wouldn't stick to his brain. Although he didn't want to be escorted to the toilet, which he clearly found demoralizing, I helped him nonetheless because he refused (or couldn't figure out how) to summon the nurse and he walked unsteadily. Sponge baths he enjoyed, and once a kind nurse even vigorously massaged his legs, after which I scratched his bed-numb back, which made him sigh with pleasure. He often tried to engage me in conversation, which in the end just frustrated and infuriated him because I so rarely understood.

"Ff-ff-fox going return?" he posed anxiously.

Latching onto the word *return*, I said: "Yes, if I go away, I'll return."

"*Noo*," he waved an erasing hand. "Mem, mem, mem, drive skutch!"

"Skutch . . . uh, Florida grass," I thought out loud. "I'm sorry, I don't understand."

He threw up his hands in irritation, and spat out: "Bog off!"

I laughed before I could stifle it. In London's Heathrow train station a dozen years earlier, as we'd hurried to a train that would carry us to Eckington and his waiting mother, Paul had collided with a Pakistani man making equal haste in the opposite direction. Both men had shifted to the left and right at the same time, back and forth, growing more irate.

"Bog off!" Paul had snarled.

"Stinkeroo!" the other man had shot back.

Then, slipping past each other, they'd pushed forward and the farce had ended. Afterward, we'd often recalled that incident with a laugh, as an example, Paul insisted, of the bygone British Empire in all its dysfunctional glory.

I doubted Paul was replaying that memory right now, just grabbing at a curse from childhood days, one he'd often heard on the lips of Eckington's coal miners.

I offered him a hand to hold, and he took it, gently squeezing, with a forlorn look in his eyes. He slumped back against the bed, a shallow and shrunken figure, digging at the mattress hard with one knuckle. His eyes said he felt lost and ridiculous. As Paul would one day, after valiant struggle, put it in words:

"Many people would be forgiven, I think, for relegating such an individual to the trash heap of history as someone who had failed and been found wanting, or who had achieved a brief prominence and then sunk into the ruck. Who is this? they would utter, who once was so demure and now is so dreadful. Is he human at all with his crossbow eyes and his elephantine stance? Is he deserving of pity or some other outlandish emotion, or should we pass him by? What is wrong with him? We would prefer not to know.

Despite whatever agony he feels, we would seek the company of happy convivial people rather than molder in his crude animal sedan."

Crude animal sedan. Yes, I could picture it well, the woolly vehicle that encloses a wild animal's spirit, the clumsy movements and barbaric yawps. The rough aphasic façade hiding Paul's artistic soul.

CHAPTER 9

A T HOME I SCOURED MY LIBRARY OF BRAIN BOOKS FOR everything I could find on aphasia, and then retreated to the bay window, literally my seat of learning. With Paul in the hospital, it became a refuge now more than ever. In I climbed with a stack of books, hoping to find some answers at least, if not solutions. Two I'd recommend for introductory reading are: *The Aphasia Handbook: A Guide for Stroke and Brain Injury Survivors and Their Families*, by Martha Taylor Sarno and Joan Peters—an essential guide from the National Aphasia Association; and *Coping with Aphasia*, by Jon G. Lyon, addressed to patients and caregivers alike, explaining what to expect, chronologically, with aphasia. In Further Reading, I've listed some other works that I found uniquely helpful, insightful—or both.

I learned of aphasia's first mention, on an Egyptian papyrus from the third century BC, the earliest known medical document, a textbook on trauma surgery. The papyrus refers to a man with a head wound, a nosebleed, "and he is speechless. An ailment not to be treated." Yet the ancient physician suggests that rubbing ointment on the head and pouring a fatty liquid into the ears will be beneficial to the patient. Paul would have loved that—including *Tea with Osiris*, he'd written two books set in ancient Egypt. I chuckled to myself as I pictured the fun he would have depicting the bleak absurdity of the scene, then somberly remembered that I couldn't share with him, as I usually would, any of this history, or the hieroglyph for "he is speechless":

To me the three symbols looked like *bird*, *whip*, *tent*, and in previous days I would have devised a silly translation ("Flip the bird at me and I'll whip you intently," or maybe a film trailer for *The Maltese Falcon*), to laughingly present to him to counter with his usual wit, but Paul was no longer able to play such games. Words had been his pastime, solace, and obsession for so many decades. How on earth would he now pass the time? More like let time pass over him. Surely his days now held more hours than before, idle hours alone and with no words as windup toys.

I imagined Paul's mind as a blackboard on which all the words had been erased, but it was more like he was being locked out of the classroom. The words were all in there, jumbled as they might be, and they had been scrambled into an alien language. His brain couldn't attach the correct word to things, and couldn't select the best words for what he felt. But he most likely heard words trickling relentlessly in his head, and was drowning in a stew of words.

The books explained that aphasia is not the *loss* of language, but a retrieval problem, a sorting problem. Words crowd one another, and very often the wrong words are the only ones the mouth can utter. Remembering a word takes two steps, pinpointing the word you want, and then retrieving the sounds for the word. It's possible to fetch only the first part, and not be able to remember how to say it, due to weak connections. Or just clutch at word fragments. I'd sometimes pursued such "tip-of-the-tongue" words myself, usually aware of their architecture (tall or low letters? beginning or ending sound? polysyllabic?), without being able to retrieve the whole word, so I appreciated his frustration. Paul knew what he wanted to say, and his brain's dictionary was still intact, but its cover was glued shut. I had to keep reminding myself that an adult still lived inside his head, only his wiring was injured, the connections were frayed.

An email to a friend at the Dana Foundation produced the name of a stroke specialist, and I contacted the doctor, who replied soon, saying he would be glad to look at Paul's MRI. But because Paul had a heart pacemaker, he couldn't risk an MRI; the force of the magnet would have scrambled the titanium pacemaker's settings, possibly triggering a fatal rhythm. Nonetheless, I could send the less precise CAT scan. All I could ask for was a prognosis. But did I really want to know? Dr. Ann had wisely advised me to "prepare for the worst, but hope for the best." The cardiologists, neurologists, and other specialists I'd spoken with at the hospital implied that he wouldn't be writing books again, and probably not speaking or understanding much either. The damage to his brain had been too sweeping. A grim forecast. What if yet another specialist told me the same? How would that affect my attitude toward Paul? If I knew his limits, would I give up hope? Would I bother trying?

Desperate for some clarity, I felt as if I were in a labyrinth, with no view beyond the narrowing hedges. If only a few could be pruned away. I longed for a prophecy from the stroke specialist, not because it would change anything, but because such foresight would bring me a little certainty at a time of agitated doubt, barely informed decisions, fear, and bewilderment. Our future and *my* life would seem less haphazard. If nothing could be done, why subject him or me to even more ordeals?

On the other hand, if I didn't know, if I could live with the indefinite, who knew what might result? A brain can learn to make do, improvise, rewire, recruit neighbors to a new purpose. Dead neurons may not be able to regenerate, but damaged ones are plastic and can grow. Healthy ones can take on new duties. New neurons can arise, even late in life, and migrate to where they belong.

A brain is a resourceful captive. We haven't fully explored its sorcery or frontiers. It can "give to airy nothing a local habitation and a name," as Shakespeare puts it so beautifully in *A Midsummer Night's Dream*. So why not try everything? Could rookie cells be drafted—however slowly, and probably with harrowing effort—and, if so, would they serve as well? Perhaps I had irrational hope for Paul. But he had a couple of important traits going for him. Because he had wordsmithed for seven decades, he would have forged more brain connections for language than most people. Also, he could be diabolically stubborn. I decided not to send the CAT scan. The knowing, I told myself, is only a vapor of the mind, and yet it can wreck havoc with one's sanity.

One of the books I dipped into was C. S. Lewis's *A Grief Observed*, a rich, precise, emotionally candid account of the ordeal he went through as his soul mate, Joy, lay dying of cancer, and the mountain of grief he felt after her death. Because he bled so intimately into the prose, he published it under a pseudonym. I identified with much of the book, especially this: "There is spread over everything a vague sense of wrongness, of something amiss." Yes, that felt right. An atmosphere of wrongness. I was stirred by the power of Lewis's grief. And yet, his experience, despite his referring to it as "mad midnight moments," didn't lead to madness. His was a mind that could cushion itself when faced with trauma, without becoming callous, neglectful, or numb to soften the pain. Despite not knowing if what he felt from moment to moment would pass or last forever, he entered fully into his shifting states of violent rage, self-pity, longing, heartbreak, cynicism, without losing the ability to think about what was happening to him. That took courage, I thought, living with the suffering in a mindful way, as an artifact of being, neither good nor bad.

I'd already noticed how my own voice had changed: losing some of its sharp peaks and bounce, and gaining firm new ridges. My phrases were smaller, slower; my rhythms thick and clumsy, not light and dancing. I now seemed to quarry words, one by one, presenting them like bright bits of jasper—not slurred in a wash of flurried adjectives—when I spoke to Paul. Sometimes with a flutter of agitated worry that felt like a beetle was trapped inside my ribs. But I savored the delicious warm touch-ribbons of silent affection, uniting and comforting us, even when words failed. And I followed the stew of sympathy from friends, whose faces flickered with unrefined sorrow-compassion-pity.

Could I continue to woo life, despite the abysmal sadness? Surely Lewis had more courage than I possessed. How tempting to live in limbo and wait for my real life to return. But this *was* my real life now. Life is a thing that mutates without warning, not always in enviable ways. All part of the improbable adventure of being alive, of being a brainy biped with giant dreams on a crazy blue planet.

"All part of the adventure," I often reminded myself, "all part of the adventure." Repeated out loud like a mantra. Felt at times like a hoax. At others it became a balm of understanding to spread across a mind in misery, one of the many transparent liniments for sprained emotions that humans rely on. Like hope. Or faith. "All part of the adventure." *One that began with blue-green algae*, I thought. *No, farther back, in volcanic verdigris on the ocean floor. No, farther back still, to where our atoms were forged in the spinning, spitting, detonating furnace of the sun. No, much farther back in space-time.* That meant picturing things before the Big Bang, when the entire universe was all in one place and solid: a small silky nugget of hydrogen floating in an endless void. The effort would gently tug my mind from suffering to curiosity. Only for moments, of course, but that's all we ever have, a mass of moments, currents of being.

Ironically, Paul and C. S. Lewis had once been in correspondence, around the time Joy was dying, still a young woman. Death made quick work of her half-quenched mind. How on earth did Lewis, as caregiver, manage to correspond with people, or even spend time with friends? Would Paul's stroke create a great distance between me and my friends because now we always had to include it in our intimacies or business, always had to include this massive sadness? At the farmers' market, for example, I bumped into several friends, as one often does while strolling among the stalls of fresh local produce, crafts, and ethnic foods.

Each person immediately asked: "How is Paul?"

In the past, they would have asked: "How are you?"

I told myself that there were going to be shifts in my relationships, meaningful shifts, and that those who loved me would shift along with what was going on. That was my hope.

To one friend, a photographer of local landscapes, I said: "I need a break from Paul; let's not talk about it. What are you working on?"

But Paul's stroke elbowed into most of my sentences; every topic seemed related to it; I was immersed, I couldn't banish it from my thoughts, much as I wished to. It was a kind of hypnosis, not just a trauma, and it bore all the tooth marks of unshakable obsession.

⸻

WHEN I RETURNED to the hospital, I found Paul listless and sad.

"Die," he said solemnly.

My already faint spirits sank even lower. I heard Kelly's voice in the hallway, on her way in for the morning's speech therapy, and I caught her before she entered the room, warning her in a whisper that he was feeling very low and didn't want to live.

"How are you doing this morning?" she greeted Paul with achieved cheerfulness.

He shrugged. In a practiced motion, she tilted his bed so that he could sit up.

"Ready for speech therapy today?" she asked anyway, flashing a small reassuring smile.

He nodded a resigned yes. Kelly was irresistible. With close-cropped blond hair, blue eyes, and petite build, she looked like a high school cheerleader. Though she seemed upbeat and hopeful, her smile always appeared genuine. No small feat that, knowing the plight of her patients. Kelly didn't expect to see her patients fully recover, that wasn't the nature of her work. She smiled the smile of someone wedded to the incomplete, used to working with badly stricken stroke victims. Paul responded well to her ease and expertise.

When she asked him to pronounce the vowel *a* on cue, even with her coaching he only managed it 50 percent of the time, often by sighing or yawning first. She showed him how to stretch his lips into an *e*, an *i*, an *o*, a *u*. As children, we learn to tug the strings of facial muscles—curling or flicking the tongue, pursing or yawning the mouth—babbling, mimicking, somehow coordinating the whole lot. We practice with gusto, parent guidance, and endless repetition, until the brain gradually stores an unconscious memory of how the tongue and mouth must dance in unison to voice a word. Even after seventy-five years of daily use, that marionette can lose some of its strings. It seemed impossible, but Paul had to relearn how to sound out the alphabet again, sculpt the mouth, aim the tongue, work the bellows of the lungs, just to say a small owlish word like *who*.

Kelly drilled him in simple yes/no questions, which he answered correctly only about half the time (and how many of those were chance?). As the questions became more difficult—"Do you write with a pen?" "Do you write with a toaster?" "Does a cork sink in water?" "Will a stone sink in water?"—he needed more time and rarely found the right answer. Next she showed him two pictures and one word, pronounced the word slowly, and asked him to point to the correct picture. Paul only answered right half the time. Did he really not know what a *dog* was? How could you lose the word that goes with a glass? She then named objects in the room and asked him to point to them, which he got right about half of the time. Body parts he could point to with slightly more accuracy, which seemed brilliant compared to his other test scores. When she asked him to print his name using his left hand (since his right was too weak to hold a pen), he wrote *P-A-U-L* in just-decipherable letters.

"That's right!" she said.

"Was it really?" he asked unexpectedly, in a tone of innocent surprise.

Where did that come from? I wondered. *So smooth and normal!*

"Now your last name, Mr. West."

He printed a legible *W*, and then the rest of the letters wormed away. When he saw the hint of disappointment on her face, he took a deep breath, as if preparing for a marathon, hesitated several times, and finally croaked: "I . . . I'm . . . s-s-sorry."

Her morning report, which distilled his progress, recorded a ten percent improvement, his two reflexive comments, and the same banners as before:

Severe apraxia of speech.
Oral apraxia.
Severe Broca's aphasia.
Dysphagia.

A dose of Ritalin helped him focus for the afternoon's speech therapy, but it also seemed to make him more agitated and angry. Or the therapy session's strains and frustrations left him that way. Or he was just tired. Whatever the reason, that became the pattern each day, and at such times I learned to leave for a few hours and return at nightfall, usually arriving in time to watch a cloud of bats, swinging right side up as they flew out from under the eaves, and feeling grateful the trials of afternoon therapy were over.

CHAPTER 10

A T HOME, WHEN I OPENED THE FRONT DOOR, A BREEZE sighed through, as if the house were psycho-sensitive, like one of those in "The Thousand Dreams of Stellavista," a sci-fi short story by J. G. Ballard, in which houses can be driven to hysteria by their owners' neuroses, walls sweat with anxiety, staircases keen if the owner dies. Pushing the heavy door closed behind me, I dropped my keys onto the kitchen counter, and their clatter smashed through the uncommon silence.

As I slouched down the hallway, nothing looked familiar. A strange disorder ruled my study, where, at regular intervals, I used to scare papers into files neat as hedgerows. Now books lay slaughtered on the rug, and, on the desk, unopened letters duned among bills and coffee cups, in a room spontaneous as a compost heap. My world was in shambles, inside and out. My body also felt derelict and unlived in. Every little thing, no matter how small—putting on makeup, changing my clothes, washing my hair—seemed to add boulders to an already unbearable weight. I felt as if a spare particle would make me collapse. I kept forgetting to eat, and, anyway, the refrigerator was bare because I hadn't the energy to shop. Whenever I finally dragged into bed, exhausted, I woke unrested to find Paul's side of the bed strangely empty, his study oddly quiet.

Sometimes I felt broad stripes of sadness, the full tarot deck of anticipated loss, and throbbing worry. I'd suffered many losses in recent years, after my father, mother, uncle, aunt, and cousin had all passed away. In her final years my mother often lamented that there was no one still alive who had known her as a girl, and I was starting to understand how spooked she'd felt. I wasn't sure I could take any more abandonments. One succumbs so easily to mind spasms, worry spasms.

In my study's bay window, my poet self stepped out of the shadows and I saw through her eyes again, the eyes of my childhood. I pulled up a cozy star-quilt my friend Jeanne had stitched by hand, and gazed out at the magnolia tree, bridging the mineral earth with the breathless blue sky. Its bark looked like unironed linen. Two wrens tried to land on the pagoda-shaped birdhouse, not smoothly but with bumps, wrong cues, and collisions, followed by the faint clamor of nestlings. A red squirrel dragged a black walnut into a redoubt among the high branches, and began shredding the thick husk as if it were flaying a woolly mammoth. The metallic snore of cicadas buzzed and quit, buzzed and quit. A fly danced at the screen.

The average lifespan in the West is 80 years, or 2.5 billion seconds. So Paul was already old by human standards. Truly ancient compared to the fly buzzing the windowpane. But young, a mere stripling, compared to some other life forms like "Methusaleh," the 4,841-year-old pine tree in the Mohave Desert, and some 200-year-old rockfish, bowhead whales, carp, and tortoises. Or the virtually immortal species of jellyfish that begins as a polyp, becomes sexually mature, grows old and decrepit, then returns to the polyp stage and matures again—indefinitely. Paul's Anglo-Saxon ancestors didn't expect to live beyond 30 to 40 years (mainly because of diseases since cured or curbed). Paul had survived longer thanks to medical interventions like the pacemaker (which would have lengthened his father's life), and drugs for blood pressure and diabetes.

Looking out over the evening skyscape, I felt some of what

Joseph Campbell must have when he spoke of feeling "a certain tenderness toward the lovely gift of light, a gentle gratitude for things made *visible*." More now than ever, I needed this pocket of calm and continuity. Losing myself in nature provided the right tonic. For me, that's always been where worry takes a holiday and the earth feels solid underfoot. After a while, I left the bay window and passed into the back garden, to stroll a while, empty my mind, and let it fill with the dew, quickening shadows, riot of pinks and purples low on the horizon, and then the silent gold fury of the sun. It was always there, always right where I left it the day before, always on time. What a relief.

Plunging into those moments with wonder and an open heart refreshed my spirit. There is a way of beholding nature which is a form of prayer, a way of minding something with such clarity and aliveness that the rest of the world recedes. It quiets the bitter almonds of the limbic system, and gives the brain a small vacation. The vivid spectacles of the sun stopped me in my mental tracks, and for whole minutes I simply *was* among the fruits of summer. I didn't always feel up to losing myself in nature like that, but whenever I could it fortified me.

Returning to the hospital after dinner, I found Paul lying awake in his bed, his forehead pinched in an expression of broodiness I was getting used to seeing. No surprise he was still depressed. I sat down in a chair on his right, with the windows behind me, as the blood-orange red sunset streaked the sky. A "clean sunset." No haze to dim its color. Nothing in my life seemed that crystal clear or elementary anymore. It was hard for Paul to see my face when I was backlit. He looked worried, childlike.

"Sc-sc-scared," he sputtered.

"You're scared?" I asked.

He nodded yes.

"What are you scared of?"

"Mem, mem, mem, you'll, mem, mem, *leave*. Would. would. wouldn't blame," he garbled. It was the longest thing he'd said thus far.

My excitement collided with his sadness, as I rejoiced over the small improvement.

I went around to the other side of the bed, so that he could see my face better, and hugged him. Even if he couldn't understand all my words, he could sort of lip-read my face, using ancient skills to decipher my meaning.

"I'm not going to leave you," I reassured, stroking his forehead. "I wish this hadn't happened to you, to *us*, but you're still my sweetheart and I love you. I'm not going to abandon you, you don't have to worry about that."

He nodded a slight yes and relaxed his gaze. He understood. I didn't know if he believed me. Or if I believed me. Who knew what lay ahead. I laughed to myself, remembering Dorothy Parker's quip: "What fresh hell is this?" It felt good to laugh, even silently and a bit darkly, and even if, for once, I couldn't share the literary allusion with him.

FIVE WEEKS IN the hospital fled as if down a sinkhole into the middle of the earth. And yet, what had I done in the hospital? Little more than keep Paul company, sleep, watch, anguish, and guard. Speech and physical therapy exhausted him, and he slept much of each day. Worry, vigilance, and trying to understand Paul exhausted me, and I dozed a lot, too. Can waiting, by definition slow, flash by? It can when the hours and days blur into a disturbing new routine fraught with uncertainty. Time becomes even more elastic than usual—minutes can stretch for ages and days suddenly snap together.

As his brain cooled and the swelling began to shrink, his speech and comprehension improved a bit more, though he still found people hard to fathom, and he mainly spoke gibberish punctuated by "Mem, mem, mem."

Kelly arrived for a routine breakfast session, and he greeted her in very communicative gestures, beginning with a cupped hand to usher her in. Then, with a sweep of his hand, he asked her to take a seat.

His hard plastic breakfast tray held a thick blue rubber mug, faded from use, and an assortment of heavy plastic plates and bowls the color of sand. Porridge for breakfast, thickened orange juice, thickened cocoa. A bowl of pudding shrouded in shiny plastic. He didn't like the thickened liquids and told her so by pretending to banish them with one hand. Again she explained why thickened liquids were important, that the stroke had affected his swallowing muscles. When he tried to drink the thick orange juice from its cup and discovered it wouldn't pour, he mimed disgust. Kelly suggested he use a spoon. Did it even rank as liquid if you had to eat it with a spoon? I didn't think so, and clearly Paul didn't either.

"What work did you do?" she asked.

I flinched at her choice of the past tense.

Pausing from breakfast, he made several false starts, then, while circling one hand in the air, he slurred: "Books."

"That's wonderful. Can you name one of your books?"

Cringing from the effort, he tried to string words together, but over and over seemed to tumble away from them, as if he were falling down a cliff, striking a rubble of nonsense sounds. A long spell of gibberish followed, during which he grew more and more frustrated.

Paul gathered himself up, looking strangely like an impostor of his old professorial self, squaring his shoulders, and stared directly at Kelly. She studied him intently. I held my breath, waiting for the words to come out. He concentrated, inhaled, opened his mouth for "Mem, mem, mem, P-pollen, rggh, mem, mem, P-pollen, MEM," followed by an even longer clotted stream of gibberish.

"I am an individual!" he suddenly blurted out. That took my breath away. It was an allusion to a film we had seen, *The Elephant Man*, about a severely deformed nineteenth-century man who begins mute and is coached to speak. In one scene, cornered by an angry mob, he cries out: "I am not an animal! I am a man!" Did other stroke victims feel like freaks? I bet some did. I bet, regardless of their life before the stroke, they just longed to be ordinary people again. That's all I wished for him as well, not to feel like his tongue was caught in a bear trap when he spoke, not to have a padlocked mind.

"Take a deep breath and try again," Kelly urged. "Use key words. Speak slowly."

After several tries and a stream of "mem, mem, mem's," he painstakingly drawled four words with a pause between them: "Place . . . Flies . . . Where . . . Pollen." Settling back, he sighed. It was the best he could do. I knew he had meant *The Place in Flowers Where Pollen Rests*, his novel about a Hopi kachina carver, but I didn't speak. In a few years, Éditions Gallimard in Paris would publish the French translation of this novel to wide praise. But for now, Paul couldn't even pronounce the title of his own creation.

Still, sitting at the sidelines, I wasn't watching passively; I was silently rooting for him and saying the correct answers in my mind. *I bet parents are like this with kids as they learn*, I thought. So much in a relationship changes when a partner is seriously ill, helpless yet blameless, and indefatigably needy. I felt old. The night before, crying, he had assumed a fetal position, and then I laid my head against his neck and gently rocked him, murmuring "Rest, little fellow, it's going to be all right." When I sang him a nursery song about Wynken, Blynken, and Nod, I felt him sinking at last into the blind trust children feel in the arms of a parent holding them high above the earth, safe from its fray. I cupped myself around him, as if I were shielding a flame. I felt responsible for his little life. At last, his breath deepened and he drifted off to sleep, while the searchlight of my vigilance burned a hole in the darkness.

I later learned that what Paul had felt was quite different: *"Here she is cuddling her overgrown baby, who had once been the terror on the cricket field. Her blue baby, her deformed baby, her armless protégé, at once older, younger, doomed, a magnet for any human task, and therefore enormously to be pitied, before being put down, buried, grave-stone naked, and maybe plundered by grave-robbers and carted away as a freak."*

Being maternal when he was in such a fragile state felt like simple caregiving. But for him it stung as a humiliation, because he was no longer someone who could take care of himself. The Paul he knew was already dead and buried, as far as he was concerned, and I was left tending a freak. He had become repugnant to himself, pitiable, a monster. And he assumed I must be feeling equal disgust.

At the time, I hadn't a clue he was thinking any of this, or even that he *could*, when he seemed barely conscious of what was going on. The animal part of him, in pain, accepted my caring. But the part of him *watching himself* in that pain didn't believe I could ever respect him again. None of this crossed my mind. I couldn't risk knowing it. No one could and continue caregiving. They'd feel so unappreciated and wronged that it would drive them away.

Instead, alternately proud and worried, I sat nearby, mentally taking the hurdles with him, frantic for his success, silently cheering him on.

"That sounds good," Kelly said. "I'll look for it."

"*You* . . . like?" he suddenly asked, cocking his chin toward her in expectation of a response.

"Oh, I bought a book by that author the Iranians are after."

"S-sal. Man . . . *Rush*die," he said proudly, sticking out his chest and grinning like a schoolboy. Surprised, we all laughed at the correct answer.

After forty minutes, Paul fell back in exhaustion and Kelly met with Dr. Ann and me in the hallway, where we discussed his gains. *Hope for the best, but prepare for the worst.* The barometer of our hopefulness had risen a little and at last the air felt lighter. Any progress, however small, was a gift, and I rejoiced. Surely this meant more improvement was still possible? Even if full speech didn't return, even if he didn't write again, even if he became easily confused, at least he wasn't doomed to spend his remaining days ranting little more than "Mem, mem, mem, mem."

CHAPTER 11

O N A SUNNY MORNING IN LATE JUNE, I FOUND PAUL SIT-
ting on the edge of his bed, waiting for me, looking eager
and excited. I'd seen this look before. He was perched like a professor with a train to catch, and despite his hospital gown, I could
picture him in a bow tie and tweed jacket.

"I have . . . s-s-surprise," he spluttered with some effort.

"You have a surprise for me?"

Smiling proudly, he straightened his shoulders, lifted his chin,
took a slow, deep breath, then proclaimed, "I speak good coffee!"

"You speak *good coffee*?" I must say I was a bit bewildered.

He nodded yes. "I speak good coffee," he repeated.

"*Coffee?*" I asked, eyebrows raised like Tudor arches, signaling,
Are you really sure—coffee?

"No," he said, laughing, "I speak wonderful English!" And so
he did.

"There's big difference!" he said gingerly. Overnight he had
indeed improved, even more than he was aware of. Since the
stroke, I'd never seen him so excited, so hopeful, so fluent.

"You're talking!" I gushed. "Well done!" We grabbed hands
and squeezed hard. For a few more moments we talked, or rather

he talked, almost normally, words handy and obedient, pouring out slowly. I found them refreshing as well water.

Kelly arrived on her usual schedule, and with an eager smile I informed her: "Paul has a surprise for you this morning—he's speaking much better."

But when she greeted him he clammed up, as if shy. Part of aphasia's bane is difficulty speaking on demand. Off-the-cuff, unpremeditated replies ("Was it really?"), uttered before he realized it, could sidestep the aphasia and flow much more easily. Kelly whisked him away for thirty minutes of speech therapy and another swallowing evaluation, while I remained in his room with his checkbook and bills, to catch up on bookkeeping. Paul had always kept track of half the household expenses, and despite the chaos I needed to find all the outstanding bills and make sure they were paid. As I sat by the window, I watched the clouds shape-shift over the lake, briefly recognizable at times—train, camel, long-horned antelope—because my brain's interpreter kept trying to ID them. Was that still happening in Paul's brain, or was his interpreter too wounded to care?

More typically, Paul came out with many sentence fragments, but was cruelly frustrated and dissatisfied with them. He could write his name legibly only in big block letters. I still greeted this with relief, as if he had somehow reclaimed a tiny fraction of himself with those four letters. Not *P-A-U-L*, but the spiral font encrypted in his cells. Or the foursome that buoys one up: *H-O-P-E*. And during speech therapy, when Kelly asked him to tell her something about himself, he thought for a moment, opened his mouth wide as if he were testing rusty old machinery, and finally said: "Many books . . . We go . . . Fl-florida . . . for fourteen, no one hundred forty, no fourteen, no four months," and "Swim." Then he shook his head at the woefully incomplete answer.

At breakfast, scrambled eggs tripped down his windpipe and he coughed violently, retching as if he were trying to expel his stomach. When he drank a little thickened milk from a cup, he uttered a cough so flannel-thick and long that it scared me. He looked terrified. Unflappable, Kelly coached him how to cough from deep in his diaphragm, while leaning forward, until he spat the milk up out of his airways, spraying white like some venomous snakes. Then she spent a long while explaining—yet again—his swallowing danger, why he had to sit up straight while he ate, why he should swallow each bite of food before putting another in his mouth, why his drinks had to be thickened. She taught him to do tongue sweeps after swallowing, to make sure that he didn't still have food tucked in a numb corner of his mouth. Nodding solemnly, Paul responded as if hearing it all for the first time, not the umpteenth, and I saw how much trouble his brain was having storing short-term memories.

Long-term memories were another cat entirely. Because it takes the brain a while to store a long-term memory—sometimes days—and his injured brain wasn't fully back in the memory-storing business yet, I knew he probably wouldn't remember any of this hospital time at all. Only I would. That startled me. Never before did I have to store someone else's trauma—not only live it at my own cost, as real gut-wrenching, but also replay it later when he asked what happened to him, as inevitably he would. I felt oddly like I was taking over some of Paul's higher brain functions (decision-making, interpreting, memory storage), shouldering the mental burden and adding it to my own. One brain laboring for two.

Not a complete novelty. Despite feeling separate, our brains regularly assign various functions to others: teachers, nannies, doctors, policemen, farmers, et al. And cede momentous and trivial work to spouses every day. *You do the taxes, I'll work on the loan application. You do the grocery shopping, I'll take the cat to the vet. You handle the garden, I'll mow the lawn and shovel the snow.* I'd always been the one who organized our travel to Florida, run the house, hired workmen. Usually I was aided by lists on paper or computer, grateful for the handy and uniquely human gift of being able to store information outside of the brain. But this was a whole new order of magnitude and of stress. I could barely remember the details of my own life and be responsible for my own fate. I wondered how much that contributes to "caregiver stress," heaping a brain with more executive tasks than it was designed to handle?

I felt pain in my fingertips, stomach, and toes. What a heartbreaking struggle for him. How would *I* fare with only a rat's nest of wrong words, an irregular heart pinwheeling in my chest, limbs tired old barn slats, the dregs of Thick-It in my mouth, senses screwy as fun-house mirrors, unable to swallow safely or dress myself, imprisoned in a noisy castle light-years from home, keyless and clueless, prickled by strangers, apocalyptically bored, and without even the words to file a petition because some fiendish constabulary raised Cain every time I spoke? And what if, no matter what I said, or how—cogently and coherently, with old-time finesse, it seemed to me—no one understood?

I couldn't imagine being in his shoes for a day, let alone weeks . . . and a lifetime? Horror of horrors, what if it were a lifetime? Could I stay buoyant in the maw of such tragedy for so long? I didn't think so. *Don't jump the gun. And don't let on*, I thought. Catching my breath, I tried to calm myself long enough to calm him.

After Kelly left, with great sadness Paul presented me with a mangled aphorism: "The word man is perhaps not the right one for the thing I see when I hear it."

"Not now, anyway," I said, "but keep trying. You're speaking, that's the main thing. . . . I know how exhausted you must be. How about a nap?"

While Paul slept, I blearily went downstairs to the cafeteria, a large room containing deli & grill, salad and soup bar, refrigerated grab-and-go foods, which opens out into a dining room with polished wooden tables, and many windows. It had been too stressful a morning, and I could feel the fabric of my being fraying. I needed a respite, the solace of losing myself once more in an equally real way of knowing, but one less devastating. I felt my mind begin to float, and the naturalist step out of the shadows and search for an agreeable tableau: lower parking lot with colorful metal carapaces gleaming in the sun; the front-door procession of people with faraway expressions; a small grassy bank and bench beside a purring creek; other diners. My eyes were drawn upward. Designed with sweeping arcs and many round inset lights, the ceiling seemed to display the starlit arms of galaxies. Not by design, I thought, but abstractly, as a kind of archetype of the night sky, a familiar sight the brain encodes from childhood and tells time by, or uses to chart its way through the world. I smiled. Even in a hospital cafeteria, we bring nature indoors with us, can't help but surround ourselves with its forms. A faint harmonious music hovered in the air, nothing loud or intrusive or even identifiable enough for my brain to puzzle over. Why do we need to fill the air with sound? Maybe because, in our deepest imaginings, we're more at home with the ambient sounds of nature. I was glad of such renegade thoughts, which tugged my mind far away from Paul and his illness. As the crust of my world continued cracking I needed more and more time-outs. Another one soon presented itself:

I shared the elevator with a female volunteer pushing a small wooden bookcase on wheels. A glance at the titles made it clear they were meant for casual readers who needed a little gem to engross them or pass the time, but nothing they wouldn't mind leaving unfinished. The lowest shelf was full of slender children's books with shiny colorful covers. I felt a wash of nostalgia, and then my mind leapt through long-dormant synapses and memory alleys to something I hadn't thought about in years—the bookmobile, which had stopped only two blocks from my house in suburban Illinois when I was seven years old. Aladdin's cave on wheels, it had looked like an unassuming trailer or bus, but inside the walls were lined with shimmering volumes that smelled of wood shavings, silver polish, and dust, just like a real library. It had solid glossy wooden shelves, a card catalogue, and moveable steps for browsing the higher books. I couldn't reach them anyway, since the steps only added three feet to me, but the children's books were shelved at ground level, so that I could sit on the carpet and choose half a dozen to adopt.

While the elevator paused and we waited for a patient in a wheelchair to slowly navigate the door, I continued to luxuriate in the memory for as long as I could before returning to the here and now. I recalled the twelve-by-eight-inch cream-colored cardboard print of a suitcase named "World Traveler," given to me the first day I started taking out books. Every week I received a new stamp to put on my suitcase, beginning with a pink one of a bookmobile driving down a country lane, then one of Norway, India, South America, Africa, Spain, Holland, the U.S.S.R., Sweden, Scotland. Somewhere along the line, I had proudly earned a blue satin ribbon that said "Reading Achievement Award," which the librarian had stapled to my suitcase with a flourish. I was especially fond of the little books with golden spines, like those on the hospital cart's lowest shelf, in which Santa rode his sleigh across the sky or Pinocchio danced. My love of books began there, in that slender kingdom on wheels. The short elevator ride beside its ghost had transported me. A sweet taste of time-travel. Proust had his madeleine; for me, wheeled bookshelves.

When the elevator doors opened again and the book trolley rolled away, I was half tempted to follow, its novels a Pied Piper for a bibliophile anxious for more escapism, but I turned in the opposite direction instead and made my way to Paul's room.

I found him awake and tousle-haired with a barely touched lunch tray in front of him. He looked like a wild child, an escapee from one of the bookmobile's adventures. Before I could say where I'd been, Kelly swept in for the afternoon's speech therapy session, and I took my usual seat in the corner, beside the windows, and far enough to Paul's right to be invisible to him.

"How are you feeling this afternoon?" Kelly asked Paul.

"Feel as like a rising just dust in ear," Paul answered. "Wasn't like this morning." Puzzled, Kelly noted it on her clipboard.

I loved the found poetry of *a rising just dust in ear.* It sounded like a biblical description of humankind. But I knew what he meant.

"Your ear is feeling tingly?" I asked. "And it started recently?"

Turning to me, he nodded yes.

Kelly thought it was a good sign, that he might be getting some sensation back in his numb cheek.

With his cramped hand, Paul found writing very difficult, so Kelly set a large portable computer in front of him and asked him to type his name. She explained that some aphasics can type what they want to say into a computer that speaks for them. Paul looked utterly bewildered, as if he were viewing a device from science fiction that would turn him into a fly or hurl him into a black hole. She pointed to the letter P to get him started. He typed *PPPPPPUUUUUUFFFFFF WWWWWES*, the letters repeating because he held them down too long. He also had trouble with spelling, and with scanning the keyboard to find the right key (he couldn't see the letters off to his right).

"Don't think trots any good," he reported glumly, and pushed the contraption away.

Despite his gloominess, over the following days his speech and comprehension continued to slowly improve. Every session, Kelly showed him pictures and asked him to describe them, and when he said anything at all intelligible, he often produced curiously quaint answers: "russet" for brownish-red, and "imposing battle scene" for forest. But he invariably tumbled letters, and "sailed away" became "selled outway," "igloo" became "legalo." Still, he produced many triumphantly lucid short phrases, such as "It doesn't look swollen" (about his numb lip), "No use at all," "Either a semester or fifteen years," "I can't speak." But asking him to *describe* a picture fetched little response. He did much better with yes/no questions. I was beyond shocked. What had become of the wordsmith? Was his lifelong lavish imagination completely obliterated?

Kelly showed him a picture of an apple. "Can you describe the picture?"

Paul looked hard at it, tilted his head quizzically, as if to dislodge a memory, but stayed silent.

Kelly asked slowly: "What *color* is the *apple*?"

Paul didn't answer.

"Is it *blue?*" Kelly asked.

Paul thought. "No."

"Is it *orange?*"

"No."

"Is it *red?*"

"Yes."

"Good! Now what *shape* is it?"

Paul remained silent.

"Is it *square?*"

"No."

"*Long?*"

"No."

"*Round?*"

"Yes!"

"Good. Now what do you *do* with an apple?"

Paul twitched his nose, as if at a bad smell. I knew he absolutely loathed fruit.

"Nothing!" he pronounced with a shiver.

Kelly explained that you *eat* an apple. Paul looked dejected. But I felt encouraged by the flicker of his old self; he had made a joke, albeit a private one, which she didn't get and he hadn't the words to explain.

Sadness stole over his face, and he glanced at me with questioning eyes.

You used to find it so easy, I thought. *What to do with an apple, other than eat it? The playful answers would have flowed. Dip the halves in paint and stencil a wall. Make a cinnamon-and-clove-studded pomander to hang in the closet. Play tennis. Carve a jack-o'-lantern. Build a beehive . . .*

I smiled at him with a closed mouth, lifted eyebrows, and nod of the head, trying to convey: *I understand. Keep going. You're doing fine.*

His face softened a little, and he returned to the cards.

Kelly showed him a picture of a man in a suit walking across a park, and urged: "Describe the person in the picture."

A long pause. "Authoritarian," Paul said.

Kelly's brow wrinkled, and her lips parted in a small smile. Patients didn't often respond with a sophisticated, polysyllabic word. All she said was, "Good. How about the next one?"

People in the next two pictures elicited more one-word answers: "Plebian," "Amateurish."

Paul seemed to be seeing the faces of the people in the pictures rather than what they were doing, maybe because the right hemisphere dominates when it comes to reading faces.

On its rampage, the stroke had seared his left angular gyrus, an injury that typically leads to *anomia*, difficulty in finding words and naming objects or describing pictures. Categories slip through one's mental fingers. If lesions disconnect the visual cortex from the language centers, a patient like Paul, upon seeing a word, can't submit the news and summon the sounds that go with it. Reading and writing crash. The brain doesn't really need them, after all. Spoken language may be an ancient delirium, roughly 2 million years old, but reading and writing are recent fetishes, only about 4,000 years old, and by evolution's standards, sheer luxury.

Paul's deficits were unique, his own aphasic signature, but that was common. It may strike impersonally, but how strangely personal aphasia is. Some aphasics only have trouble naming things. Others invent words, or parrot back what people say, or snag on a word and keep repeating it. Stranger still, I'd read of patients who whistled compulsively, or began speaking English with a strong French accent. It all depends on the whereabouts of the lesions. I thanked my stars Paul wasn't whistling nonstop and channeling French. But that was the least of my concerns.

As I waited for Kelly and Paul to finish, I recited my litany of fears to myself. With his vision so impaired, I was worried about his being alone. For him, anything to the right of center inhabited another universe. Direct his gaze at it and he'd notice it with a flinch of surprise. For seventy-five years he had scanned the world in a familiar way, one his brain processed automatically and he didn't have to think about. Pivoting his head through a wider arc to see what used to lie in front would take time to become habit. What if he didn't glimpse a doorstep, or a pot on a hot stove?

Also, he teetered when he walked, and could easily fall and not be able to get up. Aphasia reduced his ability to summon help. His damaged right arm, hand, and leg couldn't support his weight the way they used to; and he even needed assistance in bathing. I'd been told some of this would improve in the coming months, but at the moment he wasn't independent enough to be left alone, even part-time. Bringing him back home *felt* right, but I knew there was no way I could manage his care all by myself. Or rather I could, but it would cost me *my* independence. Our lives had changed forever, but I didn't want to vanish into his illness—and it was hard not to, since he really needed someone by him most of the time to act as a guardian and bridge to the outer world. I couldn't discuss this dilemma with Paul, who didn't seem to understand the scope of his injury, nor that for right now at least he wasn't as self-reliant as before. This was deeply frustrating but not too suprising, given the whereabouts of his stroke.

After injury to Wernicke's area, the brain tends to ignore its perceptual deficits and believes it's acting normally. Paul's impaired thinking shielded him from fully grasping what had happened, an irony for which I was partly grateful. He needed the rest, and sometimes it's merciful to be a little confused and not fully aware of what's at stake or has been lost. But how do you communicate with someone who doesn't know he doesn't know? In a sense, his aphasia was more apparent to me than to him. Comparing himself to the early post-stroke days when he could only say "mem," he felt emboldened by success; he was communicating. But I knew how far that was from what once had meant success to him. And so, while also cheering each small utterance, I tried to assess the vanished, the wayward, the misplaced among the familiar pieces of his mind.

Not that I could assess my own. My thoughts often sifted through the scraps of previous days, feverishly replaying conversations and events, searching for answers. Try as I might to ground myself and live in the moment, my mind grew more and more unbridled. It seemed to have its own appointments to keep, wandering from clarity to confusion, grasping any tidbit that might help.

From what I'd read, Paul's best chance for recovery relied on my seeming hopeful, positive, supportive whenever I was with him. This masquerade meant splitting my personas between hospital and home, leaving despair outside his room and sharing it only with friends and doctors. Yet I found myself shutting down and drifting on autopilot, losing resiliency in my voice and animation from my face, as my brain tried to spare me unbearable pain by making it less thinkable. A normal reflex caregivers go through, while they adjust to the new disorder of their world. The brain struggles to shield itself from shock, and it's just as well. One needs to become the mental equivalent of aerodynamic, create as little drag as possible and strip down to essentials.

Even so, the stress muddles the mind, affecting attention span and memory, and I found myself constantly forgetting things. A small regatta of colorful Post-it notes on the kitchen counter reminded me of most things before I left the house each day, but I kept misplacing my car keys, losing the notes, and forgetting calls I needed to make.

One I remembered. We're fortunate to have a well-respected speech therapy department at Ithaca College in our hometown, and I phoned a therapist about home visits. Paul was barely physically stable enough to leave, and he didn't seem to be making much more progress in speaking. But he was now refusing to go to physical therapy, a real bugbear with the nurses, and he kept demanding to go home. *Home*, from the Indo-European *tkei-*, which also gave rise to the word *haunt*. He desperately wanted to haunt his old life again.

"See, can walk . . . sit . . . Good dog. Now home!" Paul demanded of a therapist, who plastered on a smile and ignored what he said.

"Let me see you walk on your own again." She stepped back just far enough to give him room, but close enough to grab him if he fell.

Walk he did, grumbling all the while, and listing to the side whenever he glared over his shoulder at her.

"Is that the meanest look you've got?" she asked. Then added good-naturedly: "You're certainly improving. You're walking better than a week ago. Now, let's take a look at that right hand of yours."

Her very suggestion scorched him and he yanked his hand back. "No, it's . . . it's . . . no . . . it's . . ." He flapped his good hand, as if mentally paging through words for the ones that were escaping him, something simple like "It's useless."

When she lifted the crooked little finger on his right hand, he wailed: "Like h-hell!"

"I'm Catholic, I should remind you," she teased, raising one eyebrow. I stifled a laugh.

"Back!" Pushing her away, Paul almost toppled over and she caught hold of his gown and steadied him. Planting both hands on his shoulders, she guided him to a small table in one corner, where there were no visual distractions, and once more helped him lift a fork, grasp a cup, wrap his fingers around a pen. But periodically he let out howls of dismay, as she flexed his bad finger too far beyond its stiff limited range. He uttered the howls partly in genuine discomfort, but also partly for show, cranky howls, as she clearly understood, persevering with a look of forbearance.

Soon he stood up without warning, said: "All done. Go away!" and lurched into motion, gown flapping, butt flashing, heading in the general direction of his room, until she caught up with him and, by now feeling worn and irritated herself, guided him safely back to bed.

Years later, he remembered: *"In my mind, I was only pretending to be there, and the howls sounded muted to me, because in my mind I was at long last among my books, and immersed in endless swims, Diane in tow. Yes, invisible laps. But also feeling strong and protective, with Diane my*

Waif of the Water Highway, putting on the helpless little girl marooned on the bank of a churning African river, as I carried her. She who had trafficked with piranhas and anacondas in the Amazon, shedding her able past and pounds of her physical being to become a plucky little creature I could rescue from marauding hippopotamuses and tigers, and with mock-bravado, always bear safely to the other side." Paul longed to be a leonine superhero once more, at home on his veldt, Commendatore de la Piscine, Knight Commander of the swimming pool.

Kelly paid a last visit, with her discharge instructions, warning us both about the dangers of eating and swallowing: "regular food, honey-thick liquids, pills crushed in puree, small bites, small sips, sitting upright at ninety degrees for all eating, chew thoroughly, swallow what is in your mouth before the next bite, alternate liquids and solids."

Paul nodded as if he understood and would follow her instructions to the letter. But we all knew that he had forgotten the list, word by word, as soon as Kelly uttered each one, and that he'd need relentless reminding, coaching, and probably nagging, too. Once more she reinforced the swallowing regimen, and stressed the need to use Thick-It in all fluids or he'd increase the risk of particles going down his windpipe and producing pneumonia. Pneumonia he understood. It had been the scourge of his village in the pre-WWII days before antibiotics, and he'd nearly died of it as a child. The explanation was for him, but the instructions were for me, since he wasn't nimble-handed enough to mix the Thick-It nor cognizant enough to measure.

Altogether we had existed in the hospital for nearly six weeks, long enough to jar our circadian rhythms. Only two times of day descend on a hospital: the starkest noon or a disturbed, disassembled night. For me, leaving its fluorescent dreamtime felt like returning from a distant planet. For Paul, leaving felt like waking from a coma—he was released into a world of light, sound, movement, and color. Miraculously, his world had an outdoors, a way to move swiftly through the landscape, and at long last a home.

Home is a sprawling one-story house right at the end of a cul-de-sac, on a parcel of wooded land frequented by deer and skunks, groundhogs and raccoons, rabbits and chipmunks, and a host of squirrels. It's also a tabernacle for birds. At a finch-feeder hanging from a rickety trellis in the kitchen courtyard, six brilliant yellow goldfinches were bickering over the best roost when we arrived. A squirrel hurled itself from the rooftop onto the feeder, caroming off but scattering seeds in the process (which was the whole point). This was a very familiar if lunatic sight, but one Paul hadn't seen for a month and a half. Peak garden season, the roses were in full riotous bloom, the smoke bush was smoking pink, ornamental grasses were waving tall stalks, and Paul wore the expression of a pilgrim landing onshore after a long voyage.

But he was trapped in the car, and I struggled to help him figure out how to climb free, an act once ingrained, now forgotten, which he suddenly had to think about. What was the exact sequence of planting one foot, then the other, pushing off, grabbing hold with one hand (where? what?), then the other, and pulling up? Awkwardly, in stages, at times falling back into the seat, he emerged at last, winded from the effort, like a creature extricating itself from a formfitting shell. Next he had to negotiate the small step into the house, which he'd taken on his own for decades. But my worries about these little things slipped away as I watched the ecstasy on his face as he stepped over the threshold. For him, *being home* shimmered with the joy of feeling the fresh air, baking his skin in the sun, sleeping in his own bed, waking to familiar surroundings.

The house smelled the way old houses do in July, when a certain steaminess invades the carpets and any breeze ushers in just enough aroma to give air the barely noticeable tang of summer. Shafts of summer sun filtered in and the pastel walls shimmied with a soft summer light. Wandering unsteadily from room to room, Paul seemed a stranger to the locale, as if visiting places only seen in photographs. Things that had grown stale from familiarity now drew his attention. In the living room: the colorful collection of Hopi kachina dolls, the heavy beanbag rabbit bookends we'd named Bertram and Bibulous, the inflatable cheetah from the Warsaw Zoo standing next to the five-foot-tall sprawling hibiscus tree we always decorated for the holidays. In his cork-lined office, he found all his tools and toys just where he left them, and the framed sepia photographs of his mother, father, and sister.

An entomologist had built the house in the 1950s, with a sloping roof that shut out the high summer sun but allowed the lower winter sun in. Picture windows brought the entire backyard into the living room, which seemed to include trees and grass and of course the pale blue pool. Long ago, amid a marathon of house-hunting, as Paul had sat on the hearth and studied the sloping ceiling, he had an abrupt premonition; he just knew that this was the house in which we would spend our lives. And so we had, traveling to teach or explore, but always returning to our little fiefdom.

The pool was open, the sun hot. I guided him onto the back porch where he sat in an armchair in the sun, tilted his head skyward, closed his eyes, and truly smiled for the first time in many weeks.

PART TWO

A HOUSE

MADE OF WORDS

NEUROLOGIST OLIVER SACKS HAPPENED TO BE IN TOWN, lecturing on things cranial and sharing tales from the splendid curiosity cabinet of his mind. We dined together with mutual friends, and learning of Paul's stroke, he asked if he might stop by the following afternoon, a time when Paul usually avoided most humans and only the Cyclops of the television felt safe and unjudging. An ephemeral splinter of day, when neither Paul nor the earth was brightly lit.

Oliver appeared at the screen door, a white-bearded man with a gentle smile, tucking a small single hand-lens into his pocket. I recognized the device because I'd thought of ordering one myself, a portable eye for peering more closely at things. He seemed a kind, quiet man, a little shy perhaps, with loam-dark eyes and a youthful face. It didn't take him long to appraise Paul's malady, and he gave us some encouragement we found valuable and comforting.

"Many people—including doctors—will tell you that there's a window of opportunity during the first months right after a stroke, and after that the window closes and you won't be able to improve. That whatever you haven't regained by then you won't, and you're going to stay that way the rest of your life.

"Don't listen to them!" he cautioned with soft-spoken fervor.

"You can continue to improve at any time, one year, five years from now. . . . I have a relative who kept making important improvements ten years after her stroke."

Just as Oliver suspected, we'd both been warned by some doctors, nurses, books, and common wisdom that a "window of opportunity" would close about three months after Paul's stroke, with further progress slowing to an imperceptible pace. A stressful, depressing, and potentially self-fulfilling message, which we were relieved to hear Oliver dismiss. What would Paul's life be without hoping that he might one day recover some lost skills, however small?

As Oliver spoke, his face conveyed concern, respect, and goodwill—all wordlessly. I was struck by just how legible a face could be, especially to someone like Paul, deprived of language. *Bless those mirror neurons*, I smiled, *toiling away while we're busy watching and listening.* I wasn't quite sure how it was possible, and I doubted Oliver was aware of it himself, but even while he spoke of serious matters, his eyes crinkled with an innuendo of lightness, hopefulness.

Out of the blue, gently tapping his hands once on his knees, Oliver invited Paul to sing "Happy Birthday" with him, even though it was neither one's birthday. Then they celebrated their successful duet with a rousing verse of Blake's *Jerusalem*, a staple from their English childhoods, which Paul sang heartily off-tune. It was a splendid scene, the two chaps rendering boyhood songs. To Paul's own astonishment he could remember and sing most of the lyrics to both. And so he discovered, as Oliver had hoped, that it's much easier to find familiar patterns than exact words, especially if they're accompanied by music. This works famously well for children learning to sing their ABC's and other lessons, but isn't only true for humans. Among humpback whales, rhyme helps the males remember the lowing diphthongs of each year's rhythmic, raga-like songs.

A few years later, Oliver would publish *Musicophilia*, a lyrical treasury of information, insight, and stories, in which he tells of doctors using "music therapy" to help aphasics communicate, especially those like Paul with large left-hemisphere lesions, because quite often "a person with aphasia may be able to sing or curse or recite a poem but not to utter a propositional phrase." He urged Paul to try singing words out when speaking words failed him. And explained that in one promising field of treatment, melodic intonation therapy, aphasics learn to speak musically, in lilting phrases, which recaptures some of the childhood fun of singsong nursery rhymes, and calls on the musical haunts of the brain to lend a hand in the effort. After singing phrases, they slowly learn to say them. It can be a long demanding therapy, but after the torments of aphasia what price wouldn't one pay for language?

There was an instant rapport between Paul and Oliver that came, I think, from Oliver's genuine understanding of Paul's lost and aphasic worlds, complete with Oxford days and the otherness felt by smart, quirky, creative boys growing up strange in a conventional society. He didn't underplay the hard journey ahead for Paul, but he was encouraging, and his belief in Paul's ability to improve lifted Paul's spirits.

After Oliver left, Paul, drained from the effort of socializing, headed straight for the pool like a boy crawling into his mother's blue arms. Climbing up and down the ladder, balancing in the water, skimming bugs and leaves, swimming the breaststroke and treading water all served as welcome physiotherapy for his body. As the visible waves oscillated happily around him and he rested his tired ears and mouth, sensing instead with the large silent organ of the skin, I took heart in watching him smile with inexpressible pleasure.

Before the stroke, the pool had offered him a lightness beyond or before words, a different kind of trance from the one in which he wrote in his star-crazed hours, most alive when alone in late night and early dawn. He used to quip that some days the pool was more lucid than he was. Or was it I who had said that? I no longer knew. A merry confabulation of ideas and phrases can arise in a twosome even if they don't speak (or think) in the royal "we."

Since returning home, Paul had spent every afternoon swimming, just as he had in previous summers. But it took on a new poignancy.

"It's only place where always happy," he confessed.

Floating on pale blue surges and swells, while mesmerized by the pool's lozenges of light, Paul found access to a mystical realm, an out-of-body weightlessness that, before the stroke, he always blended with the nonstop purl of music. Classical music, especially that of the Impressionists and Romantics, had not only filled his life with pleasure, it had stirred memories of his mother, a splendid pianist who had taught piano to every child in his boyhood village. After his stroke, though he could still sing simple songs like "Happy Birthday," Paul abruptly lost his emotional response to music, and the pleasure of swimming no longer included the shimmery trances of Claude Debussy, the melodic quilts of Ralph Vaughan Williams, Fritz Delius's lush pastorals.

The house was quiet now, where previously music had seeped from his study, and although I liked being able to hear birds throughout the day, the soundscape had pointedly changed and I sometimes found myself startled by the silence. Why no music? Different elements of music (pitch, rhythm, emotion, etc.) are widely distributed around the brain, and there are many anecdotal accounts of cases such as Paul's, in which music suddenly loses its appeal after a stroke (this happened to me briefly after a concussion). Paul seemed actually irritated by music now; it may just have been sensory overload for his bruised brain.

The CAT scan of Paul's brain hadn't offered many clues. We knew he'd had a big clot in the left middle cerebral artery, with multiple areas of "subtle decreased attenuation," within the frontal and parietal lobes—that is, a thinning or weakening, so that neurons now spoke to one another less often and with less intensity. And there were other tracts of tissue which had withered from lack of blood supply. That sited the damage in a few general areas, without revealing an MRI's details, which could be read as one person's fingerprints of loss. But it's hard to judge exactly what happens where, because just as all people have feet, with the same basic parts, though no two are exactly alike, we all have a brain, but its folds and grooves may vary wildly. Because brains are wadded up tight like too many clothes jammed into a gym bag, everyone's brain looks a little different in its shape and pattern of folding. All the basic landmarks may be the same, but a small eventful area might lodge halfway up a groove in one person and nearer the ridge in another. During imaging, one zone may show activity when the brain is doing something—but that only means it's more focused on the task than its neighbors; other widely distributed neurons could be equally involved.

If it was hard to pinpoint where Paul's brain had been injured, it was harder still to guess the full results, because a healthy brain stages elaborate checks and balances. In that strange tug-of-war, injury to one lobe can affect the dominance of another lobe simply by not putting up a struggle. For instance, some neuroscientists propose that artists have more activity in the rear of the right hemisphere to begin with, in areas that orchestrate our complex sensory response to the world. As a result, artists are born with sharper, more easily aroused senses, the theory goes. That tangle of smells, tastes, touches, sights, and sounds is usually strained and restrained by the dominant frontal lobes of the brain, but if the front is damaged during a stroke the balance of power shifts. With nothing to curb the sensory fantasia, the back of the brain may zoom with sounds and colors, and a torrent of creativity may ensue. That can be good or bad, depending on degree—bad if it overwhelms (maybe a bugbear of some schizophrenia); good if it offers heightened awareness (the mainstay of art). Would that happen to Paul? A stroke in Broca's area meant frontal lobe damage. Without a doubt, Paul was finding the world noisier, brighter, and spikier to his senses.

When Impressionist composer Maurice Ravel wrote his famous *Boléro*, he had reportedly sustained just that sort of brain damage. *Boléro* captures the signature of Broca's aphasia: seventeen minutes of compulsive, repetitive, simple staccato phrases. It contains just two bass lines and two melodic themes repeated obsessively over

340 bars, accompanied by mounting volume and thickening, lay-ered-in instruments. Some say it captures the tempo of sexual inter-course, which is how it was employed in the male-erotic-fantasy movie *10*. But it was written to accompany a ballet in which a female dancer leaps onto a bar in a Spanish inn and swirls with abandon, her petticoats foaming and flouncing over the dark wood, until they stir up a froth of longing in the carousers. Ravel described his piece in a 1931 newspaper interview as "consisting wholly of orchestral tissue without music—one very long, gradual crescendo. There are no contrasts, and practically no invention. . . ." Ravel felt proud enough of his work to have it performed, and yet recognized that its source might be partly "without music."

As an adolescent, Paul had bought a recording of *Boléro* and played it endlessly, much to his mother's distress. But *Boléro* hadn't been Paul's favorite Ravel to swim by before his stroke. As a life-long champion of the moody and picturesque, Paul had much pre-ferred the plush harmonies of *Daphnis et Chloé*, Ravel painting the rich watercolors of orchestration that gave his lyrical work such passion and poignancy. Combining technical virtuosity with a childlike sense of wonder, Ravel excelled at conveying a shimmer-ing, dynamic sense of nature, including the many moods of water, leaves rustling, cats meowing, the moon rising like a cold white god. Creating perfect miniatures, he adopted "complex but not complicated" as his motto, which echoes violinist Albert Einstein's dictum that physics "should be made as simple as possible, but no simpler." Like a wood sprite, Paul had submerged in waves of Ravel, waves of water, and waves of light as he swam.

I relished how readily Paul had sung "Happy Birthday" and *Jeru-salem* with Oliver—it was like stumbling on a hidden sliver of the old Paul, one who hadn't lost quite all of his own musicophilia. Even if the nonstop classical score to his life was gone.

CHAPTER 13

ONCE AGAIN WADING FOR HOURS IN A SUNNY TRANCE, Paul scanned the surface of the water for errant bugs or leaves or evergreen needles, which he dutifully scooped up. It gave a sort of tai chi rhythm to his afternoons. This was one of the few ways he could restore order to his surroundings, like a monk raking perfect rows of gravel in a Zen garden (where waves of stones represent water). But Paul's stroke-humbled eyes didn't always see the slight "water maid" bees that fell in thrashing, stingers armed. The bees were on a harmless mission—collecting tiny buckets of water with which to cool their hives in a corner of my neighbor's backyard, but they had about 90,000 siblings, and some apparently didn't care for the neighbor's lovingly installed, bee-friendly water fountain.

I waded beside him, supervising, no longer sharing the blue undulations in a mystical dreamtime of my own. I was the one now skimming away bees and wasps. In the pool, as I floated while keeping Paul in eyesight, I felt my life spanning time. I slid my mind into being at summer camp as a thirteen-year-old, learning lifesaving skills for fun. Now I was relieved I knew them, lest Paul venture too quickly into deep water.

To my surprise, the stroke had brought Paul unexpected sensory bonuses. Everything looked brighter than before (though he was easily dazzled), sounds seemed louder (though noises could be more distracting), and his sense of touch actually improved. Diabetes and dermatitis had so dulled the nerves in his fingertips that for years he couldn't judge whether things were hot or cold, sharp or dull, rough or smooth. The skin on his fingers had peeled as if sunburned, becoming quite raw, and in time his fingerprints simply sloughed away. But they serve a purpose, those loopy weather systems. Detecting life's finer textures, they report on a minutely sculpted world of geography and architecture too small to see. As a finger glides across a fabric, a tribe of touch receptors (for pain, pressure, shape, temperature, etc.) fire and fade, filtering information as they go, providing the brain with a vivid three-dimensional map. Silky, warm, springy, wispy, corrugated like bark: a shawl of ruched cashmere fine enough to pass through a ring. A receptor will only fire when the surface is perpendicular to the fingerprint ridges, but since they ripple and swirl, it doesn't matter which direction a finger moves in, at least some of the receptors will be activated. Hence the amplified delight of caressing almost anything. Criminals who erase their fingerprints, hoping to make no impression, sacrifice pleats of delicate awareness in the process. Pre-stroke, Paul could still divine many textures, but not all, and not with the same finesse as healthy fingers. After the stroke, his whole brain grew so agitated that his senses perked up, and he would touch things reverently, appreciating the sheer feel of life.

"Skin . . . so . . . soft," he said one day, stroking my freckled arm as we basked in the sun. "Sun . . . so . . . *hot*." And later, in the pool, "Air . . . so . . . *smooth* . . . water . . . so . . . so . . ."

"Furry?" I offered. Trying to second-guess him was a mug's game. But it's hard to resist completing an aphasic's sentence when it's fluttering like a kite tail. Especially if he's struggling fiercely to communicate.

He shook his head no.

"Velvety?"

". . . *Silky!*" he blurted out at last.

Admiring the blooming pink hibiscuses beside the house, he asked if they were new—they'd been there for at least a decade. He studied their flouncy petals with lingering delight. He rejoiced in hearing the birds singing, especially the tuneful wren in the evergreen next to the back door, which serenaded without letup. Paul whistled back to it in encouragement. Still, the garden, the water, the sky—out of the wintry white of the hospital, he beheld nature with an unspoiled eye, as if he were on an expedition to a planet orbiting a distant star.

A fresh concern: walking the few yards to the pool one day, he tripped and fell into a flower bed, fortunately cushioned by a mattress of phlox. Another time, climbing up the pool ladder, he lurched after the last rung and sat-fell down on the grass. Try as he might, he couldn't get up by himself. Fearing for his safety (What if he fell when no one else was home? What if I didn't hear him?), I contacted a garden service to install a railing, one that led from the back door to the pool ladder. It would have been easy for me to tell the workmen what height to make it, but then Paul would have had to watch passively while his sense of liberty weakened even more. A subtle shade of difference separates a crutch you design and the one imposed upon you. So he mutely oversaw the installation of the solid, pipe-like railing, taking his time to judge the absolutely perfect height for the grip bar, and demonstrating it to the workmen.

When the weather was nice, he insisted on walking down the driveway to fetch the mail, but on one occasion he fell, bruising himself badly, unable to get up. Hearing him cry out, I ran outside to help. So now I hurried to the front window whenever the screen door gave its telltale slam, and kept a watchful eye on him as he negotiated the short walk. Indoors, he bumped into furniture and caught his toe on the wall-to-wall living room rug, falling several times, not always telling me, until I noticed a new bruise or rug burn on his knees. I learned that this was not unusual. According to many studies, a frightening two-thirds of stroke patients fall during the first six months, and they're four times more likely to break a hip, whose sequelae can include another stroke. And so a new assassin shadowed him: *falling.* When a stroke weakens the body, it also sears the confidence. No more insouciant striding of the cricket player across the lawn. No more breezy upright ape.

"Use your eyes as searchlights," I urged, thinking he might respond to the WWII image from his childhood as we navigated the front walk.

He seemed to understand, fixing his eyes sharply on the ground before him, but instead of sweeping his head back and forth, he was staring right in front of his toes and inching forward.

"No, like this." I demonstrated, moving my head side to side in an exaggerated sweep of the ground about a yard in front of me as I walked a little, turned, and did the same returning. Paul watched intently. Didn't move, just watched, clearly puzzled. I repeated the exercise.

It reminded me of how a bird teaches a chick to fly. Wings cupped and tail feathers spread wide, it stalls into the nest with a *Like this!* Then hops onto the squishy rim of twigs, tilts forward, and drops clear before flapping. Over and over until nightfall, the same *Watch and do as I do,* sometimes for days. And all the while that coaching whistle to the chick. *I'm here. You can do it. I'm here.*

"Try again," I whispered. "You can do it. I'm here."

Paul mumbled to himself, walking, scouting some, walking a little more. Then he stared at me with a look that said: *What kind of man has to be taught how to walk?*

Our next lesson was indoors. By now we knew that Paul had to relearn how to pick himself up from a fall, and after much cajoling, he finally agreed to practice.

Together, holding on to the couch, we lowered ourselves to the rug.

"Not bad so far!" I joked.

"Hrrumph!" It was less an attempt at speech than a comment on the likelihood of his succeeding.

"Okay. Let's give it a try. Lie down like you just fell." I felt a bite of foreboding at the words.

He lowered himself onto the rug, face up like a stargazer. Struggling to find the words for something, he finally made do with a gravelly ". . . *Woof!*"

"Woof?"

"You know . . ." He swept a hand parallel to the ground, and with a flourish pointed to the brilliant sunlight spiraling in through the picture windows.

"Oh, you want to *spaniel.*" *Spaniel* was the term I'd coined for curling up in a warm pool of sunlight on the rug, with pooch-like dereliction, on a chilly day. We'd often spanieled together in the fiercely cold upstate winters.

"Sorry, no. The art of standing, please."

"Ah," Paul sighed, eyes brightening in recognition. The strum of a familiar chord. I heard it, too.

"Or the *heart* of standing," I said, alluding to a poignant poem by British poet and literary critic William Empson. About a brief affair in wartime, it kept chiming the refrain "The heart of standing is you cannot fly."

"Remember Empson?"

"Oh yes!" He laughed.

Many years before, Cambridge-educated Empson had been a visiting professor at Penn State, where Paul was teaching. Empson had arrived in town without his false teeth, which were being repaired, he'd said, and would be sent by sea mail. At least that's what we thought he'd said, since he gummed his jaws together as he spoke, and did a Cambridge lisp, pronouncing all *r*s like *w*s. Students were finding his garbled diction hard to follow, and in any case, he spent most of each day up to his gills in sherry. Paul had spotted him staggering to campus through deep snow one afternoon—a thin tousle-haired figure in tweed coat, college scarf, and bedroom slippers—and felt sorry enough for him to purchase a pair of galoshes, which he dutifully delivered to Empson's office, a few doors down from his own. As he arrived, he witnessed something only slightly more shocking than sad. On first glance, Empson appeared to be holding office hours, with one young man seated beside him at a large oak desk. Empson still had on his coat and scarf, and was reciting something drunkenly, with surprising affability, as the student playfully spun him round ever-so-slowly in his chair. The boy fled when Paul knocked on the doorjamb with the galoshes.

One evening we'd invited Empson to dinner, and since he told us he could only eat "slops" until his teeth arrived, I'd made vegetable soup, haddock fillets baked until they flaked apart, and English trifle (a layered dessert of sherry-soaked ladyfingers, vanilla pudding, strawberry Jell-O, and whipped cream). He arrived tipsy. To my dismay, he drank the soup by sucking it up off his spoon, cooling it in his mouth, and spitting it back out, then drinking it again. I couldn't interest him in anything else but scotch, while he reminisced about Paul's old mentor at Oxford, Freddy Bateson. After dinner, noticing our telescope, Empson had asked if he might see Saturn's rings, and we were happy to oblige, since it was a clear night, with Saturn a diamond-yellow spark above the rooftops. At first he had trouble balancing over the eyepiece, so Paul held his shoulders steady.

"There! Saturn—it's beautiful! I see the rings!" he'd gushed excitedly. And we were delighted to provide this small glint of the universe, a cold sherbety world as a digestive, until I realized that he wasn't looking through the eyepiece at all, but below it, at the porch light across the street.

Oh my god, I'd thought, catching Paul's eye. With a tilt of my head, I directed his gaze to the porch light, and Paul's brow lifted, though he said nothing.

Before leaving, Empson stood at the door, wearing his new galoshes, and slurred: "I'm going up to Hartford by bus next week, to pay a call on Wallace Stevens."

Paul and I had exchanged looks that said something like: *It would be laughable if it weren't tragic.* Poet Wallace Stevens had been dead for many years.

Not wanting to embarrass Empson and not knowing what on earth to reply, Paul had said only: "You'll find him changed."

I remembered the pain of witnessing the wreckage of a once-great mind. Had Empson been ill? Senile? At the very least, he was being pulled down by a whale of an addiction. I thought: *Poor soul. Why wasn't I more compassionate?*

All I said was: "Remember Empson at the telescope?"

"I see the rings!" Paul chuckled. "Hey . . . look for p-planets? If we s-stare at ceiling . . ."

"Sorry, no more stalling. Time to practice." I visualized the diagram I'd studied in the doctor's office, depicting the easiest way to rise from a fall, and began coaching:

"Turn your head to the side, honey. *Other* side. Now, roll your shoulder in the same direction, and let your hip roll, too. *Great.* Now bring your right arm across like this and put your palm on the floor." I demonstrated, feeling a bit overwhelmed, as if I were coaching a giant sea tortoise how to right itself. But with a little effort, he followed suit.

"Good! The next step is to get onto all fours, like you're going to crawl."

He did, looking quite proud of himself. "Easy as pie. Now what?"

"Tuck your knees under." I bent my knees.

Tottering a little, Paul did the same, and I held an arm out, ready to steady him.

"Then you use your arms to push yourself up." With that, I stood up, and Paul toppled onto the rug.

Looking down at him, I smiled encouragingly, and worried if he had the strength to pull this off.

He grumbled. "Okay . . . *again!*"

"Wait now, catch your breath." This standing stuff wasn't easy. "Okay, here's another plan. You get on all fours and crawl over to a chair, or the couch, or even a wall. Want to try that?"

"Do I have a . . . ch-choice? I'm on the floor!" Losing patience, he crawled to the couch, grabbed it with one hand, then the other, and pulled himself up.

"Wonderful!" I whooped in delight. "You're breathing hard. Are you okay?"

Paul nodded yes, then said: "Breathing hard—better, better . . . better than . . . oh, you know, the other thing."

"The other thing?"

"The other thing," he insisted.

Breathing hard, better than . . . the other thing, the other thing . . . What does he mean?

"Than hardly breathing!" he finally blurted out.

I hugged him. "Congratulations! You stood up, and you found the words you wanted. Two bull's-eyes."

He fixed me with a gaze that didn't need words, about how far he'd really fallen, and how quickly the yardstick of success can change.

"Remember the title of that Richard Farina book—*Been Down So Long It Looks Like Up to Me*?" I asked.

His eyes closed, as he nodded in desolate agreement, "Bull's-eye."

Because he was no longer patrolling the hallways of the night, watching old movies reserved for night-dwellers, or working on a manuscript, he became diurnal for the first time in his life. We rose and retired together, like two breaths bound by the same rhythm. Our nights started early, at 10 p.m. or so, and collapsed into the sleep of bone-weary fatigue, the heavy rubbery sleep one finds on especially arduous expeditions. Paul, who used to go to sleep at 5 a.m. and sleep for six hours, now slept for ten and woke refreshed. I slept for nine and woke tired.

In most of my dreams, I kept anxiously trying to reach *home*, a cloud-draped empire of calm and safety. Bedraggled from travel, I felt lost and alone, and Paul could no longer help me navigate. A typical one found me in England, out shopping and laden with a bag of fresh produce, as rain pinwheeled down. I was drooping with fatigue, so I decided to flag a taxi to take me home, then realized to my alarm that I didn't know the address, had never stayed there before. Paul was already at the flat, and I phoned him on my cell phone. But, for the life of him, he couldn't remember the address either. As tired as I was, I patiently asked him to try to remember, then to check for envelopes that might be lying around with his address on it, or to look at the number on the front door. Growing impatient, I knew even in my dream that losing my cool would only fluster him, and there was nothing he could do about his condition. So I spoke calmly. But I worried if I would ever find my way, and it was telling, I suppose, that in my dreams I was adjusting to Paul not being able to help, let alone direct, me.

Nor could we any longer divide up territory in terms of time. His turf had been the somber, secluded, star-spangled night, when he would do his writing; and my territory the bare-faced, incandescent assemblages of morning, when I enjoyed the frisson of waking early, before household and neighbors, and having the world to myself.

My routine was to slide into a green velour robe and stagger to the kitchen, barefoot, in a waking dream. I'd turn on the stove, then follow steps constant as the heavens: unscrew the brass espresso maker, fill its wide hips with filtered water, nestle the coffee sieve into it, open a bag of ground espresso beans, inhale the aroma of smoky-vanilla almond butter, inhale the aroma again, measure two scoops into the sieve, tamp it down with the scoop's flat side, screw on the top of the coffeepot, place it on the gently luminous stove ring, begin preparing the foamy milk by plugging in a milk frother, filling its reservoir with filtered water, plugging together three small pieces of the frothing nozzle, attaching the oval milk silo, half filling it with skim milk, waiting for the red ready light to glow, listening for the huffing and chuffing of the espresso maker to begin, sliding a stainless steel cup under the frothing nozzle, holding the flow button down with one hand while lifting and rotating the cup with the other as steam rasped through the milk, which it heated and whisked until it leapt out billowy, building a rising white soufflé, and I lifted my finger off the button, just in time, before the cup runneth over, while hearing the espresso maker begin chugging unevenly like a steam train straining upgrade in the Andes, and at last coughing tubercularly as it finished perking. Then I'd scoop dollops of froth into a large yellow cup, after which I'd pour a chaser of thin bitter espresso right through the center, and follow up with another layer of frothy milk. Such routines focused my mind, inviting the muse to dine. Making cappuccino at home was my equivalent of the oriental tea ceremony, and helped to seal my attention, something I needed before padding down the hallway to begin work.

Now that Paul was waking with me, I couldn't afford so much personal time at breakfast, and I switched to a quick mug of green tea spiked with ginger. No longer beginning the day in solitude was a big loss. It took away a peaceful oasis, it narrowed my sense of self. In those solo hours, I had been able to expand, fill up the space, sprawl a little. Or maybe it wasn't as passive as that. Maybe I widened it and used it in the ways I commanded, filling the space with writing or whatever else I was doing. As the day dawned, I sometimes felt like I was the only person in the world, and it gave me a glorious sense of freedom. I wrote between the tick and tock of the clock, between dream and wakefulness, wading into lagoons of perception and thought, and by the time I emerged from the bay window for a second cup of coffee or tea, I would have written a page or three, barely knowing what they were about. Often I would drift outside for a spell and patrol the morning, surrounded by ancient forces much greater than I, feeling a kinship with lichen and deer, dawning with the rest of nature.

It was quite shocking, suddenly, to have Paul join me in the kitchen.

"Honey, it's early," I'd tell him. "I don't think you've had enough sleep."

And some mornings, to my relief, he would trundle back to bed for a few hours. If not, he demanded breakfast, "But *hungry.*" Which I could not ignore. So my half-awake Impressionist world with its spell of bright crinkled edges and dawn light would be broken, jarred, as I brought myself into focus with a snap, ready and able to test Paul's blood sugar, give him medications, inject insulin, fix breakfast, fret about his catching bits of breakfast in his throat.

For decades before Paul's stroke, I'd traveled on my own, and we'd spent semesters teaching in different cities, our time essentially our own again, our relationship alive in the dimensions of telephone, letters, packages, and not-too-often, warm skin, fingertips, and breath. I didn't wish to go back to those days of *telegamy*, as we called it, marriage at a distance, didn't prefer leading separate lives. But I knew I'd need to find a way to reclaim some cherished solitude, and I wasn't quite sure how.

It was also arduous for me not to feel impatient and resentful at times in the role of teacher, attendant, nurse: *caregiver*. That word should weigh more than others on a page, sag it down a bit and wrinkle it, because the simple-sounding job frazzles as it consumes and depletes. Not that it's only gloomy. Caregiving offers many fringe benefits, including the sheer sensory delight of nourishing and grooming, sharing, and playing. There's something uniquely fulfilling about being a lodestar, feeling so deeply needed, and it's fun finding creative ways to gladden a loved one's life. But caregiving does buttonhole you; you're stitched in one place. With children, this labor is an investment in their future, and they sponge up lessons. With a stroke victim it's also a relic of their past. While children learn following an upward arc, like wide-winged and clumsy albatrosses, stumbling at first, but rising and growing stronger and sleeker each day, Paul wasn't on a learning curve but seemed trapped in a circle. He'd swoop forward only to loop back again and fall to earth.

One day, for example, we rehearsed over and over his answering the telephone: lifting up the handset, pressing the big pink button to turn it on, speaking into the perforations. Two days later, he stood beside the ringing phone, finally picked up the receiver, ignored the pink button, and immediately pressed a slew of wrong buttons, only to hear a robotic voice announce: "The answering machine is OFF."

"Hello?" he said, thinking a caller was addressing him.

Once again I demonstrated how to use the phone.

Words for learning tend to suggest feasting on the world—*digest, absorb, soak up, assimilate, grasp, take in*. Paul slipped, went astray, blundered back to square one, groping for tidbits a toddler would have scooped up and assimilated with ease.

His working memory had been damaged, and without that temporary mental clipboard on which we scribble a few chunks of information while we're using them, it's impossible to remember a telephone number long enough to dial it, or even how a sentence you're uttering began. It's usually limited to seven elements, which is why telephone numbers have seven digits. I realized Paul had to relearn what he'd "learned" only the day before, unable to remember instructions, especially ones with a couple of steps.

Learning seems like such an elite skill, but even the lowliest vinegar worm, blessed with only 302 neurons, can learn from experience which bacteria to eat and which could make it sick. A fruit fly can learn to avoid orange jelly spiked with quinine (researchers can be so strangely creative and so cruel); a blue jay can learn that biting a monarch butterfly's wing will make it vomit; a firefly can learn the flashy Morse code of its mate. Any creature with a nervous system can learn, if it has enough time, and doesn't quit from boredom, and isn't overwhelmed by competing stimuli. This gave me such hope, but how much could Paul relearn?

Yes, caregiving had its hopes and charms, but on the downside, this meant that every hour was interruptible. My days no longer contained adjoining hours in which to work. Yet I had a new book to write, situated in WWII Poland, blessedly far away in time and space. So while Paul was straining mentally to reclaim language, I was straining to learn the peculiar skill of concentrating on my work in attention gulps. A trick parents learn from the get-go with kids; they pretty much have to. Plus they learn to work while keeping one ear open for signs of discord or trouble. Such parenting skills, though new for me, came with many others: teaching him how to hold a spoon or fork, where the light switches he'd used for decades were located, how to climb into a car, step over curbs, open a pull-tab carton of milk.

One morning he complained, "I can't even wipe my ass right," and so I found myself patiently explaining that he was still using his right hand, the one half-paralyzed, and he might try to use his good left hand instead. Later in the day, I saw him seated on the toilet, following my advice.

"Better?" I asked, and he nodded his head yes.

So much now dumbfounded him, especially household gadgets, in part because his vision had suffered and gadgets tend to have many insufferably small black buttons. I tried to reinvent the house so that he could live in it safely with as much independence and as little frustration as possible. A raised toilet seat. Big red dots on the microwave panel marking #1 or #2 minutes, so that he could warm things up. The stove was off-limits. Because it was impossible for him to remember a simple series of numbers, I bought a telephone with big buttons and programmed in phone numbers so that he could speed-dial my cell phone, 911, his doctor, and two friends. A larger, simpler TV remote. But he still couldn't work the TV remote well; the symbols looked like geometric faces. Inevitably he pushed the wrong button, which began a cascade of button-pushing that only made matters worse. Embarrassed, he often summoned me just to turn the TV on or off, or show him yet again how to change the channel or volume.

Shaving ham-fisted with a safety razor left him so bloodied that I bought him an electric razor. He struggled to use that one, too, and would emerge from the bathroom, thinking himself shaven, with only two-thirds of his stubble gone, wild white tufts poking up among clean patches, and the right side of his right cheek (which he couldn't see) still growing strong. It never seemed worth sending him back to fix.

Such little oddments contribute to the texture of a relationship. Paul still wasn't realizing all that he'd lost, but one day, out of the blue, he told me that he felt like something important had fallen out of his life.

"What?" I asked. He didn't know, couldn't remember, but he felt something missing. And all he wanted to do was sit and stare out the windows.

"Are you sad?" I asked.

"No, just . . ." He tried to continue but the next words seemed to be snatched from his mouth and carried away. Finally he came out with: "Just sitting and staring."

And I believed him. For voluptuous brooding you need an array of words. So in a way it was still a blessing that he didn't know what he was missing.

In *The Immensity of the Here and Now*, a book whose title I've always coveted, Paul wrote about a philosopher who had lost his philosophy after 9/11, and whose best friend provided him with a new one: that of the philosopher Ludwig Wittgenstein. What was I to do with a wordsmith who had lost his language?

We modern humans are distinguished from our predecessors by lavish, sometimes outlandish, spells of self-awareness. Our scientific label says it all. We're not just *Homo sapiens*—knowing man—but rather *Homo sapiens sapiens*—the man who knows and *knows* he knows. Today, all that knowing requires language, speech, and written words—three distinctly different tasks. Paul's global stroke had nearly stolen from him the second *sapiens* of *Homo sapiens sapiens*. Paul was learning more words, but to *know* you know requires many more connections, much more than a heap of nouns. Knowing the names for things like *parachute* and *candelabra* and *uncle* won't save you if your uncle attacks you with a candelabra for stealing his parachute. That requires a web of understanding: how heavy the sterling silver candelabra is, the grudge your mother's brother always held against you, knowing what a parachute is used for, being able to compute the speed at which he's running after you and whether you can outrun him, remembering that your mother warned you about him, and many more wordy twists and turns that reveal the intricate relationships between yourself and the world around you, and the people and objects who inhabit that world.

Unlike most other animals, we're not locked inside a fast, reflexive, yet limited world of immediate sensory experiences. To live in the present is refreshing and fascinating—if you're a human and it spares you a conflagration of self-sabotaging doubts. Probably not so for animals forever bound to each vanishing moment. We live in vanishing moments, too. We're also curbed by our senses. But we can *imagine* the luminous spirits of worlds that are not physically knowable to our senses in the here and now, worlds imperceptible yet thinkable because people once spoke and/or wrote about them—the lands of history, fantasy, religion, the future, might-have-been, doesn't-exist-yet-but-could-just-work, and so on. We imagine the possible through words. We use words to help us remember who and what we are. We refine how we love in words. We use words to solve problems—partly because a language that offers the word *problem* by necessity must include the word *solution*. Both words include the absorbing idea that a human is an animal who can act upon the world in such a way as to solve a problem. Using those words teaches us that we can master the world by understanding it. The more complex our words, the more layered our story, the more refined our understanding. Some grains of knowing are only possible when passed through the sieve of carefully arranged words. In *Life with Swan*, Paul wrote of us:

> One of our favorite words was *salience*, for how something shoots out at you and "gets" you. We were always surrounded by saliences: the world bristled and sparkled, came out to meet us, and we went toward it. . . .

Sitting and staring at the yard, Paul could no longer say: "It's a bright but foggy day. Not like yesterday. Maybe it will burn off or blow over." Instead, his mouth stiffened, then relaxed, stiffened, then relaxed, until he finally managed to say: "T . . . t . . . trans . . . trans . . . trans . . . trans-*lu*-cent." Then he settled back into the folds of the sofa and smiled in pleasure. He had grown thinner in the last month, and the cushion behind him fitted comfortably into the curve of his neck.

Oh! I thought. *He knows the difference between* translucent *and* transparent—*between a well-lit but unclear state, and light passing through something with clarity. His brain still knows how to use words to express fine distinctions. And the smile? Because he knows he knows.*

"My little *Homo sapiens sapiens*," I said, much to his amusement, as I hugged him tight.

CHAPTER 14

THE HOUSE WAS FULL OF WHISPERS, BECAUSE PAUL'S BRAIN had trouble coordinating lung and face muscles to blow resonant breath back into speaking. We made rubbery faces to practice sounding out letters, and we rehearsed *w* by puckering up for kisses. In the evenings, as we sat in the comforting depths of the old rose-covered couch, finding a word could take as much as half an hour for Paul, as I tried to guess his target. I learned to ask him sorting questions.

"Light house keeper," Paul said, pronouncing each word in the same flat rasp, with no gesture, pitch, stress, or facial expression to act as a guide.

What on earth did he mean? If he meant a person who operates a lighthouse, he would have emphasized the word *light*. If he meant someone who cleans a little, he would have emphasized the word *house*. If he meant a light-haired domestic, he would have emphasized the word *light* and paused before saying *housekeeper*.

"Is it a person?"

"No . . ." He slapped the couch impatiently.

"Does it have to do with you?"

"Yes." He leaned forward, and I had the sense that we were closing in on it.

"Your pills?"

"No . . ."

"Food?"

"No . . . *inferior* . . ."

"Is it a feeling?"

Now his face twisted a little in a mobile expression that usually means "sort of," and he stretched his fingers wide on both hands and waved them back and forth.

"An object?"

"No . . . *light house keeper* . . ."

Roundabout, we finally drew closer to what he meant, maddeningly closer, with Paul making do at last with a synonym rather than the exact word. How close he came, I couldn't know, except by how triumphant he looked after uttering the word "replica." All I could figure was that his brain felt like a replica of its old self. Or: once a lighthouse keeper, it now was reduced to doing light housekeeping. The exchange made him concentrate so hard that he worked up a sweat.

"Are you too hot?" I asked.

And to my delight he answered: "No, a tiny zephyr roamed through the yard for about a minute and a half and it felt good."

I laughed, and he laughed too, but only after a pause, when he realized that he'd said something amusing. I squeezed his arm appreciatively.

All he meant was that a breeze had wafted through the screen door. Unable to say that, he made do with kindred words—any he could grab. *What a picturesque tumble of words*, I thought. *As a poet, I'd have to labor for an image like that.* Looking out at the yard, I imagined a tiny humanoid zephyr, a barely visible wind with eyes.

I felt tired as wet sand, but that didn't matter. Few things are as delicious as sitting quietly under a canopy of stars and opening your senses to the world. The moon was lighting lamps across the eastern sky. As more stars blinked on, the black velvet sparkled with their diamond-backed catastrophes. When I heard a tapping, I traced the sound through the wall to the bedroom on the other side with its two large windows. Branches were rapping against the glass like poltergeists. In my mind's eye: a crooked bony finger, a twig, a finger, a twig, *tapping, tapping, tapping.* A cat stole like wind through the bushes. Or maybe it was the wind conjuring up a cat. Hard to say, when the sun fades and the brain loses its brilliant lens on the world. We weren't born to roam at night; our senses falter. Not like the yard's covenant of garter snakes, sporting long red ribbons down their backs, nesting somewhere between the warm pool liner and the food-fragrant soil.

I wondered what Paul was thinking, and sensing, but didn't bother asking him. He'd fought hard enough for words all day, and deserved to rest a spell. Fortunately he loved to sit and stare, too, and never grew bored. In *Life with Swan,* a novel loosely based on our life together, he once wrote:

> A couple who can spend half an hour watching a female cardinal sit inside a bird-feeder . . . can do other things too, such as sitting by a table covered with amaryllises and dahlias, pretending it is already spring, or staring at the curvature and convolutions of a nail clipping.
>
> This contemplative savoring was always ours, not something we aspired to or had ever read about, but a natural twitch to be reckoned with, its main implication a simple one: There will always be more to gaze and marvel at, even on the level of the commonplace, than we will ever be able to attend to. For us both, it was a matter of being plonked down amid an ongoing miracle whose component parts could not be counted. *Staring at stuff,* I always called it; the account of this activity needs no fancier phrase. So we could often be spotted staring overlong at sheep, birds, grasses, or a harvest mouse. . . .

Staring together was easy, communicating was brutally hard, and not just with me. After a few weeks, I acquired Durable Power of Attorney so that I could speak legally on his behalf and help him pay his bills. He'd completely forgotten how to write checks, so I wrote them for him, and he signed, left-handed, in a strange craggy scrawl. It brought back memories of my father teaching me how to write my first check when I was college-bound. All one day, Paul tried, in increasingly agitated ways, to say that he expected a check to come in, a reimbursement from his medical insurance company, but he didn't have the words. I finally understood when it arrived days later. Addressing an envelope, paying a bill—all posed fatiguing challenges. And when he spoke—to me or to a bank teller—any random word could dash out of his mouth before he had time to find the right one.

Most confusing, perhaps, he didn't use pronouns correctly, and they're often the first word in a sentence. I would try to interpret what he was saying, only to discover in time that he was referring to a woman, not a man. Or that he was referring to himself as "he," not "I." Was this merely a language problem, or was it something graver, a loss of a coherent sense of self? What with feeling foreign to himself, and all the people dealing with him as a thing to be fixed, was his sense of self flickering from "me" to "him"?

When the speech therapist visited to do her initial evaluation, she recorded the following among her notes, underscoring Paul's limits by repeating the single word *severe,* until it lost its impact and she had to fortify it with bold type:

The patient presents with **severe** verbal expression deficits . . . The patient presents with **severe** reading comprehension deficit. Given large print single words the patient was able to read words out loud, however he was not able to demonstrate comprehension of the words. The patient presents with **severe** written expression deficits.

Paul's speech therapy followed a standard program which included sounding out letters and syllables, learning the names for common objects, communicating basic wants, reading short sentences, and comprehending talk. But as I quickly learned, it's designed for acute problems, in the hopes of teaching stroke patients how to navigate the chief activities of everyday life. It's not intended to help aphasics regain their lost treasure of words, express subtleties, or be nuanced listeners. I understood the therapists were trying to rebuild Paul's vocabulary, beginning with the rudiments, but Paul found it taxing, boring, and disturbingly condescending. His loss of language didn't mean he was any less a grown-up with adult feelings, experiences, worries, and problems. After all his years of education, Paul was now toiling over the equivalent of a first grader's lesson book, which he found demoralizing. And yet, because of where his brain was damaged, he couldn't connect even simple objects to their names. At night, in the familiar refuge of his study, he labored over the day's homework.

As I peered in at him, unobserved, the light fell across his desk from the side. It looked like a scene in a Dutch master's painting, of a man cramped over his workbench, struggling to master a few stubborn diagrams. So engrossed was he, he didn't sense my presence, and he could no longer see things off to his right, anyway, so I craned my neck a little closer. Solemnly, as if they were sketches of family members he used to be able to recognize on sight, he considered the drawings of a chair, a lamp, a dog, unable to match them with the words in a column on the opposite side of the page. At last, with strain cutting shadowy creases on his forehead, he connected the chair with the word "dog." Looked at it a moment. What was it, the four legs, that confused him? It reminded me of René Magritte's painting *The Key of Dreams*, in which three out of four objects are incorrectly labeled, with a horse called a door, a clock called the wind, a pitcher the bird, and only a valise the valise. Magritte meant to confuse viewers, on purpose, by connecting unrelated words and images.

On the next page, some categories made sense to him, while others ("name five fruits") proved such a bugbear that when I quietly stole away and returned in half an hour, he had only thought of four, three of which were wrong. Half an hour later, I returned to discover that he had revised the four, nearly mummifying them with Type White and strips of correction tape, and the revised versions were still wrong.

He reluctantly turned a page to even more categories, as if slaying one dragon only to engender a dozen offspring. Sighing, he rubbed his eyes with both hands, then picked up the felt pen, whose barrel had been widened with a rubber easy-grip saddle. In two determined swipes of black, he mismatched "Monday" with "month" and "August" with "day," and turned the page.

The brain's sorter was injured and off-duty, making thinking in categories a nightmare; and yet categories are essential for language, which otherwise would be a stream of nouns and verbs without any conceptual lakes uniting them. We're not alone in this. Other animals—from chimpanzees and parrots to border collies, chinchillas, macaques, and quail—group important things, too, obsessively sorting the chaos into helpful mental bins. A brain stores those bins in different physical locations, where a small lesion can wreck havoc. Some patients have startlingly specific category deficits: they can't say colors, or the names of animals, fruits, famous people, vegetables, flowers, or tools.

Drawing in a breath, Paul puffed his cheeks out like the North Wind on an old map, and then exhaled thoughtfully. Next to "opaque" he circled the category "color." A color? It could certainly function as one, just as glare seemed to paint a new color in the Antarctic, and that's something he might once have fancied. But he wasn't playing with ideas now, he was groping for words in a mental blizzard.

Paul finally stopped from sheer fatigue, his mind blunt as a pencil after a long exam. The homework drained his whole brain of spare energy; he couldn't speak as he tottered down the hallway and into the bedroom. Normally, sleep after study helps to seal facts in memory. But in his case, he barely had enough wattage left to run the city-state of his body. Instinctively, the way a whooping crane seeks home, he sought the tonic of sleep to revive him.

While he catnapped, I paged through his corrected workbook in disbelief. Told to circle the right word, he'd put an X over it instead, gotten three out of five wrong and hadn't even guessed at four others. On another sheet, he had mismatched "radio" with something to be watched, "weatherman" with conducting traffic.

Yes, he had marked, *salt is green*.

He wasn't sure if one could see *through* a mirror.

No, he had answered to "Can you see your shadow at night?" I smiled wryly. No was the correct answer. But something can be accurate without being true. There are moon shadows. And night itself is a shadow, nothing that falls, but the darkness that gathers as the rolling earth turns its face from the sun. These were subtleties he once might have sported with, maybe in a yarn, certainly in our mealtime chitchat. Now he struggled just to fathom the basics.

"Say an appropriate word to complete the phrase," another exercise instructed, offering the first half of well-known sayings:

"Time waits for no ——."
"Look before you ——."
"The early bird catches the ——."
"Practice makes ——."
"Don't put all your eggs in one ——."
"You can't see the forest for the ——."
"A dog is man's best ——."

Paul had dutifully filled in blanks with misspelled clichés which, before the stroke, would have horrified him to repeat. Now they came easily to mind, because they're usually stored in the right hemisphere's library of overly familiar expressions, the verbal automata of everyday life, which may also include the Pledge of Allegiance, Christmas carols, favorite curse words, and advertising jingles. The oddest relicts may be preserved in an uninjured right hemisphere. "The golden touch of the Pennsylvania Dutch," Paul would suddenly singsong in a Pennsylvannia Dutch accent, remembering a commercial for egg noodles he used to hear when he lived in State College, Pennsylvania.

THE FOLLOWING DAY, he found me in the kitchen and pointed into his open mouth.

"Hungry?" I asked.

He nodded yes and parted his lips to speak, but nothing came out. Two more false starts. Then he took my hand, as if steadying himself on a narrow path, and shaking it gently for emphasis, said: "Nice ice."

At first glance, or listen, *nice ice* may sound rather cute, whimsical, childlike—which feels more comforting than the truth, that he was a very intelligent adult compensating as best he could for lapses, finding ways to make up for what wasn't available. Thus he drew on a word for a feeling, *nice ice*, and used rhyme to remember it. I brought him a small cardboard dish of sugar-free lemon sorbet.

"Thank you . . . you . . . ah . . . ah . . . oh . . ." His voice dropped down into a deep sadness.

"Diane."

He shook his head in shameful disbelief, and repeated "Diane."

Names of people—including mine and his mother's—were devilishly hard for him to lasso from the arroyos of his brain: a furtive herd of mustangs that kept bolting away.

Later he would tell me how *"on rare occasions, the word I sought lay like an angel, begging to be used, even if only to be used in spirit ditties of no tone. I had the beginnings of a word. Was I merely deluding myself with this childish phantom, or was there something to it, maybe miles away, maybe too far for customary use, and it would remain, a delusive harbinger of night, a word unborn, doomed to remain unsaid as* humm—*or* thal—*unable to complete itself because of my aphasic ineptitude."*

Many of the speech therapy exercises—matching word with object, filling in the blanks—emphasized the detailed, linear thinking that meant visiting the gaping ruins of Paul's private hell, his damaged left hemisphere. Good practice, designed to exercise his weakest areas, they nonetheless brought a steep sense of failure.

A lifelong overachiever and exceptional student, he knew that half wrong was a dismal result. And failing so miserably at simple exercises, he began to sink into a depression again.

Walking into the living room on a dazzling blue day fleeced with fair-weather clouds, I found Paul staring dismally at the floor. Earlier that morning, we'd lost patience with each other. I was dashing out for an appointment when he waylaid me with a request.

"Bring . . . bring . . . thing . . ." His face glazed with concentration, then he drew a square in the air. ". . . a long horse . . . *no!* not a long horse, the other thing . . ."

"Envelope?" I asked hurriedly.

". . . No . . . no . . . the other thing . . ."

I interrupted him. "We're not out of Slim Bears. I know that. Stamps?"

"Too fast!" He collected himself slowly, as I felt the minutes evaporating. I began edging toward the door, and he followed. "No . . . you know, the . . . the . . ." Again he traced a small square in the air.

"Paper?"

"*No!*"

"Cheese?"

"*No!*"

"Can you draw it on a sheet of paper?"

"Too fast! . . . What?"

I slowed way down. "Can you draw it on a sheet of paper?"

"*No!*" His eyebrows rose like brown smoke, and I could almost see steam venting from his ears, but I couldn't linger.

"I'm late. I'll be back in two hours. You can tell me then, okay?"

"WFFH!" He waved me away with an angry glower. "*Women!*"

I'd felt annoyed, but also guilty about foiling his effort. Indignant as he'd been, Paul felt even angrier with himself for failing to connect with me.

By the time I'd returned he'd completely forgotten what he'd wanted me to pick up, but not that he'd unsuccessfully tried to tell me something. I apologized for my rush. He nodded a resigned, gloomy yes. As we sat together on the couch, silence settled every-where like frost. According to an old adage, the secret to a good marriage is communication. How do you manage that when your loved one has lost most of his language?

I took his hand and said in a measured voice, "I know you're trying hard to communicate."

Desperate to buttress his spirits and buoy up my own, I had a series of points to make, and I didn't want to confuse him.

"But talking and communicating aren't the same thing," I went on. "We can communicate even though your talking doesn't work. . . . Yes, it takes longer, it's harder, it's not as complete, but it *is* possible! . . . Improving means staying together, and staying together means communicating, even if all the parts don't get said. . . . Who you are isn't tied solely to what you say, even though it may feel that way to you now. . . . We'll work this out together." Lurking unsaid was the fear that if he *didn't* improve he'd need institutional care.

My script, inspired by a residential aphasia program in the Mid-west, was supposed to bring comfort. I'd borrowed it from *Coping with Aphasia*. But Paul's sense of identity as a writer and a professor required words. Over a lifetime, he'd clung to them for solace, worked them to earn a living, juggled them to express himself, pinned them like butterflies to capture fleeting ideas and feelings. Via letters and phone calls, words always connected him to his family an ocean away, and to me, whether by his side or at the end of a phone line. Words were how he had always organized his world. He had chosen to live the proverbial "life of the mind" to the exclusion of all else, reserving his energy for writing and for his equally word-passionate wife. Taking words from Paul was like emptying his toy chest, rendering him a deadbeat, switching his identity, severing his umbilical to loved ones, and stealing his manna.

Words are such small things, like confetti in the brain, and yet they color and clarify everything, they can stain the mind or warp the feelings. Novelist William Gass, speaking to the students at Washington University (where I once taught), had extolled "the words the poet uses when she speaks of passions, or the historian when he drives his nails through time, or when the psychoanalyst divines our desires as through tea leaves left at the bottom of our dreams."

We snare things in words, if only for an instant, by ripping them from their compound relationships and freezing them in time. For instance, twenty clusters of wisteria are hanging right outside my bay window, each one a tidy tumble of gray-purple faces with lavender bonnets. I think they look like turn-of-the-century ladies seated in church pews. The word *wisteria* doesn't capture the vine's connection to the redbud tree, around which it spirals and climbs, choking it with fragile beauty, and the clay soil and southern dose of sun, and its dangling and swaying, and the rain and wind and multifiore garden, and this house and occupants, and the birds, bugs, and neighbors, and all the other *and*s that should trail invisibly from the word *wisteria* in an endless string of relations that evolves during the whole of its vigorous and purposeful life. When I call it *wisteria*, it becomes smaller, a symbol I use to communicate with others of my kind, whose own version of wisteria may be different from mine. And yet, words are the passkeys to our souls. Without them, we can't really share the enormity of our lives.

Paul used to write for hours in a dreamy state, tapping into the keg of his unconscious and letting words pour. I remembered his gluing oddments at the kitchen counter, whistling, and bending one leg like a stork, while Copland's Third Symphony boomed for the fifth time in a row in a full-scale echolalia. I remembered how he had daubed a sheet of brown butcher's paper with a blue wash, and finally held up his impromptu map: salt flats, Red Sea, desert zones. Chuckling, he had flagged a dune where the Danakil tribe and two lost airmen would meander and clash. Then he had hummed the Copland yet again, off-key. In time, the new novel, lurching around his psyche, dragged itself away and became real. How I had loved to see him shanghaied like that, careening down the rum-soaked wharves of imagination, where any roustabout idea might turn to honest labor. How on earth could Paul survive without his words? How could we?

CHAPTER 15

WHILE PAUL SLEPT, I MET MY FRIEND JEANNE FOR LUNCH at Moosewood, a vegetarian restaurant downtown serving my idea of comfort food ever since I was a student. There we sat at a shiny oak table beside a mantelshelf of moose memorabilia, presided over by a blackboard offering the day's specials. A novelist with short blond-flecked brown hair and hazel eyes, Jeanne had grown up nearby, in the small town of Geneva, New York, where she went to parochial school before moving to Ithaca and marrying a painter, Steve, who taught art at Cornell and moonlighted as an aerobatic biplane pilot and aerial artist (trailing smoke as he drew four-dimensional objects in the sky). She knew more about the texture of everyday life in past eras than just about anyone; excelled in kitchen and garden; and hand-stitched exquisite quilts. But, best of all, Jeanne could go from silly to serious and back again in a wink.

As I filled her in on Paul's condition, her eyes held me in a worried hug.

"He's able to say a few more words, though they tend to be odd or arcane."

"Like what?"

"Well, let's see . . . One of my favorites is *eldritch*," I said with a fleeting smile.

Jeanne looked amused. "That sounds like a cross between an elf and a witch!"

"It does. But it means *strange, eerie, weird*, as in: 'A flying saucer arose silently from an eldritch swamp.'"

"When did he learn *that*? Or where, for that matter."

"Heaven only knows."

My memory flitted to the day before, when Paul had stood at the living room window watching evening's grays smoke through the treetops. For long moments, he'd looked pained as he'd groped for the right words. Finally, turning to me with a satisfied look, he'd uttered the one word: "eldritch." Though it rang a distant bell, I had to turn to a dictionary, after which I'd found Paul again, still standing at the window, watching the sprinkler's rhythmic salaams to the garden. Taking his arm, reverently, I'd repeated: "eldritch."

"But he still doesn't understand much of what anyone says to him," I continued. "Reading, writing—all that's going so slowly. He's not accomplishing much with the speech therapist. And he's still having trouble swallowing. . . . But I don't want to sadden you with my grief," I said abruptly, cutting my account short.

"Are you kidding? You're my oldest friend in town. I'd be hurt if you *didn't* tell me what's happening. It's awful. I can't imagine how I'd cope if, god forbid, something like that happened to Steve." I watched her face blanch in fear, then soften once more, bearing sympathy.

"How are *you* doing?" I heard her ask.

A titanic question, and unanswerable, or so it seemed. I hadn't the faintest idea how I was. Token pleasantries wouldn't do ("I'm-fine-how-are-you?"), and there were no fresh bulletins from my overwhelmed psyche. I was moving in a narrow range between busy distractedness and a pervasive sadness whose granules seemed to enter each cell, weighing it down, one grain per cell, just enough in sum that I walked with head lowered, shoulders rolled into a slump, feet shuffling at a gait I associated with my parents when they were elderly, not a woman of still-reconnoiterable years. I ghosted between islands of anxiety (*I'm doing so little of my own work*) and a fatigue that dulled my zest, decanted it. Sorrow felt like a marble coat I couldn't shed.

"I don't *know* how I am," I said, idly stirring a mélange of French lentils, cabbage, and diced tomatoes. "I'm probably in shock, or traumatized. Sometimes it feels like I'm in a slow-motion car wreck, where the spinning never stops, and I keep trying to remember what to do—take my foot off the brake, yes, turn into the spin, yes—but nothing is working, and the car keeps spinning out of control."

"Oh, honey, that sounds terrifying!"

"It's that *churning* in my chest and stomach without the visuals. And then other times I'm in a sort of zombie haze, yet somehow speaking, moving, functioning, even making decisions about Paul's care—but all that's happening while I'm sleeping inside this real-life nightmare that keeps unfolding at new angles and growing deeper. Sometimes I feel so feeble, like a rag doll that's been shaken day after day. . . . See? I told you, I really don't *know* how I am. Except that I'm a mess."

Jeanne's eyes clouded. "You know, I bet a big source of stress comes from feeling like you're responsible for his recovery."

"I do feel like I'm responsible. He used to be able to look after himself. Now he can't. That's so different, so strange. The big question is: Is more improvement really possible, or should I stop pushing him?"

I couldn't remember the last time my vigilant selves could leave their posts and swan around.

"What do his doctors say?"

"They don't really know. It's still early days. So little is known about the brain. Even less about broken brains."

Leaning forward, she stared straight into me. "What can I do to help?"

I thought about the question for a while, as I submerged my

spoon and let it fill with the fragrant stew. Finally, I met her eyes, which still held their concern.

"I haven't a clue."

AT HOME, I flickered between denial and anguish. In one of the denial moments, which occurred often and briefly (but at other times could upend a whole afternoon), I saw signs of the old Paul, the familiar spouse, returning home to his historic self after a sojourn away in the wars.

There he was at his desk, cackling to himself as he looked at a photograph of the Versailles Conference of 1919. A sick old man and a young boy peered side by side from his eyes. I didn't have to ask what he was up to—I knew the mist his brain gave off when it was dreaming up a new story. He must have sensed me at his side.

Revolving toward me, unexpectedly, he said: "Gorgeous . . . name some flowers. . . ."

"Roses, lilacs, daffodils, tulips, peonies—?"

"Peonies," he cut in. "The yellow ones."

My mind chased around—which peonies? Oh, *our* peonies, the ones out front. "They really are gorgeous! I love their big fluffy yellow cuffs."

"Cuffs," he repeated slowly, savoring the word, perhaps picturing men in long-sleeved shirts with ruffled cuffs and onyx stickpins at a Manhattan soiree in the early 1900s. The perfect setting for a novel by Henry James.

"I planted that bush five years ago, and do you know I moved it to three different locations before I found the right combination of soil, light, and neighbors for it. High-strung plant, but beautiful—like one of those toy show dogs."

"You're plucky! And I'm . . ." He smiled, amused by what he was going to say next: "lucky. You're plucky and I'm lucky." He chuckled at the rhyme.

Normally, it would then be my turn to nudge the game of word dominoes forward, as in: "You're plucky, and I'm lucky, ducky." To which he'd reply: "You're plucky, and I'm lucky, ducky, not mucky." And so on. Whoever ran out of add-ons first lost. This time, I didn't press him to continue; I wasn't sure he could.

Still, in that moment fragrant with hope, I believed life hadn't really collapsed all around me, that I wouldn't just be grateful for the few crumbs of our relationship that remained, but could return to *How It Was*, that just-so land lost in fog.

Lying in my bay window a little later, I faced the loss more squarely. Then it crushed me with its heavy machinery, and nothing, not even a glorious vineyard of wisteria or a wren's long cantata, could save me from feeling flattened beyond repair.

Faith is a liquor that comes in various strengths and is often flavored by chance. When I looked out over the grass where the midday sun had created a cartography of light and shadow, I had faith that each of the clover blossoms contained nectar. But my faith in Paul's improving, healing back into language, changed from moment to moment, day to day, and when it vanished nothing filled its hollow. I found playing through my mind the last line of a favorite Robert Frost sonnet, "The Oven Bird":

> There is a singer everyone has heard,
> Loud, a mid-summer and a mid-wood bird,
> Who makes the solid tree trunks sound again.
> He says that leaves are old and that for flowers
> Mid-summer is to spring as one to ten.
> He says the early petal-fall is past
> When pear and cherry bloom went down in showers
> On sunny days a moment overcast;
> And comes that other fall we name the fall.
> He says the highway dust is over all.
> The bird would cease and be as other birds
> But that he knows in singing not to sing.
> The question that he frames in all but words
> Is what to make of a diminished thing.

What to make of a diminished thing, that was the question. The injury was permanent, I told myself, and Paul needed to understand that. With any luck, his skills might continue to improve some, though if they did, it would probably take years. But the lesions in his brain wouldn't disappear, he would never return to his life before the stroke. That wasn't a realistic goal, for me or for Paul. He needed a new perspective on who he was: not a hopelessly faded photograph of his old self, but a work in progress. And I knew I needed to come to terms with this, too.

I hadn't realized how much hope was still woven into my consciousness, how much denial of the obvious, overestimation of small triumphs, and a hard refusal to admit that Paul, his gift, our life together as it had been, was gone. I saw that clearly now. What remained would gradually acquire its own shape and dimension, but many of our favorite things, my favorite ways of being a couple, had vanished and it was no use pretending, hoping, wishing that he would return to his old self, and me to mine. I mean to the *us* that once lived in our house, once furnished so much of my life, the symbiotic self spouses evolve together and cherish. There was no going back to how things were. A hard truth to accept, even if no one and nothing is ever what it was.

Everywhere I looked, nature flowed indivisibly as one stream of atoms. Paul had merely borrowed 4×10^{27} carbon atoms from the universe, which he must one day return, maybe as lichen or tree, either one the journeywork of stars. "I bequeath myself to the dirt to grow from the grass I love," Walt Whitman wrote in *Leaves of Grass*, "If you want me again look for me under your boot-soles." Nothing, not anyone, is an unchanging event, no blade of grass or self exactly what it was a moment ago.

I tried my best not to compare his new state to how he was before the stroke, but rather to how bad off he was *at the time of* the stroke. Before the stroke no longer existed. But it was hard to hide my anguish. And he often looked at me with eyes clearly saying: *Who are you kidding, you fond fool.*

CHAPTER 16

A MIDDLE-AGED HOME HEALTH AIDE I'LL CALL FRED HAD joined us at first, a quiet man with a shaved head, freckled face, and genteel manner, who collected antiques and loved to cook. He had ways both strong and delicate, could hoist a grown man out of bed or arrange flowers in tiny pots with tender precision. One day, after he knew us for a while, he confided that when he was in high school his mother, learning that he would never be in a traditional marriage, encouraged him to take a course called "Housekeeping for Bachelors," which he had relished. A knowledgeable aide with an understanding of the health care system, he often prepared Paul's pills and routines and helped him dress and safely roam the house. Fred was a real character, but I'm going to tell you very little about him, because in time we discovered that he was stealing cash from Paul, using Paul's credit card for personal expenditures, and other misdeeds, and we had to let him go. This was our first experience with "elder abuse," and it took me the longest time and clearest evidence to accept. Paul suspected Fred sooner, and I've since learned that some people with left-hemisphere stroke, like Paul's, actually improve their skill at interpreting people's faces and catching people in lies. Unfortunately, I've also learned that elder abuse is all too common, and not always easy to spot since one isn't expecting it and the abusers can be charming. It seems all the more grievous since the victims are the most sick and vulnerable among us.

Fred's larceny soured Paul on the idea of aides. It was hard for him to understand why home help was so important for *me*, that, just as he found struggling to talk exhausting, I found it exhausting to interpret. It meant changing my mental gait and slowing way down, not peacefully, allowing moments to gather and stream away, but strenuously, as a sort of code-breaking that took total concentration. I was a spy in the service of love. There was no way to do it nimbly, or hastily, or indefatigably. After several hours, I'd blow a mental fuse, my brain would stop decoding, my head would ache, and I'd need to rest. Casual couple's chitchat that used to wash over me without working the brain too hard had become strenuous. I reminded myself how frightening and formidable it was for Paul. Sometimes, guiltily, waiting for five or ten minutes for him to find words to express one simple thought, I might feel antsy, the physical equivalent of *Get on with it!* When rushed, I didn't always have the patience to *sit, sit, sit*, waiting for him to make himself known. But mostly I understood, felt sorry for him, and sat.

Fred could wait for longer spells while Paul cast about for words, indeed spend most of the day in quiet reveries. He didn't talk much to Paul, and I knew that Paul needed an "enriched" environment every bit as much as lab rats do to prompt his brain cells to grow more connections. I wanted him drenched in words every waking hour. And he needed to enjoy the chatter and try to pay attention, not let the words become background noise. I remembered Liz, the energetic nursing student who had nimble skills, a real gift of the gab, and had gotten along so well with Paul. When I phoned her, I explained that the dress code was ultracasual, chatter essential, and she'd be in the pool with Paul a lot.

On one of those summer days whose pristine blue skies make you stand and gape, the blue of calendars, David Hockney swimming pools, or Paul Newman's eyes, Liz arrived wearing a sunny red dress with a tropical floral print. Oddly enough for someone who only ever wore swim shorts or velour jogging suits, Paul had a savvy fashion sense, and as she entered he glanced at her dress and back at me, nodding his approval. The dress was sleeveless and showed off very muscular, able-bodied arms. Her face was deeply tanned, and she had the look of someone who really enjoyed the physicality of life.

Liz would become Paul's part-time nurse, literary assistant, and gal Friday, and from the outset, she seemed uncommonly cheerful. Every morning, she would test Paul's blood sugar and inject him with Lantus, a long-acting once-a-day insulin, if his fasting blood sugar indicated he needed it. Self-monitoring was out of the question, though he probably could have injected himself. He couldn't read the fill lines on the syringes or safely interpret the numbers on the test meter. Numbers no longer made any sense to him at all. An 8 could just as easily have been a snowman, a 1 could have been a telephone pole. He didn't know his address, phone number, birthday. Numbers didn't just perplex him, he impressively mangled them.

While Liz sat at the kitchen table filling syringes, holding each one at eye level so that light shone through it, sighting tiny silver bubbles and dislodging them with a fillip or two, Paul and I stood at the picture window watching a flock of starlings plaster the sky, back and forth, in synchronized swipes. Then they funneled down and settled on a fence.

"How many birds?" I asked.

"Four hundred . . . no, fifty," he said uneasily.

"Which is more," I slowly posed, fifty . . . or four hundred?"

He thought for a long while, and was about to speak when, on a hunch, I said gently: "Try not to guess. Do you know for sure?"

"Fifty."

"No, four hundred is much more than fifty."

"Fifty is *m-more* than than four hundred," he stridently insisted.

Paul used to be an ace at math, and had naturally assumed most of the numerical chores in the household, from calculating taxes to reading the water meter. We used to joke about my getting a 100 percent on my Airman's Written Exam—which included many navigation and loading problems that had to be solved using a circular slide rule, not a calculator or computer—even though math didn't come easily to me. I was by no means fluent in arithmetic, algebra, or geometry. I could do my multiplication tables, but not at speed or under pressure. So, keeping airspeed steady while flying the required "teardrop-shaped" holding pattern in gusty winds, while also re-computing my heading, was a living nightmare, and in practice at least, I usually got it wrong, drawing amoebas, not teardrops, across the sky.

Paul, on the other hand, had enjoyed math, which neither captivated nor intimidated him. Once, during an unusually boring seminar, he had even translated what he was being paid per hour into cans of Campbell's soup! Was a lifetime's practice with numbers, ratios, measurements, degrees—all of it erased? And to what extent was his right hemisphere singed by the stroke? A network in the left hemisphere identifies the words we assign to numbers, but then the right hemisphere helps picture the magnitudes that are involved, and those also seemed now to elude Paul.

He edged closer to me, close enough that our arms could touch, and I heard him whisper: "Two dollars."

"Two dollars?"

Crooking a finger backwards, he pointed to Liz.

"We owe Liz two dollars for something?"

He cast me a slanting glance, and uttered a *What do you use for a memory?* sigh of exasperation.

"*Cuisine,*" he whispered emphatically, as if wondering how I planned to help him recover when I couldn't even remember something that had happened an hour before.

"For picking up the Indian food?"

"Yes!"

"That cost *twenty* dollars, not *two, twenty.* Two plus a zero."

Grimacing, he shook his head. "No—*two* dollars."

No, for the time being at least, he couldn't safely do his own blood sugar readings and insulin. Numbers might be shaped differently than words, but they no longer functioned as meaningful symbols.

On top of that, instructions of more than a couple of steps confused him. His *procedural memory*—the "how-to," long-term memory of skills—was too damaged during the stroke. We couldn't trust him to reason that IF his blood sugar was over 150, THEN administer insulin; IF less than 150, DON'T. Nor trust him to understand which pills to take when. I hated watching him feel so helpless. But we prefilled the syringes in groups of ten and stored them in the fridge.

We developed a standard breakfast routine which began with sugar-free, cold "hot cocoa" (a childhood favorite) thickened with Thick-It, a tonic surprisingly difficult to prepare. Thick-It clumps in hot water, and cocoa powder clumps in cold water, so we tried a variety of whisks, blenders, right- versus left-handed stirring, shaking while doing the Morris (English folk dance performed by men wearing bells around their knees), the shimmy, flamenco, strange versions of the rumba. After much trial and error, and laughter, we learned to mix the chocolate powder in hot water, stir out the lumps, then add prethickened milk. Still, getting him to eat much wasn't easy.

For good reason, Kelly and the other speech therapists had alarmed Paul about the danger of food or liquid straying into his lungs and causing pneumonia. The hazard frightened Paul so dreadfully that now I couldn't get him to eat much food, or even drink much, a more dangerous refusal. Altogether, he'd lost forty-five pounds, and since he started out very much overweight, he looked healthier and his blood pressure was lower. But we were getting to the point where he needed to maintain his weight. Constantly dry-mouthed because he couldn't drink regular liquids without choking, he craved milk, and often tried to snatch it from the fridge. He needed to have it explained over and over (because he forgot immediately) why he wasn't allowed to drink cold quenching milk, the satiny liquid with sheets-on-a-line freshness, a hint of vanilla, and a smart finish. He'd once told me that he loved the way it coated the mouth and lingered after swallowing. He loved that it came from female breasts. He couldn't get enough of it, but had made do with a half gallon or so a day. Now, with the required dose of Thick-It, he refused to drink it at all.

After he had some blood work done, Dr. Ann phoned me.

"He's still dehydrated," she said with concern.

"Look, he's just not eating or drinking," I lamented. "I've tried everything." Somehow it felt like my fault.

"Do you think it would be helpful if I spoke with him?" she offered. "I could drop by on my way home."

A family doctor making a house call is now an antique custom, and I appreciated her kindness.

"Yes," I sighed with relief. "Could you possibly?"

And so she did later that day, sitting on the couch with Paul as Liz and I hovered. Paul cast us the look of someone being cornered by gentle gorgons.

"I don't want you to worry if there's a conspiracy going on," she assured Paul with touching directness. "I'm just going to tell you, there *is* a conspiracy going on. We're conspiring to get you to eat and drink so that you don't have to go back to the hospital! You *need* to eat. That's really important, you need the nourishment and fluids now more than ever. I know you're scared about maybe aspirating food, but not eating isn't the answer. Just sit upright or lean forward, and take your time swallowing."

Paul had trusted Dr. Ann with his life many times in the past. I thought, as I watched the scene, how dear and tribal it seemed: a sick boy fussed over by three caring women.

The next day, try as I might, I couldn't hide my sadness and fatigue. I felt as if I were becoming Paul's coach, cheerleader, teammate, teacher, translator, best friend and wife all rolled into one. No one can play so many roles without burning out.

"What's wrong?" Paul asked

I tried not to say, but confessed anyway: "I'm overwhelmed."

And a little later, to my surprise, he offered: "Do you . . . mem,

mem, mem . . . ebb outhouse—no! silly, not *outhouse* . . . out*side* . . . house. out for dinner?"

"Yes, I miss our dinners out together," I sighed, touched that Paul was trying to cheer me up. I did miss them, and was overjoyed he felt brave enough to go out, but it was also a ploy to get him to eat again. Off we went to a local Japanese restaurant, with Paul haphazardly shaven, in a pair of plaid flannel boxers and a short-sleeved blue shirt. Never a dapper dresser, in our early days together he had worn slacks and a shirt, belt, thin socks, lace-up oxfords. During one notable year in the 1980s when he was a visiting professor at Colgate, he'd risen to the sartorial splendor of a blue velour sports jacket, wheat-brown corduroy slacks, white shirt with lightly starched collar, and a colorful tie. He'd often lamented how blandly men were obliged to dress, while women could express themselves through sumptuous colors and textures.

But gradually, he began wearing less and less, as if sloughing off dead skin. Now only a short-sleeved cornflower-blue shirt would do (fortunately he had two). Loafers. No socks. White walking shorts gave way to long boxy swim shorts that almost passed for regular shorts. Since the stroke, the swim shorts yielded to plaid flannel boxer shorts in differently hued tartans. With or without button fly. Sometimes—if the buttonholes sagged open—he wore the shorts backwards. He insisted on dressing as comfortably as possible. Nor could I *gently* persuade him to dress otherwise, and I refused to wage war over something so trivial. *Pick your fight* was a marriage rule I'd long lived by. So, like a shrine to past attire, his closet held jackets, slacks, long-sleeved shirts, and dozens of ties and ascots he never wore. Including, in 2010, a favorite he picked out himself: a jazzy tie sporting, of all things, the H1N1 flu molecule.

At the restaurant, I steered him around chairs and tables, into a secluded booth where he might sprawl a little. The menu offered glossy photographs of perfect entrees, and he studied them intently, as if they were mail-order brides.

"Anything appeal to you?"

When he looked up nervously, I realized he didn't know what to do. Would he make a scene? Run out? Frustrate and embarrass himself when the waitperson arrived? I wasn't sure. Taking his hand reassuringly, I said: "Would you like me to order for you today?"

His forehead furrowed as he struggled to disentangle my sounds from all the others, including a television set high on the wall and a sizzling hibachi grill surrounded by celebrating students. I'd learned the value of repeating anything of importance.

"Would you like me to order for you today?"

Try as he might, he couldn't seem to isolate my voice amid all the warring sounds. Leaning across the table, I mouthed the words slowly and loudly. With a grateful sigh, he laid down the menu.

I ordered dishes he had relished before the stroke: *shumai*, little clouds of shrimp-filled dough, and skewers of bite-size shrimp and vegetables. And we dined mainly in silence, with exaggerated wide-eyes and smiles for *It tastes good!* He was happy to restore a little normalcy to our life, and I was relieved to see him eating more solid food.

On the drive home, to my delight, he politely stammered, "Thanks . . . for the Japanese . . . bouquet," trying to say "banquet."

Although Paul did return to regular eating, he now insisted on exactly the same foods every day, without even minor changes for whim, holiday, health, or perverse fun. I provided what I knew he wouldn't be able to resist. The dinner menu, a health addict's nightmare, a British eccentric's dream: white potatoes out of a can, mashed, topped with bottled gravy, and either canned chicken or ham. Breakfast: Egg Beaters, stove-fried toast in olive oil, and soy-based Smart Bacon. During the evening, he ate vast quantities of sugar-free vanilla ice cream right from the half-gallon container. This wasn't the low-salt, diabetic diet he was supposed to follow, but I was just happy he was eating. With all the ice cream, he started putting on weight fast, so in the interests of portion control, he scientifically taste-tested his way through a dozen sugar-free ice cream sandwiches and bars, most of which he dismissed (as flavorless) with a sour face. At last he settled on "Klondike Slim Bears," individually wrapped squares of "No Added Sugar" vanilla ice cream in a milk-chocolate-flavored coating. But the name "Slim Bear" wouldn't stick in his head, and he kept substituting words for it.

"Skinny elephant," he said, hungry for dessert.

I chuckled at the image. "A skinny elephant?"

"No," he crooned, both annoyed with himself and amused by the picture he had created. Wiping the words away with one hand as if they'd been sky-written, he said: "Not skinny elephant."

He drew a square in the air with both hands.

"A . . . a . . . a . . . skinny elephant! NO . . . skinny elephant . . ."

The next day, in complete seriousness, sure he'd get it right this time, he requested: "Minor Bear." His request was matter-of-fact. In his mind he was saying the right words, not asking for a winter constellation.

"A minor bear isn't what it's called," I explained with an amused smile. "But a minor bear *is* Ursa Minor, the Little Dipper."

He pondered this and smiled. "*Ursa*," he echoed, and nodded in understanding.

Yet another oddity about aphasia is that it's possible to lose access to words in a native language, but still retain those in any foreign languages you may have learned. Paul had studied Latin and French more than half a century before, and he'd had a keen interest in astronomy. *Ursa* is Latin for bear, and the Little Dipper is known to astronomers as Ursa Minor, the Big Dipper as Ursa Major.

"Slim Bear . . ." I said with that special inflexion that means *Repeat after me*.

"Bear," he repeated. "Bear."

"Slim . . . Bear."

"Slim . . . Bear."

But his brain simply refused to store the brand name, only the paradox of something big being described as small. So he continued to refer to his nightly treat as everything from "Enormous Mouse" to "Midget Elephant." As soon as he said it, he'd laugh, realizing it wasn't what he meant, then ask for the right words, which I'd provide. But they had no sticking power. I might have tried "Klondike" instead, but after a while we gave up and enjoyed the nonsense words the slot machine of his brain kept tossing out.

Sometimes he'd just pantomime, drawing a square in the air with both hands. But he used the same pantomime for almost everything he couldn't find the words for, regardless of shape— postage stamps, FedEx envelopes, misplaced manuscripts—so that didn't help much, even though, in this case, it was accurate. In time, I began thinking of the square as a *templum* (the origins of our word *temple*). In ancient times, a soothsayer would hold aloft a square of four sticks (the *templum*) and foretell events based on what he saw fly across or into that space, be it sparrow, bat, star, sun, or dragon-headed cloud. It was more of a sacred corral than anything concrete, an aerial shrine or sanctuary, not an edifice. He didn't have to use four sticks for divination. An augur could also outline a space with his staff, and wherever he drew that square it framed the future. Whatever Paul yearned for—a Skinny Bear or a chunk of cheese—seemed to exist in a similar kind of consecrated space in his mind, a perfect square of desire.

I felt relieved that Paul was eating, but drinking still posed dia-bolical problems. Over time, Paul progressed to honey-thick liq-uids, but still found them unnaturally viscous, like motor oil. Pitchers of thickened sugar-free lemonade were his main thirst-quencher, along with the Thick-It steeled cocoa and milk. A cou-ple of times a week, we'd mix a fresh batch, tossing the stale leftovers down the sink. Little did we guess how much trouble that would stir up.

One day the drain backed up and I summoned the plumber for what I assumed was a routine call. Sitting on the kitchen floor, he fed yard after yard of his coiled metal plumber's "snake" down the open maw of the drain, and marveled at the seemingly endless amount of sticky black sludge he cajoled out, over and over, until the steadfast snake finally reached the street 100 feet away. As the buckets filled, it looked like a scene from an oil rig or a whaling ship, with stinking wads of tarry black. The plumber just kept shaking his head and muttering how strange this was. *Never seen it before . . .* It was only after he left that the laughter began as we realized that we'd created a huge gunky bog by subjecting the drain to gobs of discarded "Thick-It," which had gelatinized everything it touched. After the plumber left, we hovered over the sink to watch the miracle of the waters once again flowing down the drain.

"I think he's cooked it!" Paul crowed triumphantly, meaning, of course: "The plumber has fixed the drain."

The ability to obsess well is an artist's stock in trade, and apparently it doesn't vanish with speech. Paul's cravings might have changed, but not his craving for cravings. Gone were the fish pastes, salmon, and trifle that reminded him of his British childhood. Post-stroke, he developed an obsessive craving for chocolate, which, since he was diabetic, had to be sugar-free. Taste-testing once again, he settled on an obscure brand of sugar-free dark chocolate bars, which weren't easy to find locally. When the supply ran low, I would frantically order them from New York City or Rochester, buying in bulk. Sometimes Liz or I had to travel overland to buy them in Syracuse or Corning, where to the mystification of shopkeepers we'd swoop in like bank robbers and demand all their supply, *including* any in the storeroom. We might leave with fifty. Paul ate one or two a night, considering them medically necessary, since they contained maltitol, with a printed warning on the chocolate bar label that it could cause loose stools if ingested in excess. Chocolate bars became the luxurious laxative backbone of his bowel regimen for a significant period of time. The swanky chocolate store in one mall came to recognize me as the habitué who bought the bars by the case. I hadn't the heart to reveal they were being used as a laxative. Then Liz started appearing at the same store instead, with the same ostensible hunger, one only a mother lode of this particular chocolate seemed to satisfy.

Long before, Liz's landlord Gustaf had recommended the easy-to-prepare dinner Tasty Bite, a prepackaged Indian curry meal he'd been packing as emergency rations while vagabonding in Mongolia and all over the world. She and her husband tasted it, and liked it well enough to start buying it in bulk for camping trips. One day Liz arrived with two Tasty Bite offerings, Madras Lentils and Bombay Potatoes, for us to try. They could be eaten cold, but tasted delicious warmed up, and I liked them, but Paul was completely hooked. It filled some craving powerful as chocolate or coffee. Maybe it conjured up his British childhood's colonial past, or reminded him of the beef curry served nearly every day in his college at Oxford. Whatever the lure, from then on he ate *nothing* else for dinner. He would empty two pouches of Tasty Bite into a bowl, add plain yogurt to tone down the hot peppers, stir thoroughly, and microwave for three minutes (by pressing a red dot three times). This became his favorite dinner every night for five years, with the occasional exceptions of Chinese takeout or a bowl of cold peeled shrimp. Fortunately it's a healthy vegetarian meal, because he's eaten it now over 1,500 days in a row. Keeping a three-month supply on hand, our pantry is an homage to curried beans, and we're well prepared for blizzards or hurricanes. In addition to its taste, Paul loved that it was manufactured in India, sealed in pouches designed for the Apollo space program, and tested to withstand extreme temperatures and heights—from below sea level to the moon. Tasty Bite had traveled up Mount Everest with the Indian Armed Forces and to Antarctica with Conrad Anker. Surely it would do for an aphasic-British-eccentric-ex-cricket-bowler-retired-professor-author?

CHAPTER 17

IN THE CUBBYHOLES OF A LIBRARY CLOSET, I STORED YARN, gift wrap, and all sorts of presents (from the nifty to the impossibly hedonistic) for friends and relations, gathered on my travels or whenever I happened upon something just right for someone. Then, when birthday or Christmas arrived, I had a perfect little gift. Whenever I entered the closet now, my eyes fell on language tokens squirreled away for Paul. What should I do with the book of palindromes, for instance? *Madam, in Eden, I'm Adam. Rats live on no evil star. Do geese see God?* He would have loved those. Or the mug from the Folger Library with Shakespearean insults written all over it? *You egg, you fry of treachery.* Or the literary guides to European cities? Such presents would seem cruel.

Once we lived in a house made of words. Our personal vocabulary had ranged from the word *flaff*, which meant utter nonsense, to *mrok*, a plaintive cry often uttered by one of us hoping to locate the other. Just as some couples mainly relate through their children, we had related through our rowdy family of words. We wallowed in codes and idiomatic privacies.

On one signal occasion, carrying an untidy armload of mail and magazines from the mailbox, I announced my arrival—for no special reason; it just swam into my head—by singing out "Post trout!"

"Post trout!" Paul had echoed playfully from his study down the hall. He soon emerged grinning.

"Is this my post trout?" he'd asked of me, glad of a new pet name, and planted a fish-mouthed kiss on my forehead. From then on, trout functioned as postmen and carriers of all desirable commodities.

> Depending on what you are carrying, you can be the Coffee Trout, the Bagel Trout, and so on, not that trout are known for their carrying capacity or even for their ability to reduce the portion of daily inconvenience. . . . [Nonetheless, trout serve as] the epitome-personification of the helpful other. . . . I don't see how a civilized household that cherishes intimacy can function without these playful oddities, which firm the bond and widen the spectrum of sounds, though what a stranger would make of the little chiming Babel . . . I have no idea.
>
> —*Life with Swan*

Every word that bended easily we warped in playful ways. Weekdays became: Mondalsday, Tueselday, Wendelsday, Thurselday, Fridalday, Egg Day (when I fried up eggs for him), and Sundalsday. Hand became *handle*, and breakfast *breaklefast*, mouthwash *mousewash*, lens *lensness*. Self *shelbst*, sleep *schluffy*, and the Johnny Carson show *Carsonienses*. A visit to the dermatologist became a "mole patrol." "Are you a cyclamen?" meant "Are you feeling ill?" (etymology: "sicklamin" = diminutive of sick, which, sounding like the flower "cyclamen," suggests a small flower-like sick person). One especially fond reference we abbreviated to A.C.H.M., often written Achmed, commemorating the tiniest mouse we had ever seen, in a botanical garden in St. Louis: *A Certain Harvest Mouse.* "Our intimate bestiary," Paul wrote, "gave us a private world as secret as that of Cockney rhyming slang."

> Quite often, in carpet slippers, she walked on top of my feet as I paddled slowly backward and we let out a noise we had linked to

the roseate spoonbill exquisitely depicted in watercolors in the laboratory waiting room at the local hospital: *Clack-clack-clack-clack*, we went, together being a bird that stepped in and out of tidal pools.

All couples evolve private catchphrases and codes, but I'm not sure why we had felt the need for so extensive a dialect, unless it had to do with how much of our work lives we'd spent juggling *normal* words and stacking them together in law-abiding ways. Or because even off-duty we loved playing with words at their most combinative, bobbin-like, and sly, jostling and recasting them at will, without having to worry about whether they bowed to literary fashion or even made sense. Or maybe because we secretly yearned to be among our prehistoric ancestors, who had the diagnostic necessity and raw fun of coining many of the words that today bind together languages as seemingly unrelated as Sanskrit, Hittite, English, and Lithuanian, words like "sun," "winter," "honey," "wolf," "snow," "woman," "awe."

The forerunners of such words were probably spoken in sparse, robust, barbaric sounds. For sport, Paul had once translated "America the Beautiful" into Indo-European and sung it at Cornell in the "Temple of Zeus," a coffee room used by the literary set, ringed with dusty plaster replicas of Greek statues (authentically missing heads, arms, and other body parts). Words had served us, and we had served them—at times we were masters, others vassals. We had lived in American society, but within the *culture* of words, which made their own demands and had their own special trappings.

EARLY ONE MORNING, I rushed out to Target to pick up an ice cream-making machine for Paul. To get to the small appliances aisle I had to go through the office supplies aisle, for once with no requests from Paul for his standard supplies (black Flair pens, manila envelopes, glue sticks, Type White, high-luminosity printer paper), and I felt my stomach twisting. *He will never need these things again*, I thought, remembering how often we had "moused" around those aisles for office supplies. It was just one more of the incidental, barely noteworthy activities that add cell by cell to the body of a relationship over time. Familiar as rain, it was an obeisance to writing, a remembered absence, a discontinued small pleasure, a lost fragment of a home life. The pain I felt was wordless—beyond, beneath, unbeguiled by words. Not even gasping *No more* a hundred times could capture that visceral and wholly new kind of pain. There, in the Target aisle—surrounded by sparkly pink notebooks, animal stickers, glitter, a forest of multicolored pens, tapes of every hue, mothers bustling by with loaded carts and excited children, awash in upbeat music to shop by—I stood stiffly in shock, stricken that our favorite stripe of play was gone, all the impromptu word games we shared, including Paul's improvised little songs.

In the avian world, it sometimes happens that two fine-feathered mates duet to produce a characteristic song, with each singing their part so seamlessly that it's easy to confuse the melody as the work of only one bird. If one dies, the song splinters and ends. Then, quite often, the mournful other bird begins singing both parts to keep the whole song alive. Without realizing it, I found myself taking over Paul's old role of house song sparrow and began making up silly ditties to share with Paul.

Sitting together at the kitchen table, we watched a vivid blue jay enter the courtyard, and hop from cherry-tree branch to the leaf-littered ground, looking for food. I began to chant:

> Blue jay, blue jay in the tree,
> will you come and play with me?
> While you dance in the impatiens,
> won't you give me a second glance?
> You are such a pretty fellow—
> are you sad you are not yellow?

Paul laughed at the rhyme, but I wasn't sure he understood the words.

"You're such a cuddly little fruit fly," I gushed, and he shot back a pleased smile, because he understood the word "cuddly" and he was still good at social responsiveness. But when I asked, "Do you know what a fruit fly is?" he shook his head no.

"I'm not *stupid*," he added for the umpteenth time, his voice balancing between self-pity and scorn.

Patiently, reassuringly, for the umpteenth time, I replied: "No, you're not stupid. You have a communication disorder. The words are still inside your head. You're having trouble sorting out the ones you want."

Then I described a fruit fly as a tiny fly that hovers around pieces of fruit. Did he know what fruit was? He did. He understood the word "hovers."

"*Drosophila melanogaster*," he announced, with the pride of a fisherman surprising even himself by hauling up a coelacanth.

"Holy smokes! Where did that come from?" Startled, I looked at him as if he'd just performed a magic trick.

My memory skipped to an afternoon in Jamaica, on one of our first vacations together, at a surfside hotel whose restaurant menu, littered with typos, had kept us laughing for days. "Chef's bowel salad" sounded gruesome enough. But my personal favorite was: "Steak grilled to your own likeness." We'd tried to picture a silhouette of Eleanor Roosevelt in beef.

A saucer of sweet fresh pineapple chunks had drawn several fruit flies, one of whom had walked slowly across my upturned palm.

"*Drosophila melanogaster*," Paul had said with a flourish, retrieving a bit of Greek from his freshman year in college. I'd liked the swooping music of the phrase, but absolutely loved its translation.

"Hey, know the English?" I now asked.

He thought for a long while. I could hear the cicadas chirping in the forests of his mind.

"Used to," he finally lamented.

"Black-bellied dew-sipper."

The light of recognition flashed over his face and he tried to say the words, making it as far as "dew" before forgetting "black-bellied" and having to start over. Then he forgot "sipper."

"Black-bellied dew-sipper. Let's just picture the image of a

black-bellied dew-sipper," I murmured, hoping to curb his frustration. For a few moments we sat in silence and imagined the egg-
plant-blackness of the belly, the spiky hairs, the brick-red prisms of
the eyes.

That morning, with increasing frustration, Paul had groped for
"wallet," "checkbook," "swallowing." When he was so at sea, I
might try to chip through the blockade by asking him what category the word fell into, but that didn't always work, because he
might decide that swallowing was in the category of spelling since
it involves the mouth. If Paul couldn't point to the thing or body
part he meant, I would ask him if he could picture it in his mind's
eye, because even without words one can still render some images
and feelings. When that doesn't happen, what is one left with? A
psychic cramp, a precisely unutterable thought or feeling. In his
mental pandemonium using one chancy word to define another
chancy word was speaking in riptides. Words had lost their moor-
ings, they drifted like boats in a storm, cleats torn loose, fenders
awry, no longer holding fast to anything.

Quite often Paul would get a running start on a sentence, do
the first half beautifully, and then stop short, stranded before the
important final noun, suddenly having no idea whatsoever where
the sentence was headed. This intruded into our simplest conversations. As his use of numbers improved a little, he knew that an
80-degree day was better for swimming than a 60-degree day. So
he'd diligently check the thermometer on the back window
before venturing outside. When struck by sunbeams, the dial
always read 40 degrees too hot. Paul would see 120 degrees and
grin, remembering his spell at the University of Arizona, in Tucson, where the heat soared past 100, the air tasted combustible,
the sidewalk burned through the soles of your shoes, and even the
cacti grew parched. Coming from a cold rainy isle, Paul had a
lifelong love affair with heat. We kept the faulty thermometer
despite, or maybe because of, its unreliability, and nicknamed it
our "optimistic thermometer" (in contrast to a more chilling one
in a shady front courtyard).

Paul would call out the temperature as he grabbed a towel. On a lucky day in June, he cheerfully announced: "It's 75 degrees! The faulty . . . hmmm. Cancel that. The phenom . . ."

I waited for his next try, arms hanging at my side, clock ticking.

"The faulty . . ." Stopping short again, his brain uncooperative, Paul blurted out an annoyed "It's not *working* . . ."

I cocked my head, letting him know I was still listening. "One more go?"

"The faulty . . . the faulty . . . mmm."

He began to look rattled, so I decided it was time to help. *"Thermometer?"*

"Thermometer. 100 degrees," Paul announced with relief, his body visibly relaxing as he strode outside, gripped the railing, and edged at last toward the pool ladder.

It was yet another 60-degree day.

These aborted sentences were the new norm. This meant my steadfast listening and his fruitless, bitter plodding. Gone were all his tidings, bywords, and frisky chitchat. He raged at himself. How could he not be angry, bound by stutters, echolalia, and paraphrasing—to his mind a torrent of wounded language, defective language? *Bitter*, I silently called out in my best maître d' voice, *party of one*.

Paul's tortured search for words reminded me of work by Samuel Beckett, the wild and woolly Irish playwright, novelist, member of the French Resistance during WWII, and literary assistant to James Joyce. In his best-known play, *Waiting for Godot*, Beckett describes God's inscrutability as "divine aphasia," and God utters such aphasic-sounding gibberish as "Quaquaquaqua." I had a new appreciation for Beckett's character *Watt*, who speaks with aphasic peculiarity, jumbling word order, letters, and sense until they're cockeyed and no one can understand him. "In his skull," Beckett writes of Watt, eerily reminding me of Paul, "the voices whispering their canon were like a patter of mice, a flurry of little grey paws in the dust."

A custodian of silence, Beckett had often created characters afflicted with language disorders, who became tongue-tied or voiceless. With humor, gusto, and impenitent absurdity, he spent a lifetime narrating the unnameable, lives of personal apocalypse, and almost every mummery of human language, literally from first bark to final silence. Paul had relished Beckett, devoured his funny aphasic-sounding fiction especially, and shared it with students. In an odd twist of fate, Paul now spoke as if he were one of Beckett's characters, as if he existed *within* Beckett's novels.

My penchant for Beckett rekindled, I stumbled upon his final creation: an aphasic poem. Of all people to wind up beyond the pother and rescue of language! After a fall in his kitchen in July of 1988 (most likely caused by a stroke), to his befuddled horror, Beckett awoke with aphasia, from which he never fully recovered. His last work, "What Is the Word," tortures itself with relentless aphasic striving. For fifty lines it compulsively echoes variations on this faltering lament: "a faint afar away over there what . . . what is the word—"

In the poem's avalanche of repeats, elisions, stumbling, and stuttering, I heard Paul's voice as he beat the mental bushes, hunting for lost words. Paul didn't know about Beckett's post-stroke aphasia or the circumstances of his last poem, and I decided not to tell him. Beckett died a year and a half after his stroke, having spent his end days aphasic, in a small, sparsely furnished room, watching soccer and tennis on television, accompanied only by his boyhood copy of *The Divine Comedy* in Italian. It was too dismal a scene to plant in Paul's skull. He still believed in the wishbone of recovery, and I wanted him to keep reaching for it. Me, too. If only we both reached with gusto, at least one of us was sure to win, and it didn't matter who.

CHAPTER 18

A WELCOME LETTER OF ENCOURAGEMENT ARRIVED FROM A friend, with the gift of the Indonesian phrase *Holopis kuntul baris* (hoh-LOPE-iss COON-tool BAH-riss), uttered to summon extra muscular strength while carrying a heavy object, or summon more energy when toiling under a mental or emotional burden. I took to whispering it to myself. In America, we have war cries, work songs, marching chants. But we could use a phrase of our own whose only purpose is to concentrate fading energy, a bolus of sound uttered just to grip one's resolve.

The big crisis might be over for Paul, but many smaller crises followed, accompanied by lingering fears. Would he fall? Would depression strike him again? Would he give up on speech therapy? Would he learn to dial 911? Would he ever agree to use a cane? Would he be safe cooking? Would a poorly swallowed pill catch halfway down his throat? That happened more often than we liked, and the burning pill would cling like a suction cup and take ages to dislodge, leaving him with a badly inflamed throat. Another epic nosebleed? Scrape his leg, pick up a splinter, or scratch a bug bite (any of which easily became infected)? Contract pneumonia (sometimes spawned by a simple cold)? High blood sugar? High blood pressure (usually heralded by a headache, but headaches could also be run-of-the-mill)? Aspirate food down his windpipe that, for once, he couldn't free? Suppose he fell and broke a bone? I never knew from day to day what medical frights might unfold.

And then there were all the lesser crises: trying to fathom bills and taxes, dialing a phone number, working the Xerox machine, composing a letter, going out (bank, restaurant, clinic), or Paul daring to speak on demand with strangers. Navigating some days felt like a sheer drop on a country road. Others like driving over a street full of hidden potholes. Which one would crack the chassis?

Coping with those trials wouldn't have been possible without our cushion of snuggling closeness each morning, when we were simply sweethearts. Paul's sleep gradually returned to its old time-table of late nights and late rising. But a new era deserved new ritu-als, so after rising at dawn, I usually crept back into bed and woke Paul at 11 a.m., and we cuddled for half an hour or so. Soon after-ward we would hear the telltale *whumph, ping, clatter, gush,* and *clunk*—which meant Liz had opened the door, microwaved water for coffee, unloaded the dishwasher, set pills, started preparing Paul's breakfast and going about her other morning chores.

Thank heavens the brain has a mind of its own, because on weekends, holidays, and during Liz's myriad travels, I became sub-marine commander and crew combined. Breakfast routine. Then maybe shaving or showering. Helping him dress. Lunchtime medi-cations. Swimming and supervising the careful transition into and out of the pool. Preparing dinner, taking dinner pills. Endless channel-changing with the insidiously complex TV remote con-trol, whose array of buttons and arrows continued to look like runes from extraterrestrial Bingo. Or reading his mail to him, doing bills. After a few days, I felt tired at a visceral, mineral level, and slept in thick geological strata, not hours.

Besides the here and now with Paul lay the household soap operas, such as my returning home from an afternoon out to dis-cover that the house had been struck by lightning, the circuit breakers had been thrown, the smoke alarms were chirping, and the TV was blown. Paul, who had been alone through the visitation, told me proudly that he'd seen a ball of lightning rise from the floor and shoot up through the ceiling, hurling a burst of energy that had thrown him back onto the couch. Our household mantra of "never-a-dull-moment" began to seem like a bizarre understatement.

For safety, I arranged and rearranged the house to accommodate Paul's loss of balance, muscle strength, and vision. Anything he could bump into or trip over was moved, especially throw rugs. I set his dishes and mugs within easy reach, and turned his spoons and forks around in the cutlery drawer so that he could differentiate them from their modern and sleek, but harder-to-eat-from, Danish brethren. His favorite foods were always in the same accessible place at the front of the refrigerator. Though he poured his own milk from a carton with a spout, he usually spilled it; washable placemats and bibs did duty, with extra dish towels on hand. The telephone cord was taped to the sideboard with pink duct tape, so that he wouldn't trip over it. I had a raised toilet seat installed, since the muscles on his right side weren't as strong as before, and rising could be tricky. Extra couch pillows provided support. Even such incidental items as kitchen garbage bags had to change, because tie-top bags were too confusing.

Scrap by scrap, fragment by iota, life continued to evolve to accommodate his illness, which took on a life of its own, and became another inhabitant of the house, a central one, complete with special foods and routines. *Like Christoph Detlev's death*, I sometimes thought, remembering a lyrical passage in Rainer Marie Rilke's only novel, *The Notebooks of Malte Laurids Brigge*. "Christoph Detlev's death," Rilke wrote, by which he also meant Detlev's illness, "had been living at Ulsgard for a great many days, and spoke with everyone and demanded. Demanded to be carried, demanded the blue room . . . demanded the dogs . . . demanded and screamed. . . . His death couldn't be hurried. It had come for ten weeks, and for ten weeks it stayed. And during this time it was more the master of the house than Christoph Detlev had ever been."

In college I'd memorized the complete passage in German, because its exquisitely ornate sentences had so stirred me. I didn't really understand then in a visceral way how someone's illness could fill every corner of a household and take on a life of its own. In its thrall, gradually everything evolves: schedules, *dramatis personae*, meals, furniture, travel, routines, climate, conversations, layout of rooms, even the definition of the words "calm," "independence," "free time," or "leisure." Tranquillity hides in small spaces, and when found needs to be treasured, because you know it's a phantom that will slip away again. The set points of daily life change. Sometimes, as in the case of Christoph Detlev, illness or death may feel like more of a presence in the house than the man himself does. This isn't a lodger one chooses, but can adapt to, like any other, until new routines become habit, new concerns ingrained, new faces customary, and the texture of everyday life feels familiar once again.

I understood this intellectually, but the slew of new routines made everything feel temporary and uncertain. Many daily chores—setting up Paul's pills, for instance—now required strict attention and a mistake might have horrible consequences. I simply couldn't afford the luxury of going to pieces. Always a mystery trip, life had changed without warning, from casual to cliff-like. I had to reckon with medical visitors and employees. Coping with the new regime meant often locating my inner submarine commander and letting her preside. But some days all I wanted was to curl up and be taken care of, and as caregivers often find, little room existed for my concerns or woes.

Stroke changes everyone in a family. I began noticing with surprise how caregiving can reduce one to a role rather than a relationship. One normally plays so many roles—from paramour to parent, monkey baby, prom queen, warrior, florist, nosy parker, servant, savant, and a dozen more—all obvious, finite, and clear as switching between camp songs and flute solos. What had changed? I'd not only lost the old Paul, I'd lost those parts of myself that had related to those irretrievable parts of him. For instance, the Escher-like paradox of each being the other's child. I now saw how lop-sided that had become.

"You're still my child, but I'm no longer yours," I confessed tear-fully one day.

He opened his arms, held me close, stroked my hair with his limp right hand, stroked my cheek with his left, kissed the bridge of my nose, and murmured: "Oh, little sweetheart." Then, putting his hand on my chest bone, haltingly, he incanted: "Safe."

My habits were mutating. I was being more affectionate than before. He needed me closer when he was in such a fragile state, and I needed to feel closer, too.

Once he said: "You don't know . . . miss you . . . go away."

"I don't know how much you miss me whenever I go away?"

Yes, he nodded. I knew he meant small excursions of an hour or two, and that I was the only constant in his newly chaotic world.

In many ways, I had become the functional part of him. With-out meaning to, I sometimes caught myself talking on his behalf to someone as if he weren't present. Easy to do, especially since, after years of living together, one can intuit how the other might finish a sentence.

"How is your hand, Paul?" Dr. Ann asked during an office visit.

When nervous, or under pressure, aphasics find speaking even harder than usual, just as stutterers do. Without thinking, I answered, "It's still bothering him a lot. But he insists on eating with it anyway, and not switching to his left hand." In a reflex of being a caregiver, I became his voice.

"Is that so?" She redirected the conversation to Paul, as she inspected his still-tanned right hand, gently opening the crooked finger and flexing the others to test their range of motion. "Are you eating with your right hand?" She made solid eye contact with him.

He nodded yes.

"That's amazing."

He shed a small proud smile.

"I think it will help retrain your hand, so keep on doing it," she said in a slow, respectful, caring voice. She was wearing a long sage dress, dark green jacket, and matching green eye shadow. A barrette secured her shoulder-length brown hair on one side. The greens suited her, and I read in Paul's appreciative eyes, as he took in the meadow colors, that he wanted to tell her how beautiful she looked, but couldn't find the words.

"It's really good for your hand to use it, even though I know it can sometimes be hard to control," she said as she continued with her exam, checking his heart and lungs. I knew Paul wouldn't understand what she was saying about the new medications and their dosing, but now she directed her comments to both of us.

In speaking for Paul, I had only meant to help. Instinctively, one takes over when a loved one stumbles, but that can backfire, making him appear helpless. So in the future I tried always to include Paul in conversations, as if he could understand everything we were saying, lest he feel ghost-like—not just silent, but mindless and invisible.

Constricted by the presence of aides, doctors, or speech therapisrts, I sometimes addressed Paul by the saint's name his mother bestowed upon him at birth, a public name, not one of the playful monikers we'd concocted ourselves. And I spoke conventionally, the way one does among strangers, not in the cozy dialect we'd personalized, as families do. This not only made our interactions sound oddly formal, it widened the distance between us. So whenever other people weren't around, I returned to our special jazzy inflections (*ass-par-AH-gus; caul-IF-o-lur*), emoticon *mrok*s and other noises, delighted we could still communicate without normal words. After dinner each evening, we sat on the couch and cuddled as we watched the flickering hearth of the TV. Those were some of the sweetest moments of the day.

"Want to hear a monkey baby sound?" I asked when we were alone one evening, at a time when I knew language had completely failed him.

Yes, he nodded.

I made a whimpery sound that went with a helpless infant's facial expression. He pulled me close and hugged me. Anyone would respond, and for that matter so would a dog. Some sounds are universal heart-tugs for mammals—especially that of an infant in distress or someone in pain—and some are particular to monkeys and apes, who manage to convey loads of data and subtle feelings through emotion-packed sounds, facial expressions, and gestures. Even a macho alligator will come running if you mimic the high-pitched grunt of a crying baby gator. Hard-wired into us, these primitive wiles automatically elicit a response. They may be how language evolved, from involuntary notes of joy, pain, pleasure, curiosity, and other lively outpourings. We spent the evening making soulful monkey baby sounds of pure emotion, grunts and mews and whimpers, happy for this new well of communication, and laughing at how silly we could still be together, words or no.

CHAPTER 19

PAUL WOULD DUTIFULLY JOIN HIS SPEECH THERAPIST IN the library for an hour each day, emerging exhausted and demoralized, having punished his brain in an effort to fill in blanks, list words within categories (how many flowers can you name? None . . . How many animals can you name? None . . .), link words with pictures, and attempt to perform other language skills. She tried teaching him to ask himself: What category is a word in? What color or shape is the object? If he could exclude many competing things, his quest would be clearer. Despite their simplicity, he found the exercises demanding and at times impossible.

Later, I watched Paul puzzling over workbook pages, trying to rack words, like skittish pool table balls, into the rigid triangle of just one concept—he was *racking his brains*.

"Can bowls swim?" a question asked. I knew the answer they wanted was *No*. But bowls could float, even heavy bowls, if flat and large enough. The large, flat-bottomed bowl of an ocean liner, for instance. If Paul thought like that, too, he'd give the wrong answer. They meant small inanimate household bowls. Not the bowl of the deep ocean, say, holding currents, coral, plants, and creatures— itself floating on the earth's liquid core of iron and nickel, whose swaying produces Earth's magnetic field. Not the bowl of the earth floating—or, with so many life-forms, was it swimming?—in space.

"Can water freeze?" That one was easy. But some other questions required only the literal meaning of a word, not the way it's used every day in slang. "Can bullets grow?" Certain kinds of exploding bullets expand, *grow*, on impact. "Can pearls fly?" If someone throws them. "Can beavers talk?" Those in the Ipana toothpaste commercials of the 1950s used to sing. "Is a siren loud?" Air-raid sirens—yes. The seductive bird-ladies of Greek mythology who lured sailors to their deaths—not necessarily. "Can stones burn?" And how. The stones on a sun-baked beach, or the stones encircling a campfire. "Can bags frown?" They often do, especially when groceries are packed unevenly. "Are parakeets tame?" Store-bought—yes. But wild parakeets nest on several continents. Paul loved the squabbling, squawking monk parakeets that nest in Florida palm trees. "Are potatoes hollow?" No . . . but the minute I read the question I imagined a hollow potato. An intricate ivory one, carved by a Japanese craftsman, its skin a filigree where, on closer inspection, a cityscape loomed. "Are vitamins greasy?" Some absolutely are. The thick syrupy gold vitamins my mom fed me when I was little slid right down. "Are coupons expensive?" I presumed they meant coupons offering discounts at the supermarket. But municipalities had to *pay* the coupons on bonds, and they could be expensive. "Is satin sticky?" If you had rough fingertips, as Paul did, then your fingers snagged easily on satin and other slick fabrics.

Choosing the *correct* answer could be as tough as herding cats. But, like most people, I did know the *accepted* answer. Selecting it, I had to ignore all other answers that sprang to mind or were truer to my experience. Could Paul do that now with a hurt brain? Could he understand the domestic use of a word, while chasing away wild game? Or had his mind become simpler than all of that? Had he lost the mental elastic that used to connect everything to everything else with the tug of a few words? There it was again. *Tug* was another of those deliciously ambiguous words. I pictured the game we played when I sneaked up on Paul from behind and tugged almost imperceptibly at his sleeve; then I pictured a tiny boat tugging a goliath tanker into port.

Bewildered, Paul handed me the homework sheets, on which he had answered a few questions, and I silently read them, shaking my head in disbelief. Some questions seemed simple, yet were fiendishly ambiguous. Only context was missing, the opera of cues we often need to guess what sentences mean.

"Do you drink *a cup of water* or drink *a cup of river*," I read out loud. My eyes clouded with memories of the Amazon River Basin, weeks of floating and walking through the vine-thick jungle, under canopies effervescent with life. After dinner one evening, carrying an underwater lantern, some boat mates and I had snorkeled in waters dark and clear as quartz. Except for the occasional stingray, there was nothing much to fear. Nothing large enough to see, that is. Out of curiosity, I'd drunk a slow, savory mouthful of river, which tasted tinny yet soft, as if it had been stirred by water hyacinths, mechanical watches, and dolphins. Bad mistake.

"Remember when I drank some of the Amazon and got that awful parasite?" I asked Paul.

"Gaaagh!" His jaw dropped, his eyes widened, and he aped the blue tribal mask I'd brought home to him along with reddish-brown bats carved from mahogany, polished to a tranquil sheen, and bark-cloth paintings of butterflies in ginger, ochre, and black. The black had come from pressed fruits of the *huito* tree, which produce a liquid like invisible ink that's painted on with clear brush-strokes, but later oxidizes to a rich, satiny black in the open air.

Then the huge sprawling Amazon vanished from my mind's eye as I followed Paul's finger, pointing to a workbook question that offered *Sit at a table* vs. *Sit under a table*. He pointed to *Cement is hard* vs. *Cement is soft*. Next he spread his fingers stiffly—all but the two droopy ones—in a sign of tortured woe. Then he mimed the weighing of produce. At last, sighing unevenly, he seemed to let all the air out of the room.

I understood. *Poured* cement is soft, *set* cement hard.

"How about these?" I pointed to *Bridges can be carried* vs. *Radios can be carried*, and *Sew your hair* vs. *Comb your hair*.

"Yes!" he said, making a darning motion in the air.

Of course one could sew with hair. Before manufacturing, people sewed with animal hair.

"Kwai," he added. Just the one word. For a few moments, I floated the word in my mind . . . *Kwai* . . . *Kwai* . . . only its bare sounds at first, until images marched in. *The Bridge Over the River Kwai* was a favorite WWII film of Paul's, in which prisoners built, while simultaneously sabotaging, a wooden bridge for the Burma railway.

"Do you imagine these things—carrying a bridge or sewing with hair—when you read the sentence?"

"*YES*," he whispered hard in exasperation, while rubbing his brow with his good hand.

Even if he understood all the words—and I wasn't sure he did—he was still too imaginative for this sort of exercise, which required a different habit of mind. The minute he heard or read about it, he automatically pictured *taking cabbage for a walk*, *wearing poems*, or discovering *a wall full of money*. The brain imagines whatever it's told about, and trying to suppress a thought results in preoccupation with it. Try not to picture a polar bear.

"Want to take a cabbage for a walk?" I teased with an exaggerated smile. "I think we've got a cabbage leash around here somewhere."

"Why not," he said in a blasé tone, like any normal spouse being asked to walk the family spaniel.

In all Paul went through five speech therapists, mainly teaching the same skills in the same way, none able to help him progress much. Number one was Catherine, a handsome middle-aged woman with tawny skin and an apologetic smile who had the habit of peeping up over her rimless glasses, as if she were repeatedly surfacing from a deep thought.

"Can you use these words to make a sentence?" she asked Paul, setting five cards on the table, one word printed on each: "Pat," "John," "down," "eats," "sits."

Paul stared at the cards for a long silent spell, without touching them. Later he would tell me that they sometimes looked like worms cavorting on ice floes, or hieroglyphics on a tomb wall. He wasn't sure which, not that it mattered much, because reading was no longer an effortless and unconscious knack. The brain doesn't swallow a word whole. It breaks it into twigs, then reassembles the separate letters, syllables, and sounds to create meaning. Some of those mental steps had been damaged during the stroke. Anyway, he didn't know what these scattered words were *for*. What was he supposed to do with them? Was it line them up? Soon they lost their novelty and he sat back in his chair and began drumming on the table with bored fingers.

"Now, now, don't give up so fast!" she said. Leaning over the cards, she arranged two of them like this: JOHN EATS. "John eats," she pronounced slowly and deliberately. "See? It's easy. Now you do it."

Then he allowed one hand to hover above the words, before slowly lowering it into action and plucking at the cards, sliding them into different arrangements, finally settling on PAT DOWN and JOHN SITS.

Toward the end of the session, their fifth time together, she surprised us by announcing: "I'm afraid I won't be able to work with you anymore, Mr. West. . . ."

I looked questioningly at Paul. Had something gone amiss? He seemed puzzled as well.

"Because I'm getting married this weekend!" She beamed. "And we're leaving right after the ceremony on our honeymoon . . . in Europe. We'll be gone all summer."

Number two, Roger, was a bearded young man, who always arrived with a hospitable handshake, though I found his palm damp and bony. I wondered if Paul did, too, but wasn't sure how to phrase it in a way he'd understand.

"For this next activity," I heard Roger say as I did chores nearby in the kitchen, "we will practice a consonant sound followed by a vowel sound." He spaced his words rather far apart as he spoke, which removed some of the natural rise and fall of his voice.

"I want you to listen carefully and repeat after me. Let's start with the consonant *M*. Ready?" Opening his mouth, he exaggerated the movement of his lips as he pronounced the sound "MA" clear as a musical note.

"M-M-MA," Paul repeated stumblingly, more like a goat's bleat. A purposeful pause.

"MAY." Said with lips rolled tightly together—grandpa without his dentures—then opened wide.

Staring hard, Paul studied how Roger's lips moved to round out the sound.

"MM-MAY," he said, elongating both parts, the *M* and the *A*. Another pause.

"MY . . . MY."

Roger continued through ME and MO and back to MA again, over and over, trying to help Paul's brain connect letters with sounds that can be mouthed in speech.

We liked Roger, who tutored Paul for another few weeks, but a new semester was starting at Ithaca College and he needed to return.

Number three was Julie, a slender twenty-something woman with bulging blue eyes, and a voice that hadn't "cracked" yet—the female equivalent of a boy's voice during adolescence—from the distinctive crinkling soprano of a young woman into the slightly lower register of middle age.

I overheard her asking Paul "yes" and "no" questions, each of which he took his time answering, thinking it through and giving his brain a chance to mobilize a reply.

"Is your name Jack?"

"No," Paul croaked.

"Is your name Paul?"

"Y-y-yes."

"Are you at home?"

"Yes."

"Are you awake?"

"Yes."

"Is the light on?"

"Yes."

"Good, Mr. West. Now I'd like you to tell me what you see in the pictures I show you. Okay? Let's begin."

The sound of several 5-by-7-inch cards being tapped on a teak table.

"What's this?"

Paul paused a long while, then said haltingly, as if groping for an unknown language: "Duck? No, smird. grap. looch, mem, mem, mem, snok . . ."

The strain in his voice tore through me, and at that moment I would have done anything to help him, including burning incense to Panacea, the goddess of healing.

"No, those are nonsense sounds," Julie said, adding a little crackling laugh. "It's a *broom*, a *broom*."

"*Broooom*," Paul repeated, with the sigh of someone reminded of a word on the tip of his tongue.

After a few weeks, Julie left for a job at a college in another state.

Paul's least favorite therapist was number four, a tall, robust woman whom he referred to only as "the Canadian" because he couldn't remember her name. Sessions with her drove him crazy. After one, Paul escorted her politely to the front door, waved bye-bye, and explained with a false smile, a swimming motion, and the word "away," that he was going to the Caribbean on vacation.

She nervously adjusted the sit of her watch, which she wore turned around, its face on the underside of her wrist.

"When might you be returning?" she asked tentatively.

"I'm . . . not . . . com-coming back," he rejoined.

"We'll phone," I said, caught completely by surprise.

That was the last we saw of her.

All of Paul's speech therapists worked hard and stayed unflaggingly polite, but he disliked what he perceived as a condescending and too corrective manner. For speech therapy to work, patient and therapist need to feel as well matched as ice dancers. The kindest and most experienced of them was Sandra, a middle-aged woman with long brown hair and a lovely maternal way about her. Despite her patience, Paul was still suffering through therapy sessions.

After Sandra left one morning, he raised his rigid hands to the heavens as if summoning a lightning strike or preparing to do a war dance.

"She failed her postillion!" he wailed.

"I don't even know what a postillion *is*," I said, "but I'm sorry to hear she failed it."

I looked it up and found that a *postillion* is the person riding the lead horse of a horse-drawn carriage, guiding it from one post-house to the next. Once again, he couldn't remember a word like *cake* or *paper*, but he knew she was supposed to lead him from one stage to another.

Sandra continued to visit us on schedule, and during her next visit, instead of flash cards she used some art postcards I'd given her to break up the routine. Seated on a couch by the window, off to Paul's right, where he'd be less likely to spot me, I watched as he grappled with a dozen of the flash cards and postcards, most of which left him speechless or uttering the wrong words. One showed Raphael's famous painting of two baby angels leaning on their chubby elbows over a balcony.

"Chair-roo-beem," Paul piped up.

"No," Sandra patiently corrected, "these are angels, AINGELS."

I chuckled softly, but Sandra heard it and turned to me.

"A cherub is a baby angel," I said, taking the cue. "But the plural is cherubim." I raised what I hoped was a good-natured smile.

Several more flash cards followed. Then Sandra went over his written homework, patiently correcting it. When the session ended and she was packing up to leave, Paul looked exhausted and glum, thoroughly disappointed in himself.

"You're coming along fine," Sandra reassured him.

Paul shook his head and grumbled: "Words come like tardigrades."

Sandra started to speak, to say something like, *That's a nonsense word*, but paused. When her eyes sought mine, she discovered I was smiling.

"Water bears," I offered. "Microscopic little animals with eight legs that waddle like bears, and can survive *anything*—hot springs, absolute zero, outer space, massive radiation . . ."

"Cute!" Paul chimed in, happy, it seemed, to have made sense to someone. With his two pointer fingers, he drew a square in midair. Another *templum*—his all-purpose pantomime for envelopes, post-cards, boxes, Post-its, stamps, Slim Bears . . . and now tardigrades.

We had once admired black-and-white photographs of pudgy tardigrades in a magazine, awed to learn that they settle in ditches, leaf litter, and ponds, living for up to fifty years, and absolutely thriving at −400 degrees Fahrenheit. If their puddles dry up, they dry up, too, becoming light and aerial astronauts, who wake at the first dash of water to swell again and waddle after food once more.

"Yeah, they're adorable," I agreed, picturing their well-padded, huggable-looking bodies. Sandra's face screwed up, as if at a large insect.

". . . if you like that sort of thing," I quickly added.

One day I happened to be walking through our home library when Sandra was showing Paul a black-and-white photograph of a table with a telephone sitting on it.

"What is this?" she asked, pointing to the table.

"Sky-LAR-ghll?" Paul whispered.

"No, that's a nonsense word," she said pleasantly. "It's a *table*. And what is this?" she asked, pointing to the telephone.

"TESS-er-act?" he ventured.

"No, that's a nonsense word, too."

At that moment, my understanding, his therapy, and the trajectory of our lives abruptly changed. Startled, I turned on my heel and walked back into the library.

"No, tesseract *is* a real word!" I said. "It's a three-dimensional object unfolded into a fourth dimension. In a strange way, he's right, that's what a telephone is."

I didn't actually mean the fourth dimension of time we associate with *space-time*, but a physical fourth dimension—like length, breadth, and width—which creates a sort of Möbius strip.

Paul nodded vehemently. *How curious*, I thought. The words he learned when he was little—words like *table* and *chair*—might indeed be stuck in the broken primary-language areas of his brain. But it was just possible that sophisticated words, the ones he learned as an adult, get processed elsewhere, more like a second language. Doctors, speech therapists, and books on stroke didn't mention this, but it made sense, and I realized how important that insight might be for his improvement. His surprising use of *plebian, postillion, cherubim,* and *tardigrade* all suddenly fell into place.

From then on, I began rethinking Paul's therapy and creating homework tailored to his lifelong strengths, words and creativity, exercises with a little fun, a little flair, and not condescending, a sort of madcap *Mad Libs* that provided some much-needed humor (tough to come by for stroke victims and their loved ones). Some were easy, lest he grow discouraged, others a little more taxing. Instead of dull and childishly written exercises, I used adult vocabulary, and referred to people he knew and things happening around him, as well as familiar household objects. Had he been a welder or a golfer, I would have tried to include those activities. Here's one of the exercises I gave him:

When the fat lady sat on the swooning couch, she ＿＿.
The last thing Robert expected to see on a farm was a chicken wearing ＿＿.
In Diane's closet, one can find ＿＿.
When hummingbirds fall in love, they ＿＿.
Despite his height and decrepitude, he carried in his pockets

＿＿.

Just thinking about ＿＿ makes my heart revolve.

Airplanes —— and ——.
If I had flour, eggs, vanilla, and seven cockroaches, I could make
a ——.
The king said: "Bring me eight bronze monkeys and ——."
Few things on earth are as beautiful as ——.

Most days, I provided such fill-in-the-blank, *Mad Libs*–type
homework to do, and he also laboriously tried to write still-
unreadable notes to friends (squiggles instead of words, words misspelled, words left out, with many strike-throughs), practiced
check-writing, time-telling, and reading.

Returning to his study one day for a round of homework, he
declared: "When the iron strikes, you will have to obey," which
meant: "I'd better get started since I'm feeling inspired to work."

All the practice seemed to be helping. Paul found the freedom of
personally designed assignments liberating. A lifetime of buoyant,
and at times zany, thinking had ill-prepared him for straightfor-
ward exercises. His answers to my quizzes, such as this one, unfail-
ingly made me chuckle:

Q: Why was smoke coming out of the man's ears?
A: <u>Sitting in tub full dry ice.</u>

Paul was beginning to spout some normal expressions, which he
understood perfectly well: "Want to go out for a dinner date?" or
"I'm bone-weary." Also, with increasing frequency as the days
passed, he would use an unusual word correctly without being able
to define it. "I'm spavined" he began saying whenever he was
pooped.

"Do you know what *spavined* means?" I asked, suspicious that he
might not.

He thought hard for a moment, his face growing red from the
effort, as if he were trying to buttonhole a star. "No," he finally
admitted in dismay. "I used to."

I explained matter-of-factly that it's when a horse or cow has legs that bow a little convexly and can't walk right, and that he had used the word correctly, that it could mean very exhausted.

Another favorite was *skiving off*, British slang for avoiding work, whose sense of freedom doesn't stem from having nothing to do, but from evading a wealth of specific, pressing duties.

People's names seemed to live in their own drawer in his brain, one that was brutally hard for him to open. And the randomness of words embedded and words sprung loose constantly amazed me. Why should *checkbook* or *wallet* keep disappearing, like keys forever sliding to the bottom of a pocket, yet *spavined* always stay in plain view? Probably because nouns and verbs are quarried in different haunts of the brain.

"Don't *chavvle* it!" he chided me as I was opening an envelope for him by sliding my pointer finger under the flap and dragging it bumpily across.

"*Chavvle? . . . Chavvle.*" Paul beamed at me as I ferreted through the recesses of my memory. It wasn't nonsense sounds, that much I knew, but where had I heard the word before? Then it came to me: his mother, Mildred, a woman with gray-blue eyes, in her eighties, standing in the kitchen of an Eckington row house that sprawled up three narrow flights of stairs. Chenille tablecloth laid with empty jam jars and mixed crockery. Few modern fripperies. Electric lights replaced the gaslights that used to beg for another penny. But no telephone, bank account, or refrigerator (food stayed cool on a stone slab in the basement). The memory glided across my inner eye: beside her a slender forty-something Paul wearing tan corduroy pants and a striped long-sleeved shirt, whittling the edge off a piece of spice cake, and Mildred mock-chiding him with, "Now, now, don't go and *chavvle* it!

Chavvle—a Derbyshire word for cutting food untidily.

An equally exotic word tumbled from his mouth on a dinner outing. We'd chosen a quiet out-of-the-way restaurant, where he needn't worry about running into anyone he knew, which would have entailed the agony of talking. I steered him safely around the large central fireplace, between the close tables, and into his chair.

We'd learned by now to practice beforehand how he would order in the restaurant. Withdrawing a crib sheet from his shirt pocket, he read off simple requests that wouldn't prompt questions from the waitress—"Egg beater omelet—*plain*. Mashed potatoes. Gravy. Skim milk"—trying, I could tell, to sound casual.

After a quiet and blessedly uneventful meal, he pulled a credit card from his wallet and offered it to the waitress. We'd rehearsed this ahead of time, too, since he couldn't see the numbers on paper money, or reliably remember that $50 was different from $5. But as she swept the card away, he whispered to me:

"How much . . . how much . . ." He pointed sharply at the table as he groped for a word, finally throwing up his hands as if to say, *This isn't the right word but it's the best I can come up with*, as he pronounced "*baksheesh?*"

Of course, *baksheesh*, the Turkish for tip or bribe. I wasn't sure where I knew it from—maybe the trip to Istanbul with my mom when I was a moody sixteen-year-old and she, already a seasoned traveler, an attractive woman of 46 with a teenage chaperone in tow.

"My, my," I said, nodding appreciatively. "I'll work out the *tip* for you."

"*Tip, tip, tip*," I heard him repeating under his breath.

"Can you say something cute?" I playfully teased as we were driving home in the declining light. It didn't matter to me what lingo he used; I just wanted him to keep trying to communicate for as long as possible every day.

"Don't know," he said weakly. His few words dropped down into a deep silence, and I forgot about my question as night's dark cocoon began gathering around us.

Then, unexpectedly, with some labor and a silent fanfare, he pronounced: "You are the *hapax legomenon* of my life." *Hapax legomenon*: Latin for a word that occurs only once in the entire written record of a language. Like *flother*, used once, in a thirteenth-century text, as a synonym for *snowflake*, or *slaepwerigne*, used once in an Old English text to mean weary with sleep. I'd stumbled upon *hapax legomenon* one day while grazing in the dictionary, that Land of Perpetual Detours.

"Well done!" I cheered.

You're still in there! I thought, my morale lifted by the flicker of his creative spirit. Despite everything, despite the monumental effort it was taking, the smithy who bends words was still keeping a forge somewhere in his brain.

He's nearly eighty, I thought, *and there's no predicting the what-will-be. For any of us. Carpe diem.* Then I smiled bittersweetly, because *carpe diem* sounded like a travel allowance for goldfish, a pun that would have tickled Paul in bygone days. Now? Could he still make the mental hop from *carpe diem* sounding like *per diem*, and goldfish being a member of the carp family, to *carpe diem* not really meaning *seize the day*, but equaling what the carp's employer will reimburse him for in a twenty-four-hour period when he's traveling on business? That's a lot of swerves. For a healthy brain, a pleasurable jaunt, but for Paul, whose mental pogo stick was missing some of its spring? Doubtful. And then he might feel bad about disappointing me, maybe slump into a discouraged low. *Let it all go,* I thought. *Seize the day.*

CHAPTER 20

ENRICH YOUR LAB RAT'S ENVIRONMENT IF YOU WANT *him to thrive.* To that end, Liz and I engaged Paul in "conversation therapy" nonstop. Almost daily, Liz regaled Paul with stories about her neighbor Gustaf, who could easily have been a zany character from one of Paul's novels brought to life, and Paul always listened raptly to the madcap adventures.

"Gustaf's back from Chernobyl!" she said. "He slept outside on the ground to save money. Sometimes under bridges! One morning he woke up scared to death by a big guy with a gun yelling at him in Russian. Remember, Gustaf's seven feet tall, and wears bright yellow bell-bottoms, so he's not exactly blending into the landscape."

On other days I overheard: "Gustaf's planning an illegal trip to a banned, deserted Japanese island. . . . He thinks he can kite-board to it. It's only about a mile offshore. If the breeze is right . . ."

"Gustaf's having the guy from Texas who puts decals on the Hooters buses apply a decal to his car with an eight-foot-long naked woman on one side."

"Gustaf bought a new toy! Anti-gravity boots with *springs*, and apparently they're super-dangerous. They're supposed to make you be able to bounce about ten feet up in the air. He's been putting a harness around his waist, his helmet on, and roping himself to the branch of a tree in the front yard. He's been practicing jumping, springing up and down. . . . The neighbors seem a bit confused!"

"Gustaf has gone kite-surfing again on Lake Ontario. . . ."

Liz was a natural natterer, for whom any topic was fair game, from paranormal military programs to avant-garde art glass or endangered toads. As a result, I never knew what I'd hear drifting in through the screens, usually scraps of conversation too amusing to ignore. Quite often Liz regaled Paul with tales of her previous jobs, an American miscellany that, she swore, had perfectly pre-pared her for our household: slaloming through traffic and riding rails under the Capitol as a bike messenger in D.C., where she had also worked for the National Rural Electric Cooperative Associa-tion and the National Institute of Standards and Technology. Lodg-ing in a Mormon trailer park in Utah while mapping volcanics and faults for the U.S. Geological Survey. Jack-of-all-trades at the Q-U-P-Q-U-G-I-A-Q café (as I heard her spell it out to Paul), a coffeehouse and hostel in Anchorage, Alaska, named for an Inuit myth about a ten-legged polar bear. Coordinating residents at an Alaskan men's homeless shelter. Shuffling contracts for a high-rise construction firm in Los Angeles. Making cheese for Maine's iconic Nezinscott Farm, and careening their organic milk delivery van up and down the stony coast. Or her first job in Ithaca, har-vesting organic herbs for the farmers' market, which she confessed she found "a little dull as herbs don't move very quickly." And then, of course, before nursing school, with all its viscera and checklists, a couple of years on a thoroughbred farm, where she did everything from mucking out stalls to aiding veterinarian and far-rier, and got used to handling half tons of snort and lather.

Or she aired tales from recent trips: Baja for New Year's on a hippie bus from San Francisco. Canoe camping in Canada with her girlfriends. Wine-tasting in Oregon with the in-laws. Cézanne at the Philadelphia Museum of Art with her mother. The Pork Pavil-ion at the Missouri State Fair. The Roosevelt Memorial in D.C. (where a runaway horse was being chased, unsuccessfully, by Capi-tol policemen on bikes). Epic dragon-boat gaiety—from the Olympic paddling course in Montreal to our own Finger Lakes International Dragon Boat Festival, where a Buddhist monk blessed the boats and painted pupils on the eyes of the figureheads to give them sight.

Paul was by no means suffering from lack of verbal input; it was verbal output that he still found oh-so-difficult.

Whenever Paul didn't know a word, Liz or I would ask him to let his brain hunt until it found another route around the roadblock. That took a while, and sometimes I could almost feel his mind panting through a labyrinth, hitting blind alleys, backtracking, and heading off in another direction.

"When is the nosebleed on? . . . No, no, not nosebleed . . . running and gunning . . . not gunning . . . ball . . . you know . . . city in England . . . kicking, kicking, yes, ball . . ."

"The Arsenal vs. Manchester United soccer match?" I guessed.

His face melted in relief. "Yesss," he sighed.

Paul adopted a verbal shorthand for letting us know when he was tired and needed to stop wrangling with words.

"Later!" Uttered with a dismissive wave of his hand, shooing us away. His eyes said: *My brain is nodding from all the work. Let me rest.*

"How does it feel to live in a sorority?" Liz teased, hoping he'd muster a response.

Paul couldn't resist the bait. "I *luv* women," he replied with an exaggerated leer, then rolled onto his side, dug his face into a welcoming crease of the couch, and plunged into a deep sleep, waking an hour later.

A born word-maven and reader, Liz often chatted around the kitchen, and I gabbled back as Paul woke up slowly over breakfast. He preferred to do one thing at a time, while Liz and I conversed easily while doing chores. Not just true of our household. Women ply the rapids of language more easily; and if we seemed to be talking double-time, we probably were doing that, too. Women can pronounce words faster than men, and utter more sentences in a given amount of time. Maybe because women use both hemispheres to comb through sounds, while men mainly use the left side. With a richer bounty of connections among neurons and a more thickly wired *corpus callosum* zooming traffic between the two hemispheres, the female brain may be better organized for language. Whatever the reason, females are less prey to stuttering, dyslexia, autism, and other language problems, including aphasia.

Most mornings Paul seemed to thrive on our prattle, vicariously enjoying my verbal high-jinks and keen to follow Liz's newsy updates about life at home and the inspired antics of her husband Will, and of course the unending adventures of Gustaf.

"Too fast!" Paul chided us. "I'm . . . not awake! Tell me l-later."

"Welcome to the planet of caffeinated women," I teased. And then, out of the blue, in his old normal tone of voice, he stopped me cold by muttering:

"Every house is a madhouse at some time or another."

My pulse jumped. A flutter in time. My old Paul was back with his cynical wit and one of his pet sayings, from a short story of Edith Wharton's.

"What did you say?" I wondered if I'd heard him right or was merely hallucinating.

Taking a moment to carefully swallow his mouthful of omelet, he repeated: "Every mouse glad mouse bother."

"Ah . . . yes, my little mouse," I patted him gently on the shoulder. "We won't bother you with our jabbering—not *yet*, anyway!"

So the perfectly rendered quotation was just a phantom of my mind born from wishing so hard. The way I sometimes startled, quite sure I saw my mother, strolling on a sunny street, years after her death. The brain searches for the fond familiars it has lost, their sounds and images and habits of mind that haunted it long enough to leave indelible traces, scant truths it could rely on in an uncertain world.

For me, one of the most disturbing aspects of Paul's aphasia was his no longer being able to find ways to describe the combinative zest of life. That was beyond odd for Paul, of all people, whose written descriptions of anything had tended to be colorful, many-layered, and jazzy. By mixing language with a free hand, his images throbbed with an acute physicality, full of life's sexy, chaotic, nostalgic, belligerent, crushing, confusing vitality. Objects could lose their identities in the identity of other objects. Sometimes the images didn't so much combine things as trail them through a slush of other phenomena, suggesting the behavior deep in our brains, hearts, and cells, so that the language of his books often echoed their subject matter. Like his countryman Dylan Thomas, he could always be counted on to see the shroud maker in the surgeon sewing up after an operation. His images weren't well behaved, nor always explicit. But they were bold, keen-eyed, wild, and voluptuous, sometimes tenderly so.

Cheese turning a pale green cheek like an albino monkey slipping into a vale of chlorophyll. Apples waiting to crack open like two clasped hands parting.

—*Portable People*

Or:

With sunset came an almost careless quiet as the saffron over the western range turned vermillion and the antennas, the dishes, on top began to resemble mutants semaphoring for help, silhouettes against an engulfing scarlet.

—*A Stroke of Genius*

Now he could sometimes describe pictures in short simple phrases, but rarely harness the vivid resemblance of analogies; adjectives were hard to come by in his frayed and burned association areas; all the beakers of categories lay in fragile ruins.

"The sky is beautiful today, isn't it?" I observed. I knew he exulted in bright delft-blue skies. "What color is it?"

"Blue," he said.

"What kind of blue today?"

He thought for a long, long while, then repeated all he could come up with: "Blue."

By late afternoon, the day had dwindled into those hours when stroke and Alzheimer's patients are sometimes described as *sun-*

downing, descending into a state of agitated confusion—usually from being over tired by the demands of the day. The rest of us mortals may just say we're crashing from a day too full of hubbub and caffeine. For Paul, *sundowning* brought a real eclipse of language, a return to the long stumbling silences he dreaded.

This time, I couldn't lead him into simple talk, and he didn't want to watch television either. We sat in silence as the moon rose like a fleshy white old scar. All day, he'd been trying to communicate without much success (aphasia's roadblocks can vary dramatically from day to day), and he seemed at last to have surrendered. He raised his fists to his forehead, palms facing inward, and tapped them gently. I gasped. I'd seen that gesture before performed by Koko the gorilla, who had been taught to communicate in sign language. It was the sign for "really stupid." Had Paul seen the same films of Koko that I had? I wasn't sure.

"Are you trying to say something?" I asked quietly.

He nodded yes, but gave up the effort of pursuing it.

Using a vocabulary adapted from American Sign Language, Koko could describe her world, express her wants, ask questions, and even share complex feelings. Evidently she experienced what we think of as quintessentially human—abstract thought—and relayed many of her states of mind to her trainers by signing such things as: "This makes me sad," "I'm ashamed," "It's fake," "I'm mad," "That hurts," "I'm sorry," "I need your help," "I want to visit," "love," "time," and a host of other expressions. She was also creative. She enjoyed painting one canvas after another and sometimes described the subject matter, even if her bright red "bird" seemed to have an awful lot of wings. Unless, maybe, she was depicting it in flight? Most importantly, she knew that she was using signs to communicate, and she could mine a vocabulary of about a thousand words. Making monkey-baby sounds with Paul had felt intimate and right, but I grew immeasurably sad when I realized that, while sundowning, Paul was operating on a linguistic level below that of Koko the gorilla.

CHAPTER 21

A BIG SURPRISE FOR BOTH PAUL AND ME WAS HOW MUCH
we'd grown to like Liz—who sometimes seemed like our
instant grown-up daughter and at others like a sibling or college
housemate. Liz was fun: bookish, chatty, opinionated, and quirky
enough that she fit right in. She threw herself into things—be it
geology or dragon boating—with an obsessive gusto that made perfect sense to us, since we were forever fiendishly possessed by things,
too. She became our familiar, in many senses of the word, but especially: (1) an intimate friend, and (2) an animal who embodies a
supernatural spirit and aids a witch in performing magic.

Stroke patients, particularly those with aphasia, often lose
some old friends. It's hard enough for a spouse to learn to communicate with them at a vastly slower pace, using fewer words in
response, without monologuing or feeling too awkward to know
what to say. A few friends, even long-standing ones, were not
able to cope with the aphasia and deserted Paul. I listened to his
sorrow, his anger, his sadness over them. But I knew this was
usual, and that he needed to make some new friends with people
who knew and liked him as the person he was *after* the stroke.
Some did, including Liz.

In the pool, clad in a cheerful striped bikini, Liz often shared medical stories with Paul, and I occasionally overheard snippets of them drifting on the breeze through my study windows.

"A severe reaction to an antibiotic . . . body covered *all* over with oozing blisters, and on his palms and the soles of his feet . . ."

Or, on another occasion, "I got to pull out a vacuum-surgical drain today, it's called a grenade! It *really does* look like a little grenade. You squeeze it to create the vacuum, hook it up, and it sucks out all the blood and nasty fluid from the surgical area. You just pull out the tubing when it's full. . . ."

Liz practiced her new medical terminology on Paul, bludgeoning him with word games, partly to amuse herself during the languid hours she spent with him in the pool.

"I have a word for you," she'd say teasingly or as though she was bearing a gift. "Do you know *anhedonia?*"

With a few hints he'd sometimes miraculously remember, pulling it out of his word hoard.

"Guess what I'm learning?!" I heard her chime merrily one day as I was passing the living room's back door. "Extrapyramidal neuroleptic side effects!"

"Have you ever heard of *akathisia?* Okay. Fine. Do you know . . . *dystonia, dysphoria, akinesia?*" "How about easy ones . . . *trichtillomania? pneumothorax?* Maybe a little geology? *Anhydrite? Ooid? Syncline? Cataclastic? Breccia?*"

"Wanna hear about the four major types of prostate surgery?" She prattled on without waiting for an answer: "Well, the least invasive, most comfortable option goes up through the penis like a Foley catheter, but it's *actually* a miniature roto-rooter. . . ."

Paul looked forward to their swimming-buddy chatterbox time. They shared a bit of a vile irreverent sense of humor. The more gruesome the story was, the better. And Liz seemed to enjoy making him grimace.

"I like to think," she told me out of his earshot, "that sometimes some of these poor miserable patients make him feel a little better about his situation . . . to use a word I learned from Paul, a little *schadenfreude.* I mean, here he is in the sun in his pool, swimming away the afternoon . . . and these poor folks are in the hospital, oozing with drains!"

From my desk window, which commands a view of the back-yard, I could hear Liz luring him into talking more by asking about things in our house:

"In the library, there's a photo of you and Diane standing next to another couple in front of a little airplane. It's a neat photo. Where were you going?"

I paid attention this time, curious how he'd answer.

Paul looked stumped, and, undeterred, Liz pressed on with a clue designed to prod his memory.

"I think it said something about the Caribbean."

I watched Paul absently drawing an arabesque on the water with one hand as he tried to haul up the right word.

She started reeling off Caribbean locations: "Dominica? Cay-mans? Virgin Islands? . . ."

Eventually she got to the Turks and Caicos, where we had flown with our friends Jeanne and Steve in 1982. The flight down, in Steve's vintage twin-engined Apache, following the Bahamian chain, had been a pastel idyll. But on the return flight we'd been vectored into the center of a fuming thunderhead, where the air glittered an unholy green, and suddenly, in a thick whiteout, with-out our feeling anything like motion, the dials had spun around. Hurled by up- and downdrafts, the plane was doing a loop-de-loop in the clouds. Fortunately, Steve was an aerobatic pilot, who read the instruments fast and knew how to recover—flying the loop blind—even though a twin Apache carrying four people wasn't the small single-engine Pitts biplane he normally barnstormed in per-formances. Equally luckily, the Apache had strong struts connect-ing the fuselage and wings—otherwise the wings would have ripped off. A fledgling single-engine pilot sitting in the copilot's seat, I saw the instruments tumbling and guessed what was happen-ing, but I wouldn't have been able to save us. However, I had abso-lute faith Steve could. I'll never forget the look of contained panic on his face as he noticed me holding my hand lightly on the yoke (the two yokes move in synchrony), following his lead.

"This isn't the time to be learning!" he'd snapped. "Secure everything!"

I quickly stowed anything that might zing around the cabin. There was even a term for the jumble of plane and human para-phernalia that fell out when you shook a plane upside down: *gub-bins*. It was a favorite word of Paul's. Then, with a strangeness one rarely encounters or lives through, a suitcase began to levitate and sail forward through the air like balsawood. In the backseat, Paul and Jeanne looked green, scared, as they grabbed the case. And then right side up at last we leveled out and flew into plain old welcome hard rain.

The postcards Steve later had printed to commemorate the trip were a black-and-white photograph showing Jeanne, Steve, Paul and me posing plane-side before the southbound flight, with the title "Trucking Through the Turks: A Sky Art Event."

How much of that sifted through Paul's memory in the pool when he heard the words "Turks and Caicos?"

"Oh yes! With friends and *gubbins*," was all he answered.

Listening to the exchange, I thought how frustrating it must have been for him not to be able to share the trip's details with Liz. That podgy little word, *gubbins*, held his brain's key to the whole drama.

Pressing on, Liz continued asking him about curios around the living room, such as where the pounded-brass cauldron came from (the trip to Istanbul with my mom when I was sixteen), why there was an inflatable cheetah standing in front of the fireplace (it came from the Warsaw Zoo), how we acquired the see-through globe of the solar system and constellations (it went with Paul's large tele-scope, folded up and parked in a corner), where we'd bought the purple faux-velvet swooning couch (a shop in West Palm Beach), if the books in the bookcase were arranged in any special way (they were, it just wasn't obvious), and where he'd found the tribe of

Hopi kachina dolls that was dancing, spell-casting, and generally mischief-making behind the floral couch (Tucson).

Either he'd remember the errant word, or she'd finally guess, or he'd end the game by saying: "We'll ask Diane."

In the pool, he spoke more ably than on dry land. Maybe the weightlessness lulled him, or maybe it was the idleness of the conversation, the lack of pressure. He'd flap his arms around slowly, and he'd sweep the skimmer in endless arcs, while Liz hung on to the side of the pool and kicked her legs, or trod in the deep end, gabbing away or waiting for him to answer. Their record was three skin-wrinkling hours in the water.

I often joined the floating fellowship. When we talked with Paul in the pool, we paid attention to his mood. Did he seem like he wanted to space out and just meditate? Did he seem open to questions? We'd ask a few. Babble on a bit. Give his brain some quiet time to rest. Babble some more. Ask another question or two. Give him lots of time to answer. Do little charades to help him with words. Coach as needed. (Something like: "Hmm. City . . . in New York. Do you mean . . . ? Upstate? Rochester? Albany? Buffalo? Saratoga?") This created less pressure than a formal speech therapy session, where he'd have to focus and perform without the luxury of frequent long rest periods. More time to answer, less pressure, less frustration, a more relaxed mood, conversation that was tailored to his life and interests, and lots of varied clues—with all of that, he found himself most fluent when half submerged.

That he didn't swim at all the first season after the stroke—however happy he might be lolling in the pool—really concerned me. Along with his inability to button a shirt, work household gadgets, or remember instructions, it suggested serious damage to his *procedural* memory, the unconscious memory for *how* something happened, or *how to* do things. Not *that* something happened, which involves a different brain system. Drawing on many areas of the brain (cerebellum, basal ganglia, various sensory and motor pathways, among other regions), subtle skills like bathing, dressing, walking, and swimming evade language, but help the body remember itself in the world. It's why one rarely forgets how to ride a bicycle, despite the intricacies of balance it requires. One needs to think about how to float only while learning; after that the body remembers how to angle arms and torso just so, without consultation. For most people, such skills lie beyond words.

Paul remembered what swimming was, and where it took place, and even the sweet spell of gliding through the water. The missing piece of the equation was *how* to thrash his arms, kick his legs, and glide—all in unison. With practice, he had relearned how to use a spoon, a chair, a comb, the toilet, but some household tasks still eluded him. He regarded a can opener as a contraption from hell. Pens escaped his fingers. Shaving required lots of energy and focus, and he was completely baffled by cleaning his electric razor, which meant taking bits apart and then reassembling them in the right order. It made me wish he'd spent more time in occupational therapy at the hospital.

The two fingers on his right hand remained clenched from the stroke, and needed to be pried open and stretched each day. Before the stroke, Paul had had dry cracked hooves instead of heels, but a routine of regular foot massage restored the circulation and kept the hooves soft. Liz did the stretching and massaging on weekdays, I continued on weekends and whenever Liz was away. No amount of stretching would ever straighten his fingers again because their problem wasn't entirely muscular. Yet stretching and massage did ease them for a short spell, long enough to grip a pen and practice writing, or hold a fork or spoon for dinner, and it felt soothing, and helped keep the contracture from getting worse.

The daily routine never varied: hand massage preceded swimming, and swimming always ended promptly at 4:50, so that Paul could get ready to watch *Judge Judy*, a new addiction and instant mainstay of his verbal rehabilitation. After an hour of courtroom drama and dialogue—money owed on used cars, unpaid loans, scam artists, angry "keying" of a rival's or a cheating lover's car, nasty disputes over minor objects between ex-spouses, evil girlfriends, unleashed pitbulls, inheritance disputes, freeloading boyfriends, and bad debts—he watched the dire BBC news, then the national news, and after that ate dinner and tried to talk with me until movie time.

We developed a habit of watching a TV or rental movie almost every night; Paul couldn't always follow the plot, but I gave him updates at regular intervals and answered questions. He found old movies we'd already seen easiest to grasp, though anything with many characters or intersecting plotlines rattled and confused him. In his sundowning state, he could still manage language in this more passive way, with the help of Hollywood's enticing images and musical scores, provided they didn't make too many demands.

Ironically, he understood better than I the canny, ornate, electrifying Shakespeare plays filmed and acted in by Kenneth Branagh, because he had studied the plays as a boy, at a time when some of the colloquial English spoken in the British Midlands wasn't all that far from Shakespearean. And he'd often heard the local miners addressing one another as "sirrah," the Elizabethan word for sir.

I also adored Shakespeare, but half the time I couldn't translate the Elizabethan spoken at such a natural, conversational clip, and, unlike Paul, I didn't know the plays nearly by heart. But in *Henry V, Hamlet, Much Ado About Nothing*, and *Love's Labour's Lost*, Branagh, Emma Thompson, Paul Scofield, Laurence Olivier, and the rest of their brilliant troupe acted so expressively that my mirror neurons helped me fathom what they meant, despite my stumbling over some of the vocabulary. Watching the plays put me, however faintly, in Paul's aphasic shoes, struggling to understand words I once knew, spoken too fast, and having to rely on the primitive cues supplied by masterful acting: facial expressions, tone of voice, and body language.

We may owe all of our cherished parlance to those aptly named brain cells, our mirror neurons, with which we mirror one another's yawns or smiles of contentment. They're plentiful in Broca's area, which processes language in humans, signing in monkeys, and communication in other animals, too. Before humans shared words, our ancestors would have used hand gestures and facial expressions to communicate, until what they needed to say grew far too subtle and complex for mere pantomime, and prodded by necessity, they made the ingenious leap to strings of words. At times, Paul now reminded me of those crafty folk—when he cobbled together words the way two-year-olds, Tarzan, and speakers of "pidgin" languages do, re-creating a sort of protolanguage. Like the time he asked for "*nice ice*," and meant lemon sorbet. In those moments, was his brain paging back through evolution and tapping the vestigal traces of how language first evolved?

Just keep his language mill churning, I thought, *that's key*. I pictured a sunlit gorge and cascading waterfalls in the Adirondacks, where we once visited an old fashioned, water-powered grist mill on our way to Cooperstown for a weekend of opera. A lumbering and indelicate image of the brain, to be sure, but practical, mercantile. His grist mill cried out for new fittings and sluice gates, help restoring the grinding stones and fixing the sieves. And it might need to outsource. But it couldn't function at all without tons of grain. So, one way or another, from waking until bedtime I tried to keep Paul drenched in words. This much seemed elemental, and it proved critically important. It exhausted him mentally, of course, so he had to take several naps during the day. But it forced his brain to harvest words and mill language nonstop, whether it wanted to or not, planting seeds for growth, I hoped, among the desolate neurons.

CHAPTER 22

SOMETHING I FOUND ESPECIALLY ODD, BUT ALSO MERCI-
ful, was that Paul's temperament had sweetened since the
stroke. No longer dealing with the frustrations of teaching or publishing, he wasn't waking up in a high blood pressure rage, or
barely containing a volatile anger. When we met, he'd been a
charming alcoholic with a violent temper, a James Joyce sort of artist with a sparkling gift for words. I'd grown used to never knowing when Paul would explode. But he wasn't always combustible;
most times he was quintessentially loving, a real sweetheart. The
lurking land mine was part of a pattern: his unpredictable explo-
sions, my fright and crying, our coming apart, his regret and prom-
ises, my forgiveness, our reunion. For years of our marriage, I'd
walked on eggshells around him, because it took so little to trigger
what he described as his "Irish temper."

Not now. Surprisingly, his temper vanished a few weeks after
the stroke, when he became mellower, more patient, deeply appreciative, and I felt grateful for his new twist of mind. His struggles
and goals weren't competitive, he was swaddled in overt love and
encouragement, and he was taking an antidepressant for the first
time in his life (50 milligrams Zoloft). The combo—plus whatever

had happened in his brain during the stroke—produced a sweeter, less stormy Paul, which I found wonderfully welcome.

Such a spirited change is not unusual. Personality can about-face after a stroke, sometimes for the better, sometimes for the worse. A placid soul can become impulsive, angry, irritable, anxious, or emotionally flattened. President Woodrow Wilson, who suffered a stroke during the Versailles Peace Conference, is one dramatic public example.

> Even though the stroke didn't paralyze him, the people who knew him saw an immediate negative change in his personality. He was irritable, inflexible, and spiteful, whereas before he was forward thinking and able to compromise. He also became less sociable. Several weeks after the first stroke, he had another one that paralyzed his left side. Despite his obvious infirmity, he denied having any problems (denial is very common). . . . Those around him became very distressed. He fired his secretary of state for trying to discuss his medical situation with the cabinet. His stroke may have involved setting the stage for World War II. After his stroke, he could no longer argue effectively for the League of Nations.
>
> —Daniel Amen, *Healing the Hardware of the Soul*

Did Paul's personality change owe more to the stroke or to the circumstances following it? Hard to say. What we call "personality" doesn't exist in isolation; it defines itself by how it interacts with others. It's not an impervious phantom, but interpersonal; and, since the stroke, his relationships had all changed. A bit paranoid before, he now found people acting more caring, forgiving, and encouraging. In this one way, Paul's changing psyche felt better for me, even despite the heart-wrenching loss of my intellectual companion, because he was able to love me more completely. So perhaps I persisted, not just to keep Paul alive, or even to keep myself from experiencing loss, but because in some ways he finally *was* more alive for me.

But as my energy continued to flag, I realized I couldn't meet my work deadlines. I would need an extra year to finish *The Zookeeper's Wife*. And I would need to cancel spring and summer talks and readings. Although I'd promised to write a regular column for *Discover* magazine, I emailed the then-editor, Steve Petranek, explaining about Paul's stroke, and that I hadn't the time or energy for work. Steve replied with an encouraging account of his father, a conductor and accomplished viola and violin player who had had a stroke at about the same age as Paul. Steve's father had also lost his ability to speak. Actually, what he lost was his English vocabulary—he could still speak the Czech he had learned as a boy growing up in a Czech community in Cedar Rapids. He never regained his mastery of the viola, his favored instrument, but after relentless physical therapy he became remarkably better than he had ever been at the violin (even though the two instruments are quite similar). Meanwhile, he began tackling children's crossword puzzles. By the time he died, he was back to enjoying his daily *New York Times* crossword puzzle. A testament to the power of plasticity and practice.

From Petranek, I learned that a person has to hear a word repeated about two thousand times before it's deeply embedded in long-term memory. On an index card, I jotted down a list of everyday words Paul was having special trouble with—such as *Paul, Diane, drink, checkbook, hummingbird, wallet*—ones seemingly erased from his universe, and I began including them in sentences as much as possible.

"Do you think hummingbirds have checkbooks?" I asked Paul one day. He laughed, nodded yes, and drew the tiniest oblong checkbook in the air. Ten times in a row I had him repeat *checkbook*. Half an hour later, he had already forgotten the word, as if his brain had written it in invisible ink.

"Look! At the feeder, there's a bird—what is it?"

Fumbling for the right word, but failing in his quest, he produced something which he didn't understand: "Zinc quadrant."

"No, it's named after the carefree sound it makes," I hinted. "Hhhh . . . hummmm . . . innng . . ."

"Hummingbird!" he chirped triumphantly.

"Right! *Hummingbird*. I wonder what hummingbirds keep in their wallets. Pin-ups?"

"Sugar?" he offered.

"Where's my . . . fool's cap?" he then asked unexpectedly.

Fool's cap? I thought. *Does he really mean a court jester's hat?* I pictured the gaily colored cap with many peaks, each tipped by a jingling bell. Or—and I feared this was more likely—did he mean a *dunce cap*, the paper cone slow students were once sometimes forced to wear?

He made a writing gesture. *Of course! Heavyweight paper.* The original manufacturer of it had used a watermark of a three-pointed fool's cap with little bells. It was years since I'd glimpsed that watermark. But surely he remembered where the paper was—I'd seen him taking some sheets from the shelf in my study only an hour before.

"Do you possibly mean *checkbook*?" I tried.

"Yes!" he said with relief, and I led him to the special drawer where he kept his checkbooks.

Sometimes these non sequiturs were funny, but at others simply awful, jamming his brain when he most wanted to comunicate.

"The second stage of yawning presses down on my feet," he complained one morning after much hesitation and false starts, in which words caromed like bumper cars. After hard digging and what he called "blockades," and many yes/no answers to questions designed to help him sort the words into general categories, I finally understood what he was trying to say, something homely and mundane—that the soft green blanket I'd added to his side of the bed the night before had felt too heavy on his feet. Simple words like "blanket" and "bed" were still eluding him. I added them to my growing list of words to repeat often during the day.

Around this time, for some reason, I began addressing him as "wombat." Though not entirely strange, since we always did have lots of totemic names for each other, "wombat" was a sparkling fresh new endearment. I showed him a photograph of adorable baby wombats, wombats digging holes with their long claws, and two fluffy wombat mates sleeping together in the sun. An Australian friend sent us a fleecy stuffed toy wombat, whom we named Woodrow, and who assumed a regal position on the purple swooning couch.

Snuggling in bed one morning, I said to him, "Good morning Mr. Wombat." And he echoed: "Good morning, Mrs. Wombat." He was often wonderfully more fluent then, half awake, with no pressure on him.

Sleepily, I posed the question: "Hey, I wonder what Mr. and Mrs. Wombat's first names are. Let's see. His name is . . . *Hydroelectric* . . . Hydroelectric Wombat. And hers?"

He thought for a moment. "*Clopidogerel*," he said.

"Clopidogerel?!" Where did that come from? It slowly dawned on me: it was a drug name he must have heard in a television commercial. "Right—Hydroelectric and Clopidogerel Wombat. Do you suppose they have kids?"

"Six," he said. "Half, half."

"Three boys, three girls?"

"Yes."

"Well, what are their names?"

At this he began giggling, and finally said "German . . ." He couldn't find the next word, so he made a diving motion with one hand.

"Airplane?"

"No." His hand plunged shallowly this time.

"U-boat? Battleship?"

"Yes!" Eyes lighting up. "But sick."

"They named their kids after sunken German battleships?"

With a wicked smile, he said: "Bismarck, Graf Spee, Tirpitz . . ."

We began laughing uncontrollably, me from the sheer relief of hearing him play with words again so imaginatively, as we pictured Hydroelectric and Clopidogerel Wombat introducing their six children named after sunken German battleships. When we finally emerged from the bedroom at last, Liz, who'd arrived for the morning to help with Paul, asked with a grin: "What on earth was going on in there?" Still giggling, we had a splendid time explaining.

After a stroke, play is the last thing on a couple's mind, but it drew us thankfully together in innocence, it felt so good to laugh and romp with words together again.

After lunch, Jeannie and Steve joined us for a short visit, and conversation turned to TV's Catholic nuns. Steve's elderly mother was devout and watched *Sister Angelica* all day long, which meant that whenever Steve visited her, as he did almost weekly, he was subjected to a *Sister Angelica* marathon, too. Paul unexpectedly described Steve's mother as a "holy constabulary," dissolving us all into peals of laughter. A banner day. Laughter really is a wonderful elixir, and it can be hard to find in the shadow of misfortune.

After they left, and Paul began sundowning, the house felt familiar and silent. We sat purposely listening to the silence, broken now and then by the liquid marbling of birdsong. The sun had begun dusting the treetops with crimson.

"Do you dwell on things a lot, brood?" I asked Paul.

"No," he replied. "Watch trees. First time I've noticed how gorgeous. So tall. Lots of different."

"So many voluptuous shades of green," I said, and he nodded yes, approving of the word "voluptuous."

"The plants are fluorescing," he observed appreciatively.

I imagined leaves with the beauty of fluorescent minerals, glowing like brilliantly colored neon flowers. Or maybe he was picturing the fluorescent fungi in the woods, whose visible part, the "mushroom," looks innocent enough, but whose tentacles invade rotting wood and glow an eerie green, making logs shimmer like they're burning inside. It always amused me that mushrooms, lightning bugs, and trick-or-treating children with "light sticks" are all lit by the same cold green fire.

When he was a boy, Paul once had a chemistry lab that included the mineral fluorite, whose crystals scintillated in the dark. Envious, one year I requested that he give me "a British boy's Christmas," and was delighted to receive a boxed chemistry lab (nothing that fluoresced, alas), a plane-spotting guide, and an Erector set (with which we built a battery-operated wagon that sometimes buzzed down the hallway carrying the mail).

All Paul meant on this occasion was: "The flowers are blooming."

I felt guilty when I wasn't with Paul at such quiet moments, just for company, although I had stacks of work to do. It was difficult for me not to imagine his being hideously bored, but I came to realize in time that, on the contrary, he was calmly living in the moment, which flowed into the next without necessarily being tethered to the one before.

As he would tell me much later, *"The casual observer must have thought me unable to think. But wrong in the extreme: I was living in the aphasic moment, silenced, but with whatever internal organ I possessed thinking hard and fast. My brain was alive and kicking me in the pants. And thank god for it, for giving me a way through my enforced silence."*

We began quietly talking, an easy togetherness that felt good.

"What is a *stroke*?" he asked yet again when I mentioned the word in a sentence. So many times before I and others had told him what had happened to him. And he knew the word *stroke*, but couldn't seem to retain what it meant, that a clot had broken free and lodged in his brain, cutting off the blood and oxygen to some regions and cells. For him, the definition was elusive, not a sentence but a cloudscape.

"In your case," I reiterated, "you've had damage in the left frontal and temporal areas, known as Broca's and Wernicke's aphasia." I pointed on my head to the regions, then launched into the familiar litany of what aphasia can and usually does produce.

—Struggling to get every word out.
—Difficulty finding the exact words you want.
—Talking in ways its hard for people to follow.
—Getting stuck on certain words or phrases.
—Thinking you're talking perfectly well, when you're not.
—Having trouble following conversations, especially if you're

tired or anxious, or if someone speaks too quickly, or uses long
sentences, or if there's lots of noise.
—Trouble understanding what you're reading, especially if it's
long or complicated; getting mired in the details.
—Inability to write things down, spell, use numbers, do math.

All the symptoms I spoke of he had experienced, and it seemed
to relieve him to discover that these features were normal, predict-
able, and much observed in the million or so people who had
acquired aphasia. I repeated that this condition was *not* curable, that
he would *not* return to 100 percent of how he was before, but with
any luck and hard work he might return to 80 percent, and that
would be great. I said he was lucky.

"My brain is fractured . . . I don't feel lucky," he countered,
looking sickened by the thought, as if from a bad smell.

"I know. And you're *not* lucky to have had this stroke. But you
could have died, been severely paralyzed, incontinent, stayed totally
wordless. People often do."

"And hard for you, too," he murmured. Stroking my hair, with
a faraway look in his eye, he said: "Poor little sweetheart, tell me
what." His voice bore a long-silenced note of regret.

I teared up, and he held me tight.

"It's been life and death with you." As the words tumbled out, I
was grateful for the chance to explain. "You've been sealed inside,
people usually *are* after a stroke; and I've had to be all outside, fuss-
ing over you, doing for you. There's been no time to work or even
be alone and relax. *No* play time, calm time, worry-free time. *No*
room of my own."

"You worry, worry too much about *me*," he said with a pronounced shiver, as if wishing to be rid of the thought. "What do
you need?"

Before I could answer, he blinked hard and opened his mouth,
ready to speak again. Then, juggling words like small sharp sabers,
he urged: "Every zenith, you, must hie to your room and author
something, anything. . . . What do you *want* . . . to chalk?"

I liked *zenith* for day, *hie* for go, *author* and *chalk* for write. Then, unexpectedly, curving toward me with a gentle laugh, he asked: "How is your new book doing?"

"I really don't know," I answered, and that surprised him. "I've lost touch."

Always a spirited supporter of my work—who used to advise me on publishing, understand my scarcity when deadlines loomed, and even enjoy helping me choose the right outfit for a reading— Paul now encouraged me to renew contact with my editor and agent, maybe go to New York and visit with them and friends.

When I finally did decide to fly to New York for a couple of days, I fretted incessantly about leaving Paul alone at night. It would be the first time. Was he safe?

"I'll be okay," he insisted. "No problem." He sounded quite convinced that he could look after himself. This was total denial. If he didn't know it, I certainly did.

"No problem? Are you kidding?! How about the meds? The insulin?"

"Liz."

"She'll only be here during the day. What if you fall?" I knew all too well that falling was the number one cause of death among the elderly. It was how his mother had died. Startled by a visitor, she'd fallen off the stool in her kitchen and broken a hip, after which lengthy bed rest brought on pneumonia.

"I won't."

"Or have an emergency?" His vision was bad enough that he could easily burn or cut himself. Since the stroke, he sometimes found it hard to pick out the details in a scene, even though he might see its general shape. Although he could detect motion and recognize what an object was, when he reached to touch it, his hand wandered in search of the phantom object. He seemed to have trouble pinpointing it in space. This misreaching meant he often spilled liquids, and couldn't be trusted to use the stove. When I asked him to look at an object, his eyes hunted to and fro until he chanced upon it. He *misreached*, and he *mislooked*, which again suggested lesions in the section of the parietal lobe that governs the brain's *where system*, the mechanism we use to locate things in space.

And there was always the risk of his heart acting up. Of course, this had been a possibility for the past twenty years, but now, especially if he was sundowning, could I trust him to have his wits about him enough to hit the 911 button?

"I won't. I'll be okay."

We both agreed the sense of independence would be good for him, and the sense of freedom would be good for me. So I decided to go, though only for one night. Elaborate preparations began. Liz would arrive at eleven, just before Paul usually woke, and stay until about 6 p.m. That only left the evening, night, and morning to worry about. We put an Ambulance Alert sheet on the refrigerator door—a form containing all of his medical essentials: medications, conditions, doctors, and emergency contacts. His medications went into a clearly labeled plastic bin on top of the refrigerator, with a list of what drugs were to be taken when. Pills would be set out in the normal way—breakfast, lunch, dinner, and late-night doses in separate small bathroom cups. Just in case he managed to spill, which wasn't out of the question, an extra set of pills sat on a dinner plate in the library. The large button phone, stationed in the living room, was programmed to call me, Liz, or 911 at the touch of a button. However, it didn't have an answering machine. That was on a cordless phone in my study. I put bright pink tape over the button he needed to push to answer, and we rehearsed his listening for who was calling, and how to answer if he wanted to speak. And we agreed that we'd talk often, just as we always had. We were well organized, but there was still the jagged uncertainty, the diabolic *what ifs* to worry me.

When separated, we'd always telephoned several times a day, and usually teased, flirted, shamelessly plighted our troth, shared news, poured out our woes. Now I phoned home often, as before, but Paul had trouble remembering how to operate the cordless phone, and then he stuttered, unable to find the right words, until finally falling silent. It became painfully clear that when I traveled, we couldn't keep in touch the comforting, chatty way we had grown used to. Paul ended up being safe this trip, and for the most part on other trips, when my book was published. Slyly, not wishing to worry me, he and Liz always waited until I returned home to reveal anything "exciting" that had happened while I was away (such as inflamed lungs from aspirated fluid, or an infected splinter or shaving cut). My thoughts nonetheless hovered around home, and as I idled in airports I often caught myself worrying if he was okay. Had he slipped on the pool ladder? Fallen en route to the mailbox? Remembered to take his all-important blood thinner at night?

I relished my free time, and Paul treasured his increased independence, but it came with a price—pockets of foreboding, worry about factors I was too distant to assess, and a painful new truth. One more link I hadn't realized I'd lost—our telephonic inseparableness. Now our phone calls were short, less playful, less intimate, and without that lifeline I sometimes felt strangely unreal when I was on the road, as if I were somehow disappearing. Knowing that a loved one's reveries enfold you can feel so reassuring. Even if they're not thinking about you at a particular moment, you still exist in their mind. Touching voices by phone, we had always insinuated our arms down the lines or across the air-miles and held each other close. Without that ethereal embrace, home felt like a distant star.

CHAPTER 23

I DECIDED TO FOCUS ON HELPING PAUL LEARN TO SPEAK, because that would most color the flow and fabric of his life. But he longed to *write* again, to enjoy the bump and clash of creating people who never were—a young woman armed with a bow-shaped mouth and a quiver of impulses, an old man with a forehead lined like a bad stretch of dirt road, a sailor with sword-shaped eyebrows, a Mediterranean beauty with pale skin and nuthatch-brown eyes. He took a twisted pleasure in baiting and goading his characters, hearing their backchat, filling their minds with whims and memories and crazy looping lanyards of obsession.

Battling hard just to speak, why did creating again matter so much after his stroke? Years later, he would tell me that it was because of the huge gap between what he could say and what he could think. Ideas inched through his speech, but they whipped around his thoughts like ice yachts.

"The contrast reassured me as to what lay ahead. It was merely a matter of lining up the two in sync, making a match between my pall-mall thought and aphasia. Would it take six months or a year, or never happen at all? This was the great unknown of my life."

I watched him each day, laboriously trying to assemble words on a page. The penmanship grew a little better, and he knew what he wanted to say, he even seemed to know the words, but the message to his hand resulted in a stream of gibberish.

"I was extremely pissed off, unable to do a single letter, which I mauled anyway. My penmanship, that used to delight me as a masterstroke of all the ages, had dwindled into an uncoordinated heap of blurred fragments, false starts, and untidy balderdash. In a word, I was frustrated beyond belief, there were no letters left on earth for me to use."

I mulled over the problem for a while. I wanted him writing to improve his language skills and help clarify his thoughts. But how we define an activity tints how we feel about it and what energy we'll spend on it. Instead of *homework*, maybe what Paul really needed was a *project*.

"You know," I idly suggested one afternoon when he was feeling especially down in the dumps, "Maybe you want to write the first aphasic novel, or a memoir."

He looked at me with a sudden sprig of light in his eyes.

"Good idea!" he said so excitedly that the old "mem, mem, mem, mem" spilled out, too. I'd seen him pounce like this before, chasing something hare-like and hazy, sparked by the idea of a new book. It meant he was able at least to see a path before him, however meandering and uncertain. Paul writing much or writing well was beyond my expectations. But I hoped the effort would provide a lifeline to his former self, an exciting form of therapy, something to lift his mood and propel us both forward.

After Liz had left for the day, and the speech therapist had come and gone, and I'd taken Paul to the clinic for his regular blood work, followed by the bank, Paul and I finally slouched on the living room sofa, both of us tired from trying to communicate with strangers all day, including the semi-stranger he had become.

"Want to try writing about the stroke?"

He nodded yes.

When I handed him a lined tablet and pen, he struggled to scrawl something, anything, legible, drawing loose loops and wayward squiggles. A roil of anxiety and annoyance swept across his face like time-lapse photography.

"Maybe a flat surface would help? Let's go to the table," I suggested.

Sitting at the kitchen table, even with a firmer hand, he fared no better. For an agonizingly long minute, he twitched his hand across the paper. His pen jerked like a pointer over a Ouija board, until at last he gave up in disgust. Then, banging the pen down in frustration, he leaned back, defeated.

"No use," he spat out.

Combing my thoughts, I tried to soothe him. "Maybe we're asking your brain to do too much at once."

With a pang of contrast, I remembered Paul happily writing the novel *Gala* (a tale of a man who builds a mock-up of the Milky Way) in the damp, cool, millipede-bedeviled basement of a house he'd once rented at Penn State. During that blisteringly hot summer, car metal burned to the touch. Water from a garden hose spurted out hot. Students submerged their hips in shallow creeks and drank cold beer. A few stores lured people in by promising gelatinously cold air-conditioning. On the door to each shop, a decal showed Willie the Penguin, the Kool cigarettes mascot, standing on a blue-white ice floe, below a banner that boasted: *It's Kool inside!* We could only afford a small window air-conditioner, which we installed in the bedroom. In the rest of the house, the stagnant air flattened you like a case of the grippe. But as he listened to Paul Hindemith's opera *The Harmony of the World*, splashing off the naked cement walls in the relatively cooler basement, Paul had barely noticed the incessant heat. The music had been inspired by Johannes Kepler's 1619 book of the same name, in which Kepler decoded the harmonics of the spheres, and Paul was imagining the sound of Kepler wheezing in tune to the sublime mystical notes of Hindemith's opera.

Wishing to taste the raw collision of the spheres rotating in their musical rounds, Paul was traveling through the absolute zero of deep space as he nailed strips of balsa wood into a four- by two-foot rectangle, which he covered with a sheet of sky-blue paper. Then he opened up his star atlas and studied his favorite constellations—Lyra, Betelgeuse, Coalsack—as if they were nudes posing for a life drawing class. With a steady hand, he painted the color of each star onto a push pin and stuck it in place. Between episodes of galaxy-making, he wrote at a large oak desk.

"Cold drink?" I'd called down the steps, and arrived with a glass of chilled lemonade.

"Listening to Hindemith?" I'd asked, stepping over a centipede on the cracked gray cement floor.

"Hindemith-ently . . . You know, what always strikes me is the silence of the universe—but when you approach its component parts all you hear is roaring cacophony!"

How easy it had been for him, then, to mix the flame of this or that composer into the celestial stew.

Compared with the fix he was in nowadays. Neither hand really functioned, and his mind kept drawing zigzags. His brain didn't know what it was doing, or if it knew, it wouldn't tell him.

To write, Paul's brain needed to organize his thoughts, connect what he was thinking to the right words, figure out how to spell those words, then instruct the hand how to move to make the letters for each word, as well as tell the eyes to compensate for the now-invisible right edge of each page. That required so many different processes. I wondered if it might help if he cut out some of them.

"Let's go back to the couch and I'll write it down for you," I offered, "and I'll ask you questions."

Then all he would need to focus on was tethering words to thoughts. If that didn't work, maybe it was too early, and if he liked he could try again in a few weeks. Or maybe it wasn't such a good idea after all.

Paul nestled into his favorite corner, and I stretched out facing him, holding one of the many journals I collected for note-taking. One with a soft, velvety purple cover. Purple, like the purple prose that used to flow from his pen. But how well could he think without language? As different as it is from the outside world, language provides a guidebook and streamlines our observations. The

Korean language, for instance, uses different words, depending on if an object fits snugly inside something (letter in an envelope) or loosely (golf balls in a pail). And, as a result, Koreans are better than other cultures at *discerning* a tight fit from a loose one.

Not that language can express everything we mean to say. Nature flows indivisibly as one stream of atoms; we divide and structure it with our words. But at the snag of every utterance, however eloquent, remains a silence buzzing with everything we've omitted.

"When you're silent, I know you're still thinking—are you thinking *in words*?" I began by testing the waters.

"Yes," Paul said decisively. "Head full."

"Head full," I wrote on page one of the lined journal, and gently riffled its otherwise blank pages—around fifty, I reckoned.

Since the stroke, I'd often wondered if he still had a running interior monologue, the way people normally do. It seemed as good a time as any to ask: "What do the words in your head sound like? A voice speaking?"

I followed his gaze to the ceiling where a small spider was descending hesitantly on a fine-spun thread.

Paul thought a while, then said: "No, *three* voices."

"*Three* voices?" I was floored. *How strange. Where did the different voices come from?* "What do they sound like?"

He screwed up his forehead in thought, then after a few moments, face clouding, he moaned, "I can't explain."

"*Who* do they sound like?"

His eyes drifted to the right as he concentrated. "One . . . a BBC announcer," he told me.

"A BBC announcer?" I thought to myself: *Now that's an answer I didn't expect!*

"Yes."

"And the other voices?"

As if opening a rusty tap, he said in a slow, jumpy spurt of words: "F-f-first there was t-tone . . . *alluvial.* and well-bred. of BBC announcer . . . John. John. John . . . Snagge, who regaled him w-with won-wonders. wonders. of world in distant, correct . . . accent. word-perfect. and slight-slight-slight*ly* snooty. This f-fol- lowed most cases by the voice sp-spouting gibberish. Then there was voice. of himself. almost . . . *lost* . . . ampule, ampersand, *amid* barrage of suppressed verbiage. But re-re-gained as other two hun- dred, no, *two*, receded into blank of servitude. He had. leer . . . learned to speak again by some m-m-magic. which. owed . . . owed . . . oh, *something* ff-first men . . . planet, and would parsnips, no, *p-perhaps* be the b-birth-birthright . . . of all those . . . sufferers from aphasia to f-fol-follow."

Paul fell silent. This was the most he'd spoken since his stroke, and I wanted to let him rest. But I was stunned wordless, holding my breath, wondering if he could possibly rattle on. Even though he stumbled and faltered, and needed help capturing some words, his tale would have been striking in anyone, let alone an aphasic. That three people haunted his thoughts was certainly surprising. He always did have an inner word-slinger busily spinning long sentences and dialogues, and I assumed *that* was the voice he identi- fied as "himself. almost," who, long ago, needed more elbow room and leapt onto the page. But, more puzzling: Who was speaking so well *about* the three voices? For that, Paul had to be engaging yet a different spectre in his head. That had struck me as especially odd, and I couldn't resist asking him about it.

"Why are you talking about yourself in the third person?"

"I sounded . . . different from *myself.* The *people* who spoke in my head weren't me."

"Can I hear a voice?"

"Saying what?"

"Anything you like. How about Snagge?"

In the diction of a BBC announcer, he smoothly said: "The Royal Air Force in this operation lost eleven fighters."

"What did Snagge *sound* like inside your head saying that?"

He paused. "He spoke . . . spoke . . . as if denying the right of the bombers to. to . . . *exist*, relegating them to chandelier stab, *no* correctly intoned v-v-voice of the lost. So didn't seem plants, no, *planes* had been lost. at all. but were p-prom-promoted to the haughty, no, high, no, *highest* ring. *range.* of mystical beings."

Then, commenting on what he'd just said, he added: "H-h-how's that for burr-burr-brand of speech which denies. what it presents? S-s-snagge really. really. spoke like that . . . achieving . . . speech mannerism . . . clo-close. to. dizendisembodied . . . without . . . any any any . . . mustard, prettiness. or effervescence."

"If you're not too tired, tell me more."

For nearly an hour, Paul groped for the right words, which always seemed to hide on the tip of his tongue, and I tried to understand, prompting him with questions. Dictating sentences isn't easy, even for seasoned non-aphasic writers; it takes a special knack. I know several writers who prefer to dictate into a tape recorder, which they say feels more like lecturing; they bloom when thinking on their feet. Paul had always been aces at lecturing, regardless of time of day; with a few notes on an index card, he could improvise an engaging talk that—most remarkable of all—came out in complete sentences. But dictating now meant using his broken short-term memory for words. Yet somehow his brain slowly spelunked for his literary self, and found the rappel of sentences, the traverse of paragraphs, the slingshot of grammar, how clauses might be felicitously rigged.

It was a painstaking process, and I quickly learned not to interrupt him or else his train of thought would jump off the tracks. He'd sometimes pause in the middle of a sentence. If he paused too long he might forget the beginning of the sentence, and on cue I would reread it back to him so that he could reorient himself.

Often his sentences merged. Or he'd omit the small articles, prepositions, and linking words. His brain found content words easier, not words whose only function was syntactical. However, much of the time, struggle plain on his face, he'd eventually hook the word he was fishing for, or at least one that would serve. Not having to guide his hand movements reduced his brain work, so that *all* he had to do was hunt through the Grand Central rush hour of words. More often than not an inexact but apt substitute worked surprisingly well. Then came pronouncing it, not a small feat.

In a formal idiom, he declared (and I inscribed): "There is. vo-vo-voice of rhetorical . . . *artifice say*. just. about. anything I want without ff-ff-fear . . . fear of contra—. contra—. *contradiction*, and other voice . . . which ff-ffear. is. much a burr, no *blur*. When. I'm on firm. form the two hundred, while staying separate, overlap.

"When one is . . . out of contra-*control* . . . and should be asleep, this out of control vo-voice which savages any.thing. you want to say . . . In almost every say . . . stone. cir-cum-stance . . . provides the wrong words . . . and even. exerts a deadly compulsion to stab, no sink, no *say,* say them incessantly. And noth-nothing you can do to cork, cork, cork, *correct* it, so you might as well shoot up shop and g-go sleep because sleep you are not com-mun-i-cat-ing on a human level. at all . . . though for me there still remains the vo-voice of rhetorical *artifice* which enables me. to make slow but intelligent conversation . . . with my . . . my . . . my coevals."

Coevals, I thought, *why coevals, which means contemporaries, instead of a word like* friends *or* others?

Before I could ask, he reflected: "Don't know oth-other people experience this, but I do know what oth-other people's life like without . . . It's a benefit gift . . . enabling those. who. lucky to survive. Feel grateful, because I don't think it's una-una-un*ique* gift. but pre-precious as rubies to me."

For a moment his voice seemed to have left his body and was standing outside himself, looking down at his effort.

"It's bowlegged but it's l-legible, whereas the other mostly nonsense. Sometimes I forget w-words, and one of these . . . *people* . . . comes up with it."

The dictation continued until, an hour later, Paul gracefully thanked me for my help: "I'm impressed with your god-given abil-ity . . . to put these . . . random. random. thoughts in order, and with your patience." Then, with monumental effort, as if he were a spring unwinding to its last rusty creak: "That's enough . . . I can . . . *do* it."

I couldn't believe it. Where on earth had that relative fluency come from? Forehead glistening with sweat, and his mind a blunt instrument, Paul slumped back into the couch like a baggy heap of clothes. *Quite a marathon,* I thought, both astonished and over-whelmed, as he rolled onto his side, nestled his nose into a cushion, and plunged into a deep sleep.

Hearing voices—a cardinal symptom of schizophrenia. Seventy-five percent of schizophrenics are badgered by edicts and jeers, spooked by conspiratorial whispers, infested with perpetual judges and wardens they can't run away from. For an unsettling moment, I wondered if I should be concerned.

And yet, even as I thought those words, I heard them *spoken* in my mind as part of the auditory hallucinations we all live with *normally,* because the brain is a born tour guide, pitchman, and jab-ber box. It blesses, it boycotts, it scolds. *See here!* It silently fumes, or: *I'll show* you*! If only . . .* it sighs. *Why did you have to . . .* it recriminates. The brain prattles nonstop to its lifelong listener: itself.

Before his stroke, Paul had often communed with his dead mother, and *heard* her answering back, her voice sparkling clear, even when there was nothing special that needed saying. He once told me of this ethereal exchange:

"Are you all right?" he'd asked her.

"So-so," came her reply, pervading the crevasses of his mind, and intoned in her perfectly unchanged, maternal way, soft and lambent with a North Country accent.

"Is it sunny where you are?"

"No."

"You haven't much to say for yourself."

"What's the point?"

"Do you want for anything?" Ever the protective son.

"Why should I? I've all I need."

"All?"

"Yes, all."

"I better say goodbye, then."

"Look after yourself."

"I do."

In such cozy chats, he'd joined 13 percent of people, so-called "grief hallucinators," who find talking with a dead loved one helps to soothe their grieving mind.

Did it matter if the voices seemed to originate outside or inside the head? The line between the two can blur, and some studies suggest that hearing voices is really a form of subconscious whispering. Researchers at NASA have been perfecting a way to hear what people are thinking by placing tiny electrodes under the chin that will pick up "sub-vocal signals" from the brain; what we call our *inner voice* works the nerves in the speech muscles, whose subtle firing a computer can decipher. Useful in space, but maybe more so for military purposes, to avoid eavesdropping. There's no plan to adapt the program for stroke victims, let alone the hoi polloi, but maybe that day will come. Then what? Suppose we shared our inner voice with others, faster than we could censor it, piquant lust and unbridled temper blazing? Using the skill recreationally might lead to serious mischief.

Years later, I would ask again about the three voices who spoke in his head right after his stroke.

"Did your three voices ever talk to each other?"

"No, they ran distinctly separate operations."

"When did the three voices merge into one again?"

"They didn't."

This surprised me, which I tried not to show. "All three are *still* with you?"

"Two of them not used much. But I can tell they're home-free, free-born . . . still *there* somewhere. Like sensing someone in the room. Mind you, hearing tones of voice is like handling quicksilver. They blur somewhat. My own sable is that I'm speaking quite normally for the most part."

"For the most part."

"Depending on time of day."

Was this an invitation to romp? "And food."

". . . And weather."

"And sleep."

"Tell me something new!" he demanded.

"Really? Am I boring you?"

"*Nooo.* I didn't mean to say like that, but . . ." Paul dipped one hand, maybe to mimic a sigh. "You're listening too hard."

"I have to . . ." Long pause. "I've grown used to it."

"I know. Big change for you. I wish you could relax your. wa-wa-watch over me. I'm sorry. . . . I could leave, and . . . furlough your life back."

A noble offer, and genuinely felt.

"This *is* my life. And I'd miss you terribly."

"More than the hardship of bivouacing *with* me?"

I thought about the comparison seriously, then took his hand. "Much more. We're joined at the heart."

"Bad luck for you, I'm afraid. My ticker's pretty wonky."

"Too much boozing."

His eyes twinkled, and he drew me close. "Not enough kissling."

CHAPTER 24

SURPRISED AND THRILLED BY PAUL'S DICTATION ON THAT
summer day, we continued the following afternoon. I welcomed hearing from his "voices" again, those ghostly speakers
haunting the mansions of his mind. Dictation had made me once
again feel like the old Paul was peering out from within, clear as a
porch light through timberland, in a way he somehow couldn't
manage in conversation. We weren't calling the project a memoir
yet. Neither of us, because who knew if or what the coming efforts
might bring. At the moment they were only sighting shots, trial
balloons of thought, any of those metaphors humans use to convey
hope, tentativeness, and not foreseeing the what-will-be. As Paul
and I both knew, the main thing was to keep him tailoring language.

Again he opened his mental book of voices and spoke haltingly,
sometimes cryptically, for nearly an hour. This time he wasn't quite
as fluent, and he battled more to find words, which came slowly,
but he pressed on anyway and together we created his second journal entry.

"The second d-day in the Rehab Unit, I h-heard. heard. this
v-voice," he said tentatively. "And it was not the v-voice of the
flimflam, but the v-voice of pellucid flim . . . no, not *flim* . . . pellucid, articulate . . . reason . . . droning. droning the absence any

s-s-sound, and. and . . . I knew. at once. that I was g-g-going to be anchors, axels, all right. even then, in s-spite of the ersatz, no, *evil-seeming* th-things that . . . happened . . . to me."

He paused, yawned his mouth wide open without uttering a sound, and seemed to compel the next words to come out: "I *mean* that . . . though I hadn't *tried* to speak yet . . . and the whole whir-whir-world was sink bottle some kind of abstract fanfare. waiting. to be led. on or off. I w-would be all *right* because my language . . . even if even if even it led to. ee-mean, emen, im*men*sely private universe . . . or . . . or . . . full panoply of speech."

His *language*? I guessed he meant that at least he could form cohesive thoughts internally, in his private universe, even if he couldn't convey them with the "full panoply of speech."

"So, that side of him . . . remains," he reasoned, surveying himself in the role of doctor-inquisitor.

Then again he abruptly changed point of view. "I can t-t-urn it on whenever I want speak. It's. very. eerie. You might say almost like having second language f-forced upon one, one the lackadaisical, partly formal voice of BBC announcer, other . . ."

He paused only an elongated breath's worth, but I wondered if his brain was going to change gears and narrate events again. It didn't. Instead it alluded to the Shakespearean characters of his youth.

". . . oth-other the rapscallion Calibanesque la-language, or substitute Falstaff . . . No need say which one I prefer."

I smiled at the exotic twosomes, *rapscallion Calibanesque*, which I took to mean "mischievous ranting," and *substitute Falstaff*, meaning "imitative fool," and he smiled back, catching that his brain had dished up something amusing.

He pressed on. "Three voices really. One, ff-faint intellectual voice of speaker.. who. until I broke to this clutch of fortune . . . didn't know whether he exited. existed or not. . . . somersault executing virtuoso . . . of my hours daily, if I'm lousy, no l-l-*lucky* . . . of joyous harmony. Second the extinct radio voice of Snagge. Third . . . rough country incoherent you already know too well. for his for his crude nonsense. and almost defiant . . ."

The sentence fell off a cliff. I watched him trying to crystallize the right word in his mind.

"I'm stunned," he suddenly said from yet another remove. "I've proven . . . that I have two three voices."

So, the voices remained. Inside his head, Paul still seemed to harbor a trio of speakers from different parts of his life: the formal BBC broadcaster John Snagge, whom he had heard on the radio during his childhood and Oxford days; the tongue-tied aphasic, who frustrated and shamed him by speaking gibberish; and the language-loving scribe with American turns of phrase. All worked to support him like durable friends, or maybe like the strongest sides of his personality. The Snagge voice, he would tell me much later, *"spoke into my inner ear, Lord knows why, and sometimes handed me the right word."* I found it fascinating, if a bit confusing, and although the speakers seemed different, he clearly wasn't experiencing multiple personalities. No, the diction was continuous and, if anything, a bit flat in tone, spilling very little emotion. While dictating, he seemed to focus deep within his head, where all the action lay and the invisible people took turns doing his internal monologue, or really, his internal trialogue. What he uttered came from that three-man theater, and could be spoken of by yet a fourth voice.

It brought to mind a book I'd read ages before, *The Origin of Consciousness in the Breakdown of the Bicameral Mind*, by Julian Jaynes. There was a time eons ago, Jaynes suggests, when we *all* heard voices inside our head, not as chat from a familiar brain, we thought, but from otherworldly beings telling us what to do. Jaynes speculates that in the days before people had modern minds capable of self-reflection, our instincts spoke to us with commands on how to survive. We believed the internal voices to be from gods because they seemed wise, stayed invisible, and yet invaded the interior mind. "At one time, human nature was split in two," he controversially suggests, "an executive part called a god, and a follower part called a man. Neither part was Consciously aware."

We forget that in ancient texts, hearing voices was commonplace—especially divine voices. Not only did the Greek and Roman gods speak to people, even their statues spoke. All of the monotheistic religions were founded by people who swore their god spoke to them, issuing bans, rules, and proclamations (and, of course, Joan of Arc's famous call to battle). Genesis proclaims: "In the beginning was the word," the word of a god who knew every dialect and engaged worshippers personally, moodily, sometimes in the give-and-take of conversation. Today we'd most likely deem mad anyone who said he heard God speaking to him from a burning bush. In a courtroom, a defense lawyer bidding for an insanity plea need only prove that his client hears voices, and that's enough to sway the jury. So, claiming to hear three voices in his head, Paul might well raise eyebrows.

Jaynes's theory argues that these vividly distinct voices arose in the right hemisphere, in the convolutions that are counterparts to the left hemisphere's language centers. After all the damage Paul had suffered to the left, in precisely those regions, could it be that his mind was compensating by unleashing the usually stifled voices in his right? To keep a continuous sense of self alive, perhaps? After all, someone had to call the shots, tell him what to do, even if his longstanding, carefully whittled "self" was temporarily fractured into several voices, not many compared to the mob reported by some folk.

"I had been splintered into a million beings and objects," Vladimir Nabokov wrote in an essay on sounds. "Today I am one; tomorrow I shall splinter again. . . . But I knew that all were notes of one and the same harmony."

"The head we inhabit is a haunted house," philosopher William Gass once wryly observed, full of "the words which one burns like beacons against the darkness." At heart lies "this secret, obsessive, often silly, nearly continuous voice . . . the silent murmur of us, our glad, our scrappy, rude, grand, small talk to ourselves, the unheard hum of our humanity."

Talk we must, we haven't any choice. As babies we babble, and we keep right on babbling as grown-ups, too—but silently, to ourselves. The words in the haunted houses of our minds never stop, even inside the head of someone with aphasia. *Not* speaking to someone you barely know is considered a slight, and if you know them well it's a blind arrow of anger or cruelty. Not talking to someone is regarded as passive violence, which is why we call it "cutting someone" or "cutting someone dead." We remember who we are, what we did, how we felt in words, even if most of the time we-don't-know-who is saying we-don't-know-what to we-don't-know-whom. We talk to ourselves all day, even while eating or making love, and at night we talk to ourselves in our sleep. We talk to cooperate and exchange ideas with others—it's how our species survived—but also to commune with that compound ghost, our so-called "self," and know how we feel, consider what we're doing, analyze whether someone may be a killer, a rival, a mate.

Some unlucky stroke patients are haunted, not with alien voices but with alien limbs, a rare neurological condition when a hand seems to have a will of its own, reaching out and grabbing things (or, most embarrassingly, body parts) unbidden, and needing to be wrestled down by the other hand. Sometimes called the "Dr. Strangelove syndrome" (after the Peter Sellers character in the movie of the same name, whose arm would suddenly shoot up in *Heil Hitler!* salutes), it makes the limb seem foreign to its owner, so beyond conscious control that patients usually give it a name, or refer to it as "It." "It" may even try to strangle its owner. The cause remains a mystery, but seems to stem from multiple lesions in the brain that, in effect, separate it from itself in too many places, more than it can overlook and still feel whole. It made sense to me that lesser lesions in Paul's brain might do something similar, not with limbs but with the speechifiers inside, the homely ghosts we talk to when we talk to our "selves."

⟝⟞

"THREE DAYS OUT of seven, I can zoom," Paul stage-whispered the next day, "the others no," by which he meant speak, converse.

His verbal ability also seemed affected by how much he'd slept, and even by the whims of weather and the time of day. True for all of us, as our brain cycles and rests. The best time of day for brainwork changes with age. A child's internal clock naturally summons it to sleep at around 8 or 9 p.m. Teens tend to grow sleepy later, at around 11 p.m.; need nine hours of sleep, even if they rarely get it; and are notoriously hard to wake up. College students often report feeling brightest at night, and the elderly say they're sharpest in the morning. Negative ions—molecules naturally produced at cascading waterfalls, beaches loud with heavy surf, or after a spring thunderstorm crackling with lightning—create more oxygen in the brain, which makes us feel exhilarated and more alert.

It made sense that his "dictating" ability might vary from day to day, just as his speaking did. Also that it would provide invaluable speech therapy, if he continued to prod his brain to craft language until it wore itself out. And he'd be focused on what had always made him happiest: being immersed in a writing project, something creative and constructive which he was motivated to continue. I know now, as I sensed then, that it's essential to tailor rehab to what impassions someone. The brain gradually learns by riveting its attention—through endless repetitions, alas.

Right after breakfast, Paul felt most fluent, and that's when he usually met me on the couch with a short list of notes on a small scrap of paper. Sometimes he sat down and studied his carefully prepared scribblings, unable to decipher his own craggy handwriting no matter how hard he tried. Other times even I could read the list, which might include a one-word cue such as "Morpurgo," and sure enough, at some point during the hour, he would slip out a phrase like the "pitter-patter of Dr. Morpurgo's feet."

The dictation was exhausting for both of us. For the hour or so I needed to concentrate hard on deciphering errant, often-wrong words, using my own language skills to do overtime, climb cliffs of possible meaning, looking for any toehold. After years of writing poetry, odd combos of words didn't faze me, and I knew Paul's habits of word and mind, so I could catch his dictated curve balls, but it became clear to me that I couldn't be his secretary. It would sap all my writing energy, change our relationship, erase my creative self, bruise my own voice, reduce me to excavating when I needed to be freewheeling. And so I gently suggested that Liz be recruited to help transcribe his outpourings, and fortunately she agreed.

Day after day, Paul continued dictating, sometimes with mountain-moving effort, and others sailing along at a good clip, freeing an account of what he'd gone through, what the inner world of aphasia felt and looked like. It was Paul's chosen regimen, a struggle that helped him to organize his mind, which also impressed upon us all just how wounded his brain had been. Composing his narrative—and relating it to someone while doing so—was the best speech therapy anyone could have prescribed. For an hour of animated slogging every day, he stubbornly forced his brain to recruit cells, build new connections, find the right sounds to go with words, and piece together whole sentences. Painstakingly reviewing the text with him the next day helped Paul clarify his thoughts and gave him the opportunity to repair some of aphasia's fingerprints in the prose. In those moments he transcended his brain injury, and was able to repossess himself, narrate and reorder his life. At times, what he said sounded nonsensical, but Liz and I were both punctilious about recording him exactly, whether he made sense or not.

We already knew that when someone has aphasia, working out a seemingly simple, yet new, practice can be incredibly frustrating. Dictation was no exception. From the kitchen one day, I overheard Paul and Liz working through a typical roadblock.

Paul requested a "new paragraph."

Liz presented him with the newly typed paragraph.

Disappointed, he insisted, "No, new *paragraph*."

She stated emphatically, "It *is* a new paragraph."

He said, "No, new *paragraph*."

And round and round they went, both baffled and frustrated, until finally Liz figured out that Paul *really* meant "new chapter."

He made other irregular substitutions as well. "Period" for comma. "Full-stop" (British) for period. "Period" for question mark. The flags of punctuation are all symbols, and they defied him. For some bizarre reason known only to his gray matter, he didn't make mistakes with the semicolon.

To add to the general confusion, Paul was now the king of malaprops and a geyser of neologisms, at times substituting the wrong word or mispronouncing to the point of unintelligibility. For instance, trying to catch the word "cloud," and pronouncing only the word "loud." "Skeleton" became "skellington." "Mold" came out as "mole." He said "pillar" when he really meant "pillow." He could only convey the idea of an umbrella if he referred to it as a "pagoda." A simple word like "hurt" mutated into the more dire "hearse." For "obsess" he'd say "abscess," as if obsessing were a sort of boil in the brain. On the other hand, we were often surprised when we tried to puzzle out what we thought were nonsense words we'd faithfully written down phonetically—*pallaisse, corybantic, halma, fatidic*—only to discover they were real if obscure words, outside our vocabularies.

What emerged in time was an aphasic's journal yanked out of the brain attic, an account of stumbling around in his scary new mental landscape, searching for hidden light switches and keys to locked rooms, while dodging cobwebs of numbers, moth-eaten garlands of logic, dusty shoeboxes full of old photographs, newsreel memories, and, scattered everywhere, disintegrating sacks of word-shells collected over a lifetime—lightning whelks, owl limpets, heart cockles, alphabet cones, fighting conchs, pearly jingles, tiger cowries, saw-toothed pens, frilled dogwinkles, banded turbans, noble volutes, and thousands more—all knuckled together in quiet inclines that were threatening to spill. The book he christened *The Shadow Factory*, a unique chronicle of his first aphasic months, and he published it with Lumen Books, the avant-garde press in Santa Fe, known for its books on architecture and design, fiction and poetry, especially in translation.

CHAPTER 25

To my surprise, Paul had the urge to create every single day. The habit of using language to express himself, despite the Sisyphian difficulties, still persisted. The language mill in Paul's brain may have been blasted by the stroke, but apparently not the pied-à-terre of the muses. Where might those fickle ladies reside?

By most accounts, the right side of the brain organizes creativity, but it's a suspected whereabouts defined mainly by loss (people with right-hemisphere strokes typically lose their gift for poetry, music, or painting). Paul's brain had always relished thinking in images, and he'd spent a lifetime being creative, in the process farming more of the neural landscape in his imaginative, intuitive right hemisphere. An ordinary feat. Every brain spirals and dovetails in unique ways, and propensity often leads to predilection—having a talent for something makes spending time at it pleasurable, which in turn shapes and fortifies the gray matter for it. Physical exercise develops muscles; mental exercise remodels the brain. Painters grow richer visual-association ranges; musicians auditory glens; writers language orchards.

Paul's lifetime as a wordsmith would have built dense language country, with more back roads between the hamlets, even if the major highways had crumbled, and more neural networks, wired as java joints and hopping to serve. My hunch was that his brain still had tillable hills and valleys, where a crop of words might yet flourish. This would help explain why he was speaking at all, given his CAT scan's grim cameo. Creative brains nimbly scout both hemispheres for raw material—it's a whole-brain enterprise. One needs the left hemisphere to inspect the results emerging from the right, and decide if the work is apt, original, and effective. So a well-built bridge between the hemispheres (the *corpus callosum*) must also play an essential role in creativity, and Paul's would be built for heavy traffic, because he'd been bracing (even frescoing) it for decades.

That seemed likely, especially since Paul had studied French, Latin, and Greek in school. Learning multiple tongues would have bolstered the language connections in his right hemisphere as well as in his left. We know from brain imaging done with bilingual speakers that most of us don't take advantage of all the language room we inherit, which can be greatly enhanced. A person speaking one language shows activity in the classic left-hemisphere language areas. But as a bilingual speaker switches rapidly from one language to another, she increases the activity in *both* the right and left hemispheres, engaging more of what's available for language, in time cultivating many more brain cells. Also, bilinguals, just like taxi drivers, jugglers, and symphony orchestra musicians, grow denser gray matter in areas related to their skills. The earlier the better, with the most changes in people who learn a second language before the age of five.

A neuroscientist friend had told me about a visit from a Norwegian colleague who was surprised by the frequency of post-stroke aphasia in the United States compared to Norway. His colleague theorized that Norwegians fare better because they learn several foreign languages as children, giving them a distinct advantage in later years. Quite often, like the Czech-speaking violist, aphasics who lose access to their primary language can still remember a foreign tongue. Paul began studying French at ten, Latin and Greek at seventeen—late by some measures, but tilling spare gray matter nonetheless, because the temporal lobes (replete with regions that process language and emotions) are still efflorescing until around sixteen, when another round of pruning begins to sculpt the topiaries of the brain. And even then, honing new skills, or even new ways of thinking, can fertilize a bed of neurons, increasing its size.

Ideally, post-stroke rehab should play to each patient's strengths, the dense knots and networks of gray matter developed over a lifetime of use, one's own private larder or offshore bank account. In college courses, a teacher often encounters the rubric of "all that must be learned," but discovering how each student learns best is far more effective. It takes longer, and ideally the student and teacher will be a good "match." The same is true with rebuilding after a stroke. Not just remodeling from scratch, but finding extra or out-of-the-way storehouses, and rewiring paths to them, bushwacking with unconventional tools if need be, uncovering lost or meandering trails, guiding by invisible and at times intuitive maps.

Since Paul was naturally creative, a wild and woolly thinker, it wasn't really surprising that he balked at conventional speech therapy, with its linear, fill-in-the-blank, right-or-wrong answers. Before his stroke, his brain hadn't worked that way; that's not where his strengths lay. In any case, everyone learns better through play—though, after a severe stroke, finding a playground may not be easy. It depends on what amused a loved one beforehand, and blazing paths, at a snail's pace if need be, to that hidden reservoir. In Paul's case, progress could only be made by pointing out the slime left by the snail, the calcium "love darts" that snails use during courtship, and any grotesque scenery along the way, since he loved weird metaphors.

To build even such a slight metaphor, the brain hunts far and wide, across neural networks in both hemispheres, and connects seemingly unrelated tidbits that nonetheless have things in common. Different domains of knowledge are slammed together. It's a pictorial kind of thinking, pre-rational and full of emotional intensity, a way of painting thoughts and feelings. When Lord Byron dubbed his wife-to-be "the Princess of Parallelograms," he very effectively combined her rare gift for mathematics with her wealthy family, strict morals, elegant beauty, and cool demeanor.

What we airily label *creativity* typically blends so many features: risk-taking, perseverance, problem-solving, openness to experience, the need to share one's inner universe, empathy, detailed mastery of a craft, resourcefulness, disciplined spontaneity, a mind of large general knowledge and strength that can momentarily be drawn to a particular, ample joy when surprised, intense focus, the useful application of obsession, the innocent wonder of a child available to a learned adult, passion, a tenuous (or at least flexible) grasp on reality, mysticism (though not necessarily theology), a reaction against the status quo (and preference for unique creations), and usually the support of at least one person—among many other ingredients.

In the throes of creativity, a lively brain tussles with a mass of memories and rich stores of knowledge, attacking them both *sub rosa* and with the mind wide open. Some it incubates offstage until a fully fledged insight wings into view. The rest it consciously rigs, rotates, kneads, and otherwise plays with until a novel solution emerges. Only by fumbling with countless bits of knowledge, and then ignoring most of it, does a creative mind craft something original. For that, far more than the language areas are involved. Hand-me-down ideas won't do. So conventions must be flouted, risks taken, possibilities freely spigoted, ideas elaborated, problems redefined, daydreaming encouraged, curiosity followed down zig-zagging alleyways. Any sort of unconsidered trifle may be fair game. It's child's play. Literally. Not a gift given to an elect few, but a widespread, natural, human way of knowing the world. With the best intentions, our schools and society bash most of it out of us. Fortunately, it's so strong in some of us that it endures. As neuroscientist Floyd Bloom observes:

> Schools place overwhelming emphasis on teaching children to solve problems correctly, not creatively. This skewed system

dominates our first twenty years of life; tests, grades, college admission, degrees and job placements demand and reward targeted logical thinking, factual competence, and language and math skills—all purviews of the left brain. . . . [T]he brain is a creature of habit; using well-established neural pathways is more economical than elaborating new or unusual ones. Additionally, failure to train creative faculties allows those neural connections to wither.

Creativity is an intellectual adventure into those jungles where the jaguars of sweet laughter croon, with a willingness to double back, ignore fences, or switch directions at the drop of a coconut.

Why was Paul doing so well, all things considered? One small piece of the puzzle, strangely enough, may be that his earlier stroke—a small one, known as a TIA—probably worked in his favor. Swiss scientists Paciaroni, Arnold, van Melle, and Bogousslavsky reported, after studying over three thousand stroke patients, that "the occurrence of previous TIAs was significantly related to a better outcome." They offered several explanations, among them that the slow blockage of an artery that leads to a TIA—like the narrowing of a hose—forced the brain to irrigate through other channels. After that, when the big stroke hit, there were backup routes for blood flow. Also, these patients were already on anticoagulants because of the TIA, a mixed blessing, preventing the use of tPA but still possibly protective.

Of course, that doesn't factor in the role of other chemicals in the brain's bag of tricks. Without a doubt, the antidepressant Zoloft was working, and the Ritalin helped Paul focus. But one of his heart medicines probably fostered creativity, too. In a University of Florida study neurologist Kenneth Heilman conducted with college students, some were given a stimulant (*ephedrine*) and some a calm-inducing beta-blocker that's often prescribed for stage fright (Inderal). Surprisingly, the students on the beta-blocker performed better on tests requiring mental flexibility. For years, Paul had been forbidden coffee, tea, chocolate, and other stimulants by his cardiologist, but prescribed Inderal to lower his blood pressure and slow the speed of his quivering heart muscle. Made sleepier by the Inderal, he nonetheless stayed wickedly productive.

As much as I might relish a mug of oily, dark French roast coffee, revving up the brain doesn't necessarily spur creative thinking. Vigilant calm works better. After all, the secret to good improvisation isn't choosing the first thing that comes into your mind, but the best thing. That usually means generating different possibilities, rotating mental images, juggling, arranging, rearranging, testing how each lurks in the mind, before settling on a solution.

So, with one thing and another—the years of foreign language, his strong bridge between the hemispheres, his luck with medications, the previous TIA, etc.—Paul remained fiercely creative, even if he couldn't process language well. Since he was motivated, it made sense to encourage his brain to recruit healthy laborers from the suburbs, and travel even farther afield to employ other gandy-dancers, however strange, who were still fit enough to hammer out a word or two.

CHAPTER 26

"MA BÊTE, MA BELLE BÊTE," *MY BEAST, MY BEAUTIFUL Beast*, I sweet-talked to Paul one day, quoting from a movie we both knew well.

In Jean Cocteau's exquisite 1946 film *La Belle et la Bête*, a rose-adoring, art-collecting, sensitive beast is the avatar for a prince, whom an evil fairy has turned into a hideous monster (until he can find true love, despite his ugliness). It was based on a popular eighteenth-century European fairy tale about a search for a lost husband. We both adored the magical film, which we'd seen eleven times, often enough for Paul to decipher the Latin on the back of the Beast's chair, which reads: "All men are beasts when they don't have love."

"Ma Bête, ma belle Bête," I whispered.

Automatically Paul responded, also quoting from the film: "Je suis un monstre. Je n'aime pas les compliments." *I am a monster. I don't like compliments.*

Just as I'd sometimes called him "ma Bête" in bygone days, he'd sometimes called me "ma Belle," but that had been one of the simplest of all his fanciful names for me. For him, playing in the sandbox of language had meant building ornate castles. As well as his dictation was going, and his speech improving, he still had difficulty combining words to forge images. And he deeply lamented the loss of decades of daily pet names and endearments. He'd loved creating and bestowing names of all sorts—wildly whimsical, just feasible, or apropos: π, *Moon*, *Paprika Cheeks*, *Bush-kitten*. We'd both relished the Native American spirit of naming, in which a Hopi female might be called "Beautiful Badger Going Over the Hill," "Child of Importance," "Spider Woman at Middle-age," "Butterfly Sitting on a Flower," "Overflowing Spring," "Beautiful Clouds Arising"; and a male "Where the Wind Blows Down the Gap," "Short Rainbow," "Throne for the Clouds," "Joined Together by Water," "He Who Whistles."

There was a time, long ago, when all names described personal attributes, origin, or the hopes of parents, when names could be allegories that determined someone's fate. A time when naming was magic, knowledge, possession, and a shaman could inflict injury by mishandling someone's name. A time when you only shared your true name with someone you completely trusted. What spells Paul and I had cast with our secret names for one another.

Passing by the back door, when Liz and Paul were wading at the shallow end of the pool, I heard her ask him, "Do you have a pet name for Diane?"

His face fell as if touched by a taser. "Used to have . . . hundreds," he said with infinite sadness. "Now I can't think of one."

It was true. Once upon a time, in the Land of Before, Paul had so many pet names for me I was a one-woman zoo. Now it was as if a mass extinction had taken place, all the totemic animals we shared had vanished. The veldt of our love was less noisy, the fauna of the watering holes sparse. He understood how much I missed the romantic, frisky hobgoblins like *Elf-heart* he used to invent for me, the strange cuddly creatures of forest and sky he tricked out with diminutives and recruited for our private fun. In our mythology there were golden baby owls, ring-tailed lemurs, axolotls, shoulder rabbits, honeybunnies, bunnyskins (a.k.a. *peaux de lapin*), hopping spiders, roseate spoonbills, and many more.

He wished he could revisit that private bridge to the supernatural world, which we had crossed and recrossed with ritual devotion. But he couldn't find it in the mob of words elbowing one another for attention.

So I began teaching him some of his old favorites—*swan*, *pilot-poet*, *baby angel*—and he recognized them. Other times he sighed "my precious," "my little sweetheart," or "my cute." Was he really once master of the *piropo*, that adorable Argentine courtship game? A street poetry of amorous, flirtatious compliments, *piropos* are public yet private, usually whispered to a woman as she passes close beside an anonymous admirer.

"If beauty were a sin, you'd never be forgiven," a man might sigh to a woman in Buenos Aires. Or: "You move like the Bolshoi Ballet." Or: "So many curves, and me without brakes." Or, simply: "Goddess!"

"My legume," Paul murmured romantically, trying to say "My Lady," and I giggled before I could stop myself.

"Legume!"

Then we both slid into laughter at the thought of his romantic inclination for a lima bean or lentil. But slowly, heartfully, the endearments were beginning to emerge again. Aphasics are often good at echoing, and if I told him that I loved being his little *bush-kitten*, thus prompted, he'd repeat in imitation "my little bush-kitten," and I'd coo appreciatively to reinforce his efforts. I knew Paul needed the tangible bond of naming during his famine of words; and he knew I needed the nourishment during my long days of caregiving.

"Why don't you make up some brand-new names?" I suggested to Paul one morning.

His first offering—after ruminating for a few minutes—was: "Celandine Hunter." Not a deliberately chosen twosome. The words just tumbled out like dice.

"*Celandine?* . . . Oh yes, buttercups. How sweet!" We had celandine sprouting wild in the garden, and I often strolled to gather them in springtime.

"Where on earth did *that* come from?" I asked.

He didn't know, but was pleased and surprised by it. This was a new pier where aphasia's merry-go-round of words could be welcomed in a colorful and creative way. Instead of trying to block wrong words from popping out, he made space for them. Before the stroke he would have had to purposefully "free-associate" to do the same thing. Now he opened the floodgates in order to create. In search of a *piropo*, he could unleash the hounds of aphasia for a second or two. One *piropo* was all he could manage at a time, he told me, it was too taxing. But I think the truth lay deeper, that it was too frightening to invite the aphasia any more than that. Turning it off and on like a valve empowered him. What he didn't want was the leaky trickle of chaotic words.

The next day, on waking, I cajoled Paul for another and he chewed his mental cud and provided: "Swallow Haven." He didn't always have a sassy sobriquet for me each day—"Sorry, later," he'd say to excuse not being in good tune—but on many mornings he was able to freshly mint a new pet name. When they started following a pattern too much, such as the "____ of ____," I'd protest and beg him to conjure up a novel variation. My intent, along with added play time, was fun practice at creative imagery, a seemingly lost gift. Since aphasics' brains often snag on one word or sentence or way of doing something, this wasn't always easy for him. (I wondered if, with the usual pathways broken, some signals looped round and round in a cul-de-sac.) But from then on names arrived, spoken as we snuggled in bed, such marvels as "Little Moonskipper of the Tumbleweed Factory," "My Snowy Tanganyika," "Spy Elf of the Morning Hallelujahs," "My Little Spice Owl," "The Epistle of Paul to the Rumanian Songthrushers," "Blithe Sickness of Araby," "Baby Angel with the Human Antecede Within," "Little Flavanoid Wonder," "Rheostat of Sentimental Dreaming," "My Remains of the Day, My Residue of Night," "Lovely Ampersand of the Morning," and "O Parakeet of the Lissome Star."

What a surprise! I cherished these riotous, spell-cast endearments and wondered what fantastic gallantry he might utter anew each morning. Even if some seemed to go awry, like "Blithe Sickness of Araby!"

"I love *Blithe* and *Araby*," I said, "but . . . could you maybe find a word other than *sickness*?" When nothing sprang to mind, he shrugged his shoulders and said: "Best can do." They only emerged as amalgams.

"My little corn-crake," he whispered tenderly, and I made contented creatural noises into his neck as he caressed my cheek and ear, then wrapped both arms tightly around me, locking me into our circle of love. In those moments, which were really hours, I came to rest, warmed by his irregular heartbeat, free of worry's albatross, feeling safe at last.

Whether whacky or tender, the names spiraled in ways that always made me laugh and feel loved, courtship restored. The old pet names and *piropos* from before the stroke—"Swan heart," or "Park" (short for "You are a park for my eyes")—had evolved over time, acquiring layers of meaning. But I also treasured the new, more hallucinatory ones, forged on demand, as aphasic telegrams from his phoenix-feathered brain.

And Paul loved playing the swain again, even if it meant difficult and tiring word-craft, and he had fun concocting verbal novelties, offered to me as miniature gifts. It also guaranteed that, whatever else might unfold, each day would begin with closeness and a dose of laughter.

CHAPTER 27

"HI, WOMBAT," I GREETED PAUL AS HE STUMBLED OUT OF the bedroom's cave of dreams, looking like he'd been waylaid by gremlins. His hair stood to attention, his flannel boxer shorts were on backwards, he wobbled as he walked. And yet he wore the expression that humans do upon waking, that of a swollen-eyed infant, which, by design, we find cute.

"You have me all to yourself today," I announced—as I always did on Saturdays, Sundays, and the many weeks when Liz was away.

He put his right hand over his heart, curled pinkie and all, as if a national anthem had begun playing, and added the day's new pet name: "My Little Bucket of Hair."

I laughed so hard I had to stop pouring a cup of milk. "Ooh, I *love* that one!"

"My Little Bucket of Hair," Paul said again in a singsong, this time grinning to the right and left, acknowledging the applause of imaginary bystanders.

Then, with a "What's new, wombat?" sung off-key to the 1965 tune "What's New, Pussycat?" he sat down to breakfast.

Well, this morning I had fun news to share with my fellow wombatophile.

"I've discovered that the Pre-Raphaelite painters were *obsessed* with wombats! Did you know there's a British tradition of wombat-snogging?"

"Wombat-snogging? Tell more." He was hooked.

Paul had once been an expert on the Pre-Raphaelite Brotherhood: the mid-nineteenth-century band of young British artists who had jolted the drab art world of their day with jewel-toned paintings full of moody women who somehow managed to be simultaneously erotic and ethereal. When the Pre-Raphaelite ringleader, Dante Gabriel Rossetti, was commissioned to paint the walls and ceiling of the Oxford Union, he gathered his motley crew of friends, and they gaily painted elaborate murals filled with heroic and supernatural scenes of Arthurian legends, complete with forests, castles, velvet-clad damsels, and dashing knights.

"You know about Rossetti painting knights on the ceiling of the Oxford Union, right?"

"And on the roundabouts," Paul added.

Roundabouts? Oh, walls. "Yes, on the walls, too. Everywhere *except* the windows, which were whitewashed for protection. But the whitewash made such a tempting clean surface that they sketched dozens of frolicking and cavorting wombats on the windows!"

Paul's gray-blue eyes opened so wide I could see their rims of agate.

"Apparently Rossetti had persuaded his clique that wombats were just dishy, the most beautiful of all God's creatures, and he threw picnics full of frolick and badinage near the "Wombat's Lair" at London's Regent's Park Zoo. One of his sketches even showed a wombat dashing past Egyptian pyramids! Fantastic!"

"Can I see them?"

"No, I'm afraid somebody washed the windows. But there are sketches at the British Museum. Shall we fly to London and hold hands in front of Rossetti's wombat drawings?" I asked impishly. *If only his health were better and he could travel, what a lark that would be.*

"Don't think so," he said. "Good idea . . . maybe . . ." He twirled round the index finger on his right hand, struggling to find the word for something. ". . . box?"

"Mailbox?"

"No, not *mailbox*, the other thing . . ." He continued the high-spirited word-hunt. ". . . Light dancing mailbox."

Light dancing mailbox. . . . light dancing . . . and a mailbox . . . "Computer?"

"Yes," he said excitedly. "Swivel?" Whirling his forefinger in the air, as if stirring up mischief.

Months before, I had shown him an Italian museum website where viewers could virtual-tour, strolling through the museum, from gilt to rococo. Did he actually remember that?

"Do you mean the museum tour . . . ?"

"Yes!" he said with relief, adding, "Of course."

In school, Paul had studied the great revolutions of the past—Agricultural, Industrial, Transportation—and how they'd edited and revised being human, from our gene pool to our ability to survive in climates and landscapes deadly to our ancestors. But that hadn't prepared him for being swept up in the next great one. It was both his privilege and bad fortune to be alive in the throes of the Information Age, too slick, fast, and silicon for his old-fashioned brain. This was a revolution he didn't fathom, didn't like, didn't use much, and yet nonetheless profited from—which made it all the more daunting *before* his stroke. After his stroke, it confused him utterly, and Liz or I served as go-between. I soon found the British Museum site, and although we couldn't "stroll through" the halls, together we browsed.

Discovering Rossetti's wombat was fun, but it also reconnected us through an activity not related to illness, the arc of learning something new together, a lively way to bridge minds. More and more now, we began to delve into subjects we could share, which satisfied both my curiosity and Paul's. The history of aphasia produced a cabinet of wonders not for the squeamish. In the second century AD, the Greek physician Galen would have diagnosed Paul's aphasia as a blockage of black bile gumming up a cranial sac believed to store his animal spirits. To our horror, in the sixteenth century, doctors would have applied leeches to his tongue. Paul relished the recipe in Théophile Bonet's seventeenth-century *Guide to the Practical Physician*, which advised a "most secret and certain remedy for apoplexy [stroke]":

> Take a lion's dung, powdered, two parts, pour spirit of wine till it be covered three fingers' breath, let them stand in a vial stopped three days. Strain it and keep it for use. Then take a crow, not quite pinfeathered, and a young turtle, burn them apart in an oven, powder them, pour on the above-said spirit of wine, let them stand in infusion for three days. Then take berries of a linden tree, an ounce and a half. Let them be steeped in the aforesaid spirit, then add as much of the best wine and six ounces of sugar candy, boil them in a pot till the sugar be melted. Put it up. Let the patient take a spoonful of it in wine, often in a day, for a whole month.

To Paul's delight, an apparently plausible medical reason for his aphasia in the late eighteenth century would have been keeping a mistress. Presumably because the worry, or the unusual sexual excitement, raised some men's blood pressure? Doctors didn't specify why, only that mistresses could lead to stroke. We chuckled together when we discovered that in the nineteenth century, phrenologists concluded that verbal memory was located behind the eye sockets, because brilliant wordsmiths displayed big bags under their bulging, frog-like eyes.

Thank goodness for medicine's steady advances. At least Paul didn't have to endure tongue leeches or linden berries stewed in lion's dung and baby crow. I'd already told him about the clinical trials with vampire-bat saliva, and those in which the brain is stimulated by coiled magnets. Maybe treatments hadn't changed that much after all.

"No bat saliva?" Paul casually asked Liz as she offered him a mug of milk.

"*Bat saliva?*" She cocked an eyebrow. Her pixie-cut hair was a new shade of red—dark chestnut with a touch of persimmon—and her shoulders were newly tanned from a canoe trip.

Deadpan, he said: "Because I'm off Tasty Bite."

"*R-i-ght,*" she drawled skeptically. "You better not be—Tasty Bite was having a sale, and you have seventy-eight boxes stacked up in the pantry!"

Her eyes lingered a moment on the unopened asparagus can next to Paul on the kitchen table. It was wearing a wristwatch. A self-winding one, which seemed all the more implausible. I smiled. Though it looked like a doubly amputated aluminum arm, I knew it was just Paul's solution for a tight Twist-O-Flex watchband.

CHAPTER 28

_____

"WILL HAS STARTED DESIGNING THE WEBSITE FOR THE Buddhist monastery," Liz announced in a breezy way as she entered the house on Monday morning. With a quick flick of each ankle, she sloughed off her street shoes by the front door and slipped into a pair of waiting flip-flops, whose raised soles were a translucent amber. Over the weekend she'd had her hair streaked sweet-potato red, and she was giving Paul a race in the tan department, hers from dragon-boat practice.

"It's a marketing thing. They plan on selling baseball caps to raise money for the new monastery, and because the Dalai Llama's coming to town."

"I thought he wore an orange golf visor," I interjected, but there was no slowing her caffeinated ebullience.

Without missing a beat, she grabbed Paul's electric razor from the counter, whacking it open for its regular cleaning.

"Hey! Remember when Will shaved his head that freezing winter night outside on the porch? I'd banned him from doing it indoors—he always makes such a mess, hair all over the place! He was standing in his sleeping bag, at midnight! And then the shaver broke, so there he was, halfway done with his haircut, dismantling and rebuilding the shaver so he could finish. He is *such* a disaster!"

Seated at the dining room table, a barely awake Paul began look-ing confused. This was exactly the sort of direction change that left him in the dust.

"Well, at least he can fix the things he breaks," I rejoined, trying to sound reassuring.

"Break?!" Paul called out. That word he caught solidly through his morning fog.

"Remember when Will broke his arm practicing kite-surfing in the backyard with Gustaf? And of course he had bought all that equipment. Different kites for different wind speeds. Endless amounts of gear." She rolled her eyes skyward. "Now in the base-ment with the ice axes, five bicycles, and six pairs of skis. Good grief!"

"*Nooo*," Paul smeared the vowel around the air, managing to give it a *Ye gads, talkative women!* tone. "It's an infestation!"

Liz and I laughed at the image of words thick as locusts.

"Need calm. For the . . . the . . . you know, the . . ." He waved a hand at himself impatiently, as if he were fanning the embers in his skull.

"Phone call?" I finally helped.

"Yes! Phone call. I'm not awake."

"Okay, we'll be quiet. Promise." I lifted a hand to my mouth and turned it like a key in a lock; Liz did the same. We knew that telephoning was nerve-racking for him.

Paul avoided the telephone instinctively, the way moles avoid light. His anxiety was understandable, since he never knew if he'd be able to find the right words, and he couldn't see the other person's face to gain clues about what they were saying. Worst of all, as wrong words kept muscling in and sabotaging him, his listener would often retreat into a confused silence. Then the common to-and-fro of a telephone call would deteriorate into long spasms of quiet.

All he wanted was to return a call from his friend Brad, novelist and editor of the literary magazine *Conjunctions*. As we stood in my study, Paul finally gave up trying to dial and sat seething in frustra-tion with the cordless phone in his hand.

"Why do I keep pressing the scurvy button when I know it's scurvy?! I can't stop pressing the scurvy one!" Paul snarled. Holding the receiver at arm's length, he looked accusingly at its dumb gray face. "It's as if someone else is guiding the machinery, and always scurvy! No . . . *scurvy* is the wrong word. *Wrong* is the wrong right word."

"Shall I dial it for you?" I tried to keep my voice on an even keel.

"I won't be able to talk anyway," he moaned.

He was dismal, self-incriminating, feeling the warp of his mental universe. How could he not grow discouraged? My study was safe and comfortable, with the plush purple armchair for him to slouch shirtless in, and a flock of brilliant goldfinches chittering outside the open window, but there was no way for him to relax. And the more stressed he felt, the more difficult talking would be.

"Are you afraid you'll have trouble finding the words you want?" I offered, hoping to help him make peace with his nerves.

"It's like having a head full of holes, in which the perfect repository of words have shamed themselves," he lamented.

"It's as if some words loom larger than others and actually repel them," he then said at half speed, thrusting his arms out, as if pushing words away. "It's as if a word, the wrong word, clings to my face like an *octopus*, and then leaves, thank god."

Sympathizing, I murmured: "That sounds wretchedly frustrating."

"Frustrating!" he echoed. "The minute I talk into the Plexiglas I'm a goner. . . . not *Plexiglas* . . . Plexiglas . . ." He paused so long he forgot what he was saying, and threw up his hands in disgust.

Doing my best to tease out his trouble, I pressed on: "What happens exactly? Does a roadblock get in the way? Can you talk around it, you know, make a little detour and find another way to say what you mean?"

Taking a deep breath to calm down, Paul stroked his ill-shaven chin with one hand, smiling absentmindedly when he discovered a tuft of hair missed by his razor.

"There's a word clamoring to be heard . . . that . . . that . . . blots out all the others. Then all grammar, all verbal structures . . . blow out the window. . . . Sometimes I see a word, spelled right, at the front of my skull, in several colors. But never the word I want. For example, I said 'Plexiglas' when I was grabbling for something else."

"Telephone."

"*Tel-e-phone*," he sighed with the relief of someone scratching an itch.

"Not to say *Plexiglas* is incredibly hard," he said haltingly, as if groping for an unknown language. "When this anarchy occurs, there is for me no way of dragooning anything else into the mix. My brain feels like suet."

"Nice image!"

Paul considered my praise a moment, agreed, and smiled with the pride of ownership. That small achievement, however slight, buoyed his confidence just long enough to risk the perils of phoning once more. This time I dialed, but after all our pre-game warm-up, Brad wasn't home. I left a message that Paul had called.

Around dinnertime, Brad returned the call and began leaving an encouraging message for Paul on the answering machine. Hearing Brad's voice, Paul pantomimed that he wanted to talk. I answered the phone just as Brad was saying "I love you, man," and handed the receiver to Paul. Although I was tempted to leave the room to give him privacy, I knew he might need my help finding words, and several times he did. He stammered a lot, but nonetheless conveyed his feelings and for once he enjoyed the pleasure of touching voices with an old literary friend. I agonized as Paul searched in vain for words, but I was also proud of him for bravely tackling the labyrinth of aphasia.

"You know Rexroth had a stroke with speaking problems, too," Brad ventured, referring to the poet sometimes called "the father of the Beats."

Paul's face seemed to wither from the question on his mind, but nonetheless he asked: "Did he recover fully?"

My heart sank. *Cure* wasn't possible, only *improvement*, and only after unbelievably long, hard work, and even then Paul was bound to feel unsatisfied.

"What hap . . . happened . . . to Rexroth?"

"He hired an assistant and did lots and lots of therapy. But just a year later he published a new book of poems," Brad replied in encouragement.

Long forgotten, I now recalled how another poet, William Meredith, had visited our home years before with his partner Richard Harteis. Ex-Navy pilot and past poet laureate, Meredith had published ten celebrated books of poetry before a stroke, in 1983, which badly crippled his ability to speak and move for over a year. Assisted by Harteis, he still traveled and "gave readings," with Harteis reading while Meredith sat in the audience. Afterward, he'd socialize, and let Harteis interpret if need be. I remembered Meredith's strange, clogged, halting speech. Yes, it made so much sense now. What a lovely guest Meredith had been, affable and smart, and, after years of speech and physical therapy, able to handle small talk and walking, albeit with great effort. In devastating hindsight, I recalled how Paul and I had felt grave sorrow for him.

Idly browsing my bookshelves while Paul finished his call, it occurred to me that Paul had joined a wretchedly distinguished club. With stroke and aphasia so common, myriad authors, composers, and other creative souls *must* have suffered similar fates for centuries. Ravel, Rexroth, and Meredith piqued my curiosity, and I resolved to do a little research, a project that might also interest Paul.

As if reading my mind, Paul asked after he and Brad hung up: "I wonder . . . about other writers . . . have aphasia? . . . Proust . . . Joyce . . . Dickens?" He quickly circled one open hand in the air, a motion that usually means *and so on*.

Despite the day's highs, as night fell, a savage wistfulness haunted me, as Paul's words, gestures, and concerns unfolded on a narrow plane, in few dimensions. All that was missing existed offstage, as shadows. Some things are much more present in their absence.

About that Marcel Proust was right. I remembered that like Paul, Proust also had a cork-lined room to shield him from the clamor of daily life, and kept a reverse sleep-wake cycle. Proust's room was a bedroom chamber where he wrote, and sometimes dined on mashed potatoes delivered by carriage from his favorite restaurant at the Ritz. In Paul's case, the cork-lined room was his study, also windowless. And for years before his stroke, Paul had had a serious mashed-potato addiction, too. He'd traveled with packets of dried mashed potatoes in his suitcase, and at home he liked to thicken soups or stews with them, a habit I found repulsive and vehemently banned from my own portions.

While Paul watched his nightly television, trying to distract myself, since I was still feeling a bit blue, I hunted through the library and online to find an answer for us about other writers afflicted with aphasia. Sure enough, Baudelaire had been stricken, as well as Ralph Waldo Emerson, William Carlos Williams, Samuel Johnson, and C. F. Ramuz. Proust was a strange case. A lifelong asthmatic and neurotic, he hadn't endured aphasia himself, but morbidly feared it. His physician father had published scholarly papers on aphasia before succumbing to a stroke at the age of fifty-six, after days of altered consciousness. Later on, while Proust was still living with his mother, he experienced its devastation first-hand when she had a stroke that left her aphasic for two years before her death.

Small wonder Proust became alarmed, in his early thirties, by the onset of slurred speech, dizziness, memory lapses, and falls. That constellation of symptoms probably hadn't come from stroke but from the collision of all the drugs he was taking in excess—for sleep, waking, asthma control, psychosomatic banes, and reappearing streaks of malaise. Paul knew about Proust's suffering—lucid, addictive, and otherwise—but not his mother's aphasia. Computer printouts in hand, I trundled out to the living room to share with Paul what I'd found.

When I read Paul this quote of Proust's—"A foreigner has taken domicile in my brain"—he nodded with empathy.

"But did you know that Emerson also had a stroke with bad aphasia?" I asked.

"No! . . . How did he transcend?"

Paul's question was serious, but we both smiled at the pun on "Transcendentalist" that had winkled its way around his brain and out through his mouth under its own power.

"I don't know. I couldn't find many details."

By the summer of 1871 Emerson had begun losing his memory and braving progressive aphasia, probably part of a degenerative brain condition. The great essayist forgot his own name, and when someone greeted him with "How are you?" he'd often reply: "Quite well. I have lost my mental faculties but am perfectly well."

"Actually, there's been shockingly little written about *any* authors who have had strokes or aphasia," I told Paul. "Isn't that odd? But quite a bit is known about Baudelaire. . . . he had a left-hemisphere stroke very similar to your own, only it didn't turn out so well."

"Tell me," Paul said eagerly, and settled back comfortably. He loved to hear about other aphasics who were worse off than he was.

Then, wistfully, he added the single word *"flâneur,"* pronounced with a good French accent and a hint of tenderness. He had taught me the word when we visited the picturesque medieval city of Tours, for a conference on Paul's work at the Université François Rabelais, on the lush banks of the wide, myrtle-green Loire. *Flâneur* is French for someone who strolls or lounges, a word Baudelaire had commandeered to mean "someone who walks or loafs around a city in order to experience it," because modern life, with its social riptides and cultural bonds, had become too complicated for traditional art. Baudelaire felt that one needed to live as a cynical voyeur on the one hand, and yet a passionate denizen of the meanest streets on the other. Paul's working-class background and rarefied Oxford education had resulted in a similar outlook.

I dived in. "Baudelaire's case is very sad. He was only forty-five when he had a left-hemisphere stroke with Broca's aphasia." I spoke under easy sail, habitual by now, pausing between parts of sentences, to give Paul time to process what I was saying. "As you know, he caught syphilis in his teens, and it kept flaring up and plaguing him with the usual miseries: pain in all his joints, hair loss, ulcers, god-awful fatigue, fevers, sore throats, rashes everywhere, depression, and bouts of psychosis."

Paul grimaced silently.

"Yep. The whole bag of tricks."

"And he was . . ." Paul lifted his thumb and first finger to his mouth, separated and tilted them in a gesture of drinking.

"No, it didn't help that he was drunk as a fish and took opium. There was this episode in Brussels where a friend found him in his room at the Hôtel du Miroir . . ."

Paul grinned.

"I know. How funny is it for a French poet to live in a hotel of mirrors? Anyway, one morning his friend found him in his room, lying in bed, fully dressed, but unable to move or speak. He recovered slightly, well enough to read proofs and dictate a few letters. But he had another stroke, this one paralyzing the right half of his body and leaving him completely aphasic."

Looking concerned, Paul asked, "Could they do anything?"

"Not much. One of his friends said that 'the softening of his brain' was obvious, and she was afraid that he would 'outlive his intelligence.'"

Paul's eyebrows leapt in horror.

"Isn't it a wretched thought? He really couldn't communicate at all, so finally he was taken to the Institut Saint-Jean et Sainte-Elisabeth, a clinic run by Augustinian nuns, where, apparently, they found him quite a handful. Not least because all he said was a curse, *Cré nom.*"

"*Cré nom!*"

"Which translates roughly as *goddamn*, right?"

"*Goddamn.* But a . . . nunnery?" Paul looked positively gleeful.

"Of all places for a perpetually cursing, decadent artist! Listen to this passage about Baudelaire from this book I bought called *Neurological Disorders in Famous Artists.*"

Paul nodded in assent, so with a deep breath, I read:

With these two words, he who had loved and practiced the art of conversation was obliged to express the whole gamut of his feelings and thoughts—joy, sorrow, anger, and impatience—and he sometimes flew into a rage at his inability to make his meaning clear, and to answer those who spoke to him. . . . [T]hought still lived in him as could be divined from the expression in his eyes, but it was imprisoned in the dungeon of his flesh, and without means of communication with the outside world.

Although I read the passage twice and slowly, I wasn't sure Paul could follow all of it. But he gestured he wanted me to go on.

"So, the Sister Superior," I continued, warming to my report, "wrote to Baudelaire's mother that the religious hospital really wasn't the right place for her son, complaining that she didn't like having such a blasphemous man in the house! Apparently Baudelaire's mother began to get concerned that the nuns might torment him."

"How?" Paul asked.

"Who knows. Maybe just engulf him in prayers and demand that he repeat them. It really must have been an awful place for someone who couldn't speak except for yelling *goddamn!* I'm sure the constant cursing got on the nuns' nerves."

Paul was chuckling to himself, and I could tell he was picturing the scene, with Baudelaire screaming *Cré nom!* and the kind sisters in wimples and flowing robes circling him with crucifixes and prayers.

"And the sisters said they found him frightening—so maybe he seemed satanic to them? Remember, Baudelaire once said, 'Men and women know from birth that all pleasure lies in evil!' I'm sure they must have thought he was totally wicked. Maybe," I drawled with exaggerated seriousness, "they *exorcised* him! Apparently he shouted his head off at them. But it was the only clinic in Brussels for patients as bad off as he was. I'll read you what one of his caregivers said about him."

As usual, I read the passage to Paul slowly and twice through:

He acts like a quasi-mute, who would articulate one single word and try to make himself understood by varying intonations. I understand him quite often, as far as I'm concerned; but it's hard.

"Still following?"

He nodded, but that didn't necessarily mean *yes*. I wondered if he was just being courteous or obliging or didn't have the energy to protest, but I continued nevertheless, skipping down the page to a quotation from one of Baudelaire's friends:

> I became convinced that Baudelaire had never been more lucid or subtle. Seeing him lending his ear while having a wash, to the hushed conversations near him and not missing a word of it, which I could observe through the signs of approbation or impatience he manifested, exchanging sustained attention and the clearest intelligence. I had no doubt that the part that illness had spared in him was completely sane and active and that his mind was as free and nimble as I saw in the previous year.

"So, with friends, he acted as if he understood. Just couldn't speak. It sounds like Broca's. He might not have known he was cursing. He didn't improve. Mind you, no one expected him to. Therapy didn't exist. Imagine. His entire poetic gift reduced to that one curse: *goddamn!* How awful."

But Paul had beaten me to the imagining. "I know how he feels," he said, then self-mockingly, as if he had a toad in his mouth, added: "*Mem, mem, mem!*"

"I'm sure you do."

"Why only poultry?"

Scrabbling around my mind for the connection, I finally recalled a friend telling us of a man she knew whose stroke, bizarrely, left him only able to say one word. Not a curse, but the word "chicken," aberrant and alone.

"Well, from what I've learned, neurologists don't really seem to know. Many aphasics can only say one word, or maybe a phrase—

and it's often a curse. Like Baudelaire. Maybe because it was some-thing really familiar, like song lyrics? Something automatic. Or was it the *last* word they thought or spoke before their stroke? And then the brain got snagged on those sounds?"

Paul nodded assent. He was with me.

"Or the *first* word the person thought or spoke *after* the stroke, with the same stuck result? Or maybe just one *syllable* of that word or phrase? Like the way you kept saying *mem, mem, mem.*"

I could see Paul grinding the gears in his head—what words began with *mem*?

"Member, memoir, memo, memento . . ." I offered.

"Memba," he added.

"*Memba?* . . . A rap-music-singing member of Mensa?"

He giggled. But did he laugh automatically because he assumed I was being cute, or did he laugh because he understood and was picturing a brainiac from Mensa, the high-IQ society, doing hip-hop hand-jive?

"Did you understand what I just said?" I suspected not. Aphasics often respond correctly, and convincingly—without understand-ing a word of what you're saying—because so many elements of conversation are automatic. They know you've probably conveyed some ideas, without being able to identify them.

"No. Don't need to."

For once, his not understanding didn't frustrate either of us.

"You just like the sound of it?"

"Yes. That's enough. Back to . . . *mem, mem, mem.*" Paul waved one hand, indicating, *Continue.*

"Why *are* people left repeating one word or phrase? Well, both sides of the brain do language," I ventured. "But some scientists think they play different roles, with the left"—I cupped the left side of my head to help illustrate—"in charge of voluntary speech, and the right"—now cupping the right side of my head—"in charge of all the words and expressions you've heard so often that they're indelible, automatic, like reflexes. Clichés, slang, song lyrics, curses, polite stuff, that sort of thing. You know them by heart. You don't need to *think* about them."

Under thought's radar they glide, I thought, *along with an armada of bad habits and a handful of well-oiled skills.* Just as Paul had lost his speaking voice, at times it felt like I'd lost my poet's voice, which I had to simplify, censor, and make more linear in order to communicate with him. It felt strange, even after two years, because linear isn't my natural gait.

"Couch man?"

"Couch man . . . Couch man . . . couch man . . ." Again I racked my brain. "Do you possibly mean Freud?"

"Yes! Freud!"

I smiled. Paul *knew* I would have researched Freud's take on all this.

"Freud was absolutely interested in aphasics. He marveled at all the people left only with curse words—which he, of course, blamed on repression! He theorized that in a healthy brain, our well-behaved speech represses all the nasty words, which would otherwise ooze from the jaggy, snarly, greedy curse-besotted id. Anyway, sweetheart, I sure am relieved you weren't left like Baudelaire."

"Jaggy? . . . Jaggy? . . . Jaggy?" he rolled the adjective around in his mouth, savoring it.

"Nice word, huh? Got it from Dr. Ann. It sounds so . . . so . . ."

"Jaggy."

"Exactly! You know, I forgot to tell you that Baudelaire's response to music didn't change a bit after his stroke. He still loved listening to Wagner. All that *Sturm und Drang.* His stroke must have spared the part of the right hemisphere that colors the sounds we hear with strong emotions."

"Not for me," Paul frankly admitted with surprisingly little regret for his paled response to music.

"No, but you're not limited to just one curse!"

"Sky's the limit!" He beamed, his inner perpetual schoolboy no doubt thinking about all the blasphemies still open to him. "Not just *MEM*!"

"Oh, right, what's 'memba'?" I was still wondering if it was a real word.

Sticking out his chest in a parody of exaggerated pride, he grinned, then drew a ragged outline of something in the air, shaped like a kite or a diamond. Not his usual *templum*. Maybe an object or a country? I looked the word up in the dictionary. Sure enough, the Memba were a tribal people living in India.

CHAPTER 29

T WO YEARS AFTER HIS STROKE, PAUL WAS NOW ABLE TO
write longhand, slowly, which he did with gusto every single day. Our mission was to keep the momentum of his recovery
going, and for Paul that meant continuing to write, regardless of
obstacles. In part because writing daily influenced his self-
confidence and mood. But also because it was his lifelong form of
deep play. Not ha-ha play, but an altered state humans seem to
crave, one of clarity, wild enthusiasm, and saturation in the
moment. This requires one's full attention, because when acting
and thinking become the same event, there's no room left for other
thoughts. Life's usual choices and relationships recede. Into an
imperfect world and into the confusion of life, deep play brings a
temporary, limited perfection. So even if what he wrote read like
a dog's breakfast, I cheered him on relentlessly, sometimes having
to draw deep to find the energy, while at other times feeling invig-
orated because it was something tangible I could do to help him.

Some of his sentences were so aphasic as to be incomprehensi-
ble, and then Liz or I, as tactfully as possible, would go over the
work with him, highlighting nonsensical phrases or misused
words, and helping him tease what he meant out of the mental
cobwebs. We all regarded his writing as vital speech therapy. Pass-

ing by his study, the door cracked open a little, I'd see him sitting at his desk, in a cork-walled corner of the room, curving over a page as he always used to, redolent with thought. But more than his mind seemed to be straining these days—his back yawed, his shoulders flexed and wilted. I sometimes stood and watched the tension of a whole body thinking. With great effort, he'd painstakingly revise every page, sometimes only to have new infelicities emerge. Though Liz and I were free with our opinions and criticism, out of necessity we simply overlooked many mistakes in the name of progress. Paul always knew how he'd like something to read; it was *his* creation, *his* deep play, not *just* speech therapy, and above all it should please him. Writing both fiction and essays, he scrawled 300 pages during the first two years, and the dogged daily work of writing and revising exhausted but satisfied him, while improving his skills.

It also allowed Paul and me to bridge our old and new life, as once again we found ourselves having discussions over word choice, consulting each other for adjectives, and comparing the sound of one phrase to another. Again our voices breached the space between our offices, which felt as welcome as a bluff of trees on the prairie. Like the call and response of two strange, literary birds, Paul would yell across the hallway to me:

"Hey, poet, what's the name of that red star . . . Orion . . . belt?"

And I'd yell back: "Betelgeuse."

Then I'd call: "Honey, how do you spell *zyzzva* [a palm weevil]?"

And he'd answer: "Three *z*'s!" His spelling was surprisingly reliable when it came to arcane words.

And we were all beyond thrilled when he began to place some essays and fiction he'd written *since* the stroke in *Harper's*, *The American Scholar*, *Conjunctions*, *The Yale Review*, and a few other literary magazines.

Every so often, if Liz and I were chatting too much in the kitchen, Paul came to scold us, holding his small navy blue talisman of a pillow, on which white embroidery implored: *Quiet*

Please! Novel in progress. Silently, he'd lift it to his chest and hold it out to us like one of the "ring girls" at a boxing match announcing the number of the round.

Over these years, Liz had become an ace literary assistant and good friend. I'd grown used to her hair color changing, from fire-engine red to carrot-orange to calico. More and more of her flip-flops took up residence in her office, a converted guest room with three walls of windows looking into the garden, floral tiles along the skirting boards, a floral sofa and matching drapes, floral rug, large blond table for a desk, and chairs whose wooden backs were silhouettes of Montgolfia hot-air balloons. In the fall, I planted spring and summer bulbs outside her windows—daffodils, fritil-larias, giant alliums, bluebells, dwarf irises, daylilies, and canna lilies—without telling her exactly what or where so that they would be a surprise.

In time, the household wombat fetish evolved from my address-ing Paul as "wombat," to his calling me "wombat," to Liz referring to us as "the wombats," to Liz merging into the general wombat-tery. When she was in Oregon, she signed her emails as "Wombat-at-large," in San Francisco she became "West Coast Wombat," in Washington, D.C., "Capitol Wombat." I might sign my emails "Wombat-in-Residence" or "Two-legged North American Long-haired Wombat." And Paul swiftly became the likes of "P-Wombat, House Wombat, or Swimming Wombat." The screensavers on her laptop and mine showed adorable baby wombats. A growing col-lection of wombataphilia entered the house: key chains, stuffed animals, mugs, baseball caps. Before her annual canoeing adven-ture with college friends, she created a notebook whose cover read: *Field Guide to the Wombats of . . .* . Inside, methodical notes and instructions explained everything from Paul's medicines to how to restart my hybrid Prius. At Christmas one year, Liz received a mug appropriately emblazoned with *Wombat Wrangler*.

So it was only fitting that I produced a quirky new work con-tract, a "Wombat Incentive Package," which included, among other things, a raise, as many weeks off as she wanted pretty much whenever she wanted them, a monthly pedicure, and last but not least, her body weight in chocolate.

Ultimately, the "body weight in chocolate," much as envisioning a public weighing-in ceremony delighted us all, was not as alluring to her as a book allowance, so together we drew up an elaborate sybaritic chocolate-to-books conversion chart. The far from button-down contract suited her, and she signed on for another tour of duty in the wombat warren of the household and the always-a-surprise-around-the-next-corner jungles of aphasia.

Self-described as "borderline OCD in a useful way," Liz was a born fact-checker and proofreader, an awesome organizer of people and closets. I was grateful that she set out and triple-checked Paul's pills, and was fanatically methodical about everything from keeping Paul's prescriptions up-to-date to bandaging a cut or scrape on his foot. Liz folded towels symmetrically, like perfect strips of colorful pastry, and only occasionally confessed to refolding the ones I'd folded into thirds, which didn't match those she'd folded into quarters. She performed elaborate *interventions* on neglected filing cabinets and the hinterlands of our dusty, junkyard-style garage, where old manuscripts lurked.

"I'm just *fully integrated*," she would say when praised, suggesting that, after a while, she knew instinctively what we preferred. But a parallel truth is that we had adapted to her ways, too.

When it came to sway in the household, I sometimes teased that she missed her calling as a dominatrix. Like most people, I have habitual ways of running the house, but I'm not wedded to them. About sharing space, I have a strong sense of "live and let live." So I gave her free *reign*. To my amusement, it astounded her that I didn't mind at all if she reorganized the kitchen drawers, turned the mudroom into an overflowing pantry, rearranged the in-their-place-for-a-decade armchairs in the living room (creating a fine basking spot at the picture windows), or devised a color-coded monthly calendar on the refrigerator with red dots for days Liz was away, yellow for days Diane had trips, blue for Paul's appointments. She established a hierarchy of Post-it notes on the kitchen counter—

ranked by size, color, shape, and level of importance—now and
then so abundant that they looked like prayer flags strung across a
Nepalese col, and other times overlapping like genteel folds of skin.

We were a shockingly good fit. Paul and I would generate an
endless stream of projects, and Liz would get to compulsively organize them, cheerfully stating she had always been "a fan of
enthalpy," by which she meant the fine art of bringing order to
chaos. Hundreds of small changes appeared in our daily life, and
although I wasn't as systematic, I appreciated the growing sense of
method in the house at precisely the time my world felt disheveled
beyond repair. Myself, I've always organized in waves. For months
on end, slowly descending into disorder, I drift with the status quo.
Then I wake up one morning with a sudden compulsion to color-
code my socks and stack them vertically. Or I have a longtime
writerly habit, more of an instinct really, of obsessively tidying my
office before I begin a new book, as if I were an expectant mom
preparing for birth. I think it soothed the bubbling inner commo-
tion a little to find my surroundings less chaotic, providing a bit of
sensory relief.

One thing we all had in common was a great respect for, even a
reveling in, eccentricity. With pride, Liz told us stories of her dad,
a small-town Presbyterian minister in Missouri and consummate
tinkerer who fervently believed in reusing and recycling. How
he'd salvaged materials from a local junkyard and cannibalized
discarded lawnmowers to build fully functional, multihued, Fran-
kensteinian mowers. How he'd unconventionally, yet oh-so-prac-
tically, painted her childhood home two-tone: dark brown halfway
up all the walls, then white above the height where kids could
leave dirty fingerprints. How he and his second wife, a former
Ukrainian nuclear biochemist who now runs a successful luxury
knitting business, were building their lakeside retirement home
complete with a small "worm factory," to provide bait for their
almost daily fishing.

So while Paul and I had such playful habits as soccer-kicking
boxes of Kleenex and rolls of toilet paper down the hallway rather

than carrying them to the other end of the house, and quacking the theme song to *Masterpiece Theatre*, Liz was hard to faze. Married to her burly, six-foot-tall, double-earringed husband (a graphic designer working at Cornell's Laboratory of Ornithology), she enjoyed the turmoil of highly creative minds. She would some-times mock-vent, while pretending to tear her hair out at the roots: "*Artists!* What's wrong with me?! I surround myself with you peo-ple at work—as if I don't get enough chaos at home!"

At times Liz reminded me a lot of my undergraduate college roommate Kathe, a woman with a Scottish complexion, cropped blond hair, and quick wit. Kathe was yards smarter than I was, upbeat, insightful, and fun. To earn money, she'd been a part-time go-go dancer at the My-Oh-My Lounge down the street from our apartment. We romped verbally all the time, and got up to endless mischief. What Liz and Kathe had in common was a certain stripe of brain. Not artistically creative, but brilliant, high-spirited, and curious, they had similar restless minds that craved stimulation. And so when Liz said of herself, "I don't *do* reflection," or regaled us with stories of the many jobs she'd had, I understood. For both Paul and me, although our passions changed as we invented new books, our career was writing. Our method was focused and dreamy spells mixed with practical minutiae. In contrast, Liz needed the variety of changing *occupations*, keeping her family and longtime friends constant, while replenishing her pool of cowork-ers and her landscape. A different sort of mental nomad, one who wanders without versus one who wanders within. My mother was similar. I had a hunch Liz wouldn't work with us forever, no matter how much she might enjoy the work or grow to love us. Her brain needed novelty to feel most alive, something it didn't generate but sought, then explored and transformed with gusto.

To her delight, in our household, unpredictability was *de rigueur*, so she never knew what to expect when she arrived each morning. One of us might be immersed in Mongolia and the other in the primeval forests of Poland, each needing her research skills at the last minute. She didn't hesitate, but I think was amused, when I

suggested we hang a few lovely photographs of bats up by the raf-
ters where they *belong*. She regularly found on her to-do list such
items as: "organize universe" (the filing system in my study), "blow
up cheetah" (the inflatable one in the living room), "don't frighten
lady garter!" (striped snake that likes to sun on the patio),
"Desdemona—safe to plant with Othello?" (two ligularias I'd
planted), "down to two endangered species; order a dozen" (referring to a brand of dark chocolate). Or "Slim Bear shortage" (indicating we were down to the last of Paul's frozen treats).

Or there might be a medical emergency requiring her care,
which over the years Paul and I provided in spades: broken toe (I
confess, mine, from an unfortunate incident with a massage table),
concussion, pinched cervical nerves, asthma, diabetes, high blood
pressure, arthritic knees, congestive heart failure, and more. Or an
unexpected publishing crisis or proofreading deadline. Then we'd
all three gaze at each other, nod our heads, and together bleat in
mock seriousness: "Never a dull moment!" Emailing old friends
from college, she'd once laughingly described her job as: "stay-at-
home mom for two writers."

"You know what's weird," Liz said in a tone of bemusement,
"Some people work in *cubicles*! . . . Of course, working with your
contrarian spouse Paul isn't all that different from working with
thoroughbreds"—referring to the racehorse farm where she'd
labored for a few years before nursing school—"except, unfortunately, *no whips and leathers*!" Her eyebrows leapt like twin dragon
boats at a starting line.

I'd never known anyone with such expressive eyebrows. They
didn't just raise or cock. Instead they vaulted, they pranced, they
sharpened into hard strawberry mesas, or curved somberly into
neolithic burial mounds—especially when Paul dug his heels in.

Liz and Paul could be equally stubborn and opinionated, and it
always amused me to see them hunched over the table, politely
arguing about all sorts of things, from the "correct" way to take his
pills without choking, or the benefits of replacing his molting loafers, to the fine points of grammar. Liz's eyebrows would hover in a

tolerant position as she listened, then close ranks to be peered under as she stated her judgment: "Well, Paul, with all due respect, I think you're wrong this time." Liz's husband frequently sent his sympathies to Paul, because he knew Liz was a "tenacious arguer."

One day when I descended into Liz's office with a look of horror and dismay, my arms piled with seemingly infinite versions of a manuscript that needed line-by-line sorting—because I'd made the behemothic mistake of working on it in different cities, on different computers, over several years—she gazed upon me with messianic mercy and declared:

"Every poet needs at least one overly linear friend."

About Paul's health issues she was especially vocal. Paul protested, as a point of honor, but he also appreciated her vigilant concern, sometimes in endearing circumlocutions. Once, when Liz apologized for nagging him about checking his feet for diabetic sores, he blinked hard, then responded cordially, without a hint of sarcasm:

"Always feel free to lecture me—I'm a friend to knowledge."

CHAPTER 30

A T THE BEGINNING OF JUNE, A FEW SUMMERS AFTER THE stroke, we opened the pool for the season, and Paul slid into its blue eye with a shiver of delight. Flailing some and looking a little anxious, he swam a tentative breaststroke across the shallow end.

"You're swimming! You're swimming!" I yelled from the patio, feeling a sudden surge of excitement.

He paused long enough to grin and call back an exultant "I am, aren't I!"

Then he suddenly turned toward the deep end and pushed off from the shallow bottom, swimming in awkward but nonetheless continuous strokes for his first lap of the season. Pausing at the far end, he gasped a bit, caught his breath, then, face beaming as if he'd astonished himself, set off on the return lap with verve.

Over the past few years, he had learned how to cope a little more with the lack of coordination, vision, and balance problems he had suffered during the stroke. Depending on where a stroke hits, one's sense of the body's scale and edges can change dramatically, the skin feel porous instead of elastic, a leg grow heavier, a wrist dangle looser. Suddenly one can have so many toes. But his brain was reorganizing and learning to compensate. He still had irritating trouble with things that required many steps, but he'd relearned how to hold a felt pen and write reliably in longhand, wield a knife and fork, button his shirt, steer a zipper, brush his teeth, and dozens of other commonplace but sublime small acts of complexity the brain teaches itself and then secretly remembers. All the stuff we take for granted, unless they're taken away from us by injury.

"A bowl of raspberry and rum space dust," I teased, on a typical morning, as I presented his usual breakfast of Egg Beaters and Smart Bacon. Then I shared with him a short article from *The Guardian* online. It reported that astronomers had identified a swirl of amino acids in Sagittarius B$_2$ (a giant dust cloud in the Milky Way)—and that if we had a bowl of that space dust to sample, it would taste of raspberry and rum.

"What do you make of that?"

"I need something to write with!" Paul picked up the pen, which he habitually kept next to his place at the table, almost as another type of cutlery.

"You're holding a pen," I replied, taken aback.

"No, I need something to *write* with!"

"You have a pen in your hand," I said slowly, with growing puzzlement.

"To *write* with!"

I took hold of his hand with the pen. "Here's a pen. You have one. Do you need a different pen?"

"*Nooo*—the other thing," he sighed, getting more flustered.

"The other thing . . . a *tablet* to write on?"

"*Yesss!*" he crooned in relief. Yet another never-ordinary conversation to start the day.

"Thank you for an absolutely lascivious breakfast," he pronounced with conviction, while chasing a last patch of soy bacon around his plate.

Since it was noon, my lunchtime, I joined him with a bowl of Moroccan Vegetable and Chickpea Stew.

"*Lascivious*, eh? I'd be happy to share my lunch with you."

"No way, too burly," he declined with a grimace. "Has that . . .

that . . . double-barreled entity sent their . . . hmm . . . their . . . *spondulicks?*"

Words crowded my mind. Stumped, I finally asked: "What's a spondulicks?"

"Money."

"Really? Truly? Spondulicks?" In my mind's eye, I pictured a spastic duck.

"Yes," he said emphatically.

"Okay.". . . *double-barreled* . . . and *sent* . . . *double-barreled* . . . and *sent* . . . Do you possibly mean: Has the Johnson and Wales School sent me my check?"

"Yes!" He nodded firmly.

"*Spondulicks?*"

"Spondulicks. It's British."

Surely he was pulling my leg. I breezed into the library to look it up in an etymological dictionary, where I found this entry:

> 1856, Amer.Eng. slang, "money, cash," of unknown origin, said to be from Gk. *spondylikos*, from *spondylos*, a seashell used as currency (the Gk. word means lit. "vertebra"). Used by Mark Twain and O.Henry and adopted into British English, where it survives despite having died in Amer.Eng.

"You're right!" I said, returning to my seat. "I think you meant to say *check*."

"Check. Check. *Check*," he repeated, pressing the word into his doughy memory.

In his early-morning fog, brain cells warming up, a simple word like *check* could slither away. But spondulicks would do, and while he repeated *check* in his mind, I repeated *spondulicks* in mine. The important thing was to find a shared vocabulary.

"What's the price of an airmail stamp?" he asked Liz.

"Ninety-eight cents," she advised. "But it's probably easiest if you use one of the dollar stamps."

"Thanks for invading my darkness," Paul replied chivalrously.

"How about the screed . . . ?" He moved his hand through the air as if he were writing in invisible ink. Since he had trouble finding the word *paper* or *essay*, Liz had become well acquainted with *screed*, the Middle English word Paul often used for any form of writing.

"The manuscript I typed for you?"

"Yes," he said. "What's the total mileage?"

"A little more than . . . eight . . . hundred . . . words." She slowed down at the numbers to give him time to manage the sum. "Just the right length. That's what *Transfuge* asked you for."

"Good."

"Oh, by the way, don't forget you have an appointment with Dr. Blemkin this afternoon."

Wanting to know if his eye doctor accepted check or credit card, Paul queried: "What does Dr. Blemkin traffic in?"

Her eyebrows arched like silk worms. Then she replied: "You'll need to take your credit card with you."

It was a typical exchange. We didn't interrupt Paul when he was trying to speak, which usually required his full attention. In his strain to communicate, he knew just what he meant, but was not aware he was substituting an odd word or expression. The three of us sometimes laughed about the word chimeras of the day, with Paul cackling over them as much as we did. It delighted the part of his personality that had always appreciated gaudiness, especially in language.

"What does Dr. Blemkin *traffic in*?!" Liz repeated with an amused smile later that afternoon, as she massaged Icy Hot into his crooked fingers.

Paul giggled. "Did *I* say that?"

"You did."

"Opium?" He thought a moment. "Nepenthes?"

"*Nepenthe?*" I said. "Where did that come from?"

Laughing, he shrugged. "Floated up." To the surface of his mind, he meant, from the lily-pad-covered word-pond beneath.

"Okay, okay, what is it?" Liz asked. Few could feign exasperation with such aplomb.

"Soporific," Paul explained.

I could tell Liz was paging through her mental pharmacopeia under the letter *N*. She wouldn't find it there, it was too esoteric an allusion from his school days, when he had had to translate books of the *Odyssey*.

"Ancient Greek," I added. "Some Egyptian herb they took to forget their grief." *How odd*, I thought. *He even remembers that the original word had an s at the end, which English translators dropped by mistake because they confused it for a plural suffix.* At some point in our decades together, he must have spoken to me about it, but I couldn't remember where or when.

Paul laughed, shook his head, grinned proudly. "I never know what I'm going to say!"

"But you can *say* what you mean most of the time. That's huge. I'm really proud of you."

"I am, too," Liz chimed in as she stretched his cramped finger until it almost straightened for a moment, and he flashed her the tortured grimace of some Inuit masks.

Wrong words still veered through his speech like errant comets. Deciphering his sentences was still taxing for me. Not as taxing as it was for him to utter, of course—it might take Paul five minutes of false starts to work a sentence free.

"The movie starts at two. No. Two. No. Two, three, four. *Four*," he'd declare with relief at finally finding the right word. Even then he might choose a word by default because he couldn't lasso the ideal one.

Once he was truly awake, he was fresher. But that's when he tended to be writing in his study, or working with Liz on revisions. I spent more hours with him in the late afternoons and evenings, when he was sundowning. By mistake, he sometimes referred to that period, quaintly, as his "five o'clock shadow." By now I knew that when he was fatigued, asking him open-ended questions ("Which movie would you like to watch?") didn't work well. Instead I used short phrases and offered him choices in pairs ("Would you rather watch *A Perfect Murder* or *A Gathering Storm*?

The thriller or the Churchill movie?" "Shrimp for dinner or Tasty Bite?"). Then, by using the words I'd already primed his mind with, he could simply model his reply on mine: "Tasty Bite. The Churchill movie."

Some of his days seemed cut loose from past and future. Out of the blue he couldn't remember something that happened yesterday, or he'd forget a routine (taking vitamins) that had been part of each day for months. To him it was unbelievable, rumor, not conscious, not real, yet another figment he must take on faith.

"We spoke about it last week," I reminded him when he complained he didn't know about the doctor's appointment that day.

"Last week is mythic to me!" he snapped in gruff exasperation.

Whenever he poured milk into a mug, half of it still spilled over the front edge. The first hundred or so times, I tried centering his hand over the cup, showing him where to pour. But he never did improve his aim (though he did improve at mopping up). People don't just calculate sums. While pouring milk, we gauge how far a stream of milk is from the edge of a cup, and while walking we compute how high a foot must lift to glide safely over a curb. For depth perception, the brain relies on visual clues *plus* the ability to recalibrate distances if the situation or landscape changes. Paul's brain had lost the knack of counting, and he also had trouble judging distances. Maybe that contributed to his spilling when he poured, and how easily he tripped over steps and curbs.

But few things continued to plague Paul more than remembering *how* things were done. Over and over, he relearned how to dial the phone, open a pull-tab carton of milk, unlatch a pillbox, push the microwave's one-minute button the correct number of times, and a hundred other feats. Check-writing proved hopeless. He'd write the wrong name, the wrong amount, the wrong date, all on the wrong lines—there seemed an infinite number of mistakes he could make with a single check. Sometimes it took an hour to get one check right. But he kept trying. If he didn't do something regularly he forgot how. It was as if he needed to reinstall lost habits, which are really mental shortcuts. The brain would grind to a halt if it had to think every time its owner tied a shoelace or wielded a fork. So, to keep household life flowing smoothly, we established simple routines and stuck to them. Doing the same things at roughly the same time each day seemed to leave Paul more energy to devote to relearning speech and the arts of once-familiar tasks.

Most afternoons we'd convene for a midday break. "Wombat Teatime!" Liz would holler to me in my study, and I'd pack up work for the day and wander down the hallway to join them, in the style of a British afternoon tête-à-tête, my mind often trailing thought-clouds from faraway atolls. As the three of us caught up on our day's doings, our planet seemed to grow smaller and non sequiturs flew. A typical teatime conversation: I emerged full of news of Nyepi, the Balinese national day of silence and introversion. We decided I should learn to touch-type when I retired—Liz and Paul agreed I'd never have the patience to do it now, plus they got such a kick out of watching me type like a mad, two-fingered organist. Liz vented about her husband. Paul announced he had been writing an essay about "George Foreman and cows." Liz popped an eyebrow in surprise. I'd do my best to horrify Liz and Paul with favorite awful puns, such as: "What geometric shape most resembles a lost parrot?" Answer, of course: a Polly-gone.

A bonus from Paul's stroke was how much time Liz, Paul, and I had spent together—"more than I've spent with my husband!" she once laughed. Time, that sweet luxury, and the close tie it inspires, usually happens in college, when days move slowly around similar events. College roommates or housemates tend to stay friends for years. I've sometimes heard professional women complain about how hard it is to make lasting friends, how there isn't always enough time for closeness to flourish. So one wonderful side effect of Paul's stroke was what cherished friends Liz and I had become.

As different as we are, she's a word-slinger who is sharp as a fang, we're both bookish, both excited by nature, both curious little ferrets who identify with Autolycus, in Shakespeare's *The Winter's Tale*, a self-described "snapper-up of unconsidered trifles." Not least, we've been thrown together during periods of sorrow and joy. We appear in many of each other's memories. We've survived scary episodes in Paul's life. And it's been a godsend for me as a wordsmith. Even though I couldn't communicate well with Paul, especially during his first years post-stroke, Liz and I could talk normally—sometimes just for the sake of talking, as humans do—and that kept me from feeling silenced by his aphasia.

Our days flowed around well-charted, often traveled courses, and yet, the underlying sense of falling out of time, out of the trajectory of one's life, not by choice, but by subtraction, was frequent and disquieting. Then I grieved for him, for the lost and previous Paul. He grieved for that man, too. Both our griefs were mainly private, internal, unuttered. Return was impossible, and there was only one direction open; and so we kept our compass pointed forward.

Physically, Paul grew stronger, thanks to lots of swimming. He divined time by listening to the planes pass overhead. *Prop-jet. four o'clock.* Using planes as sound clocks, he seemed infallibly to know exactly when five o'clock came around and it was time to go inside. He was continuing to improve his speech, writing, and walking, and to compensate for his faulty vision. But the slow progress had a tinge of black shadow. I could still feel the hot breath of what-could-go-wrong. Falling still posed a threat, as did pneumonia. Swallowing pills and liquids continued to make mischief with his airways. But, as usual, concerns were tempered by moments of levity. Every day seemed to include the unusual juxtapositions of fun and worry, laughter and fear, hilarity and danger.

Toward the end of that summer, as Paul continued to roast himself in the sun on the patio, sprawled in his favorite chair before and after his swim, he grew browner and browner, and we started calling him the names of coffee beans.

"Good morning, Sulawesi," I'd greet him.

"Hullo, Java Blawan," Liz would teasingly chime in with another favorite dark roast.

One day I noticed something odd about Paul's robustly brewing tan. His chest, underarms, and pubic hair had begun, ever so faintly, to blush green. Then, one hot afternoon as he climbed out of the pool after a skinny-dip, his body hair glowed the green of ghostly ectoplasm. He looked like an aurora borealis surging up from the blue, though he hadn't seemed to notice.

Mystified, I yelped in mock horror: "It's the Green Hulk!"

"Where?" he cried, looking around, a bit confused.

"On *you*, you're bright green!" *What on earth is that?* I wondered, and *Is it unhealthy? Where have I seen that green before?*

Paul inspected his hairy green arms, legs, and groin—the last especially picturesque—and let out an uneasy chuckle.

"Giant sloths! You look just like the three-toed sloths with green fur I saw in the Amazon. The ones that move so slowly whole tribes of algae and bacteria take up residence in their fur!"

"The same tree-huggers that shimmy down their stanchion to vote?" Paul asked.

Stanchion = tree. Vote = cast a ballot = defecate. I got it.

"Yes, fertilizing their tree once a week. Creative exchange of goods and services, don't you think?"

Paul surveyed his arms and legs as if they didn't belong to him. I could tell he was picturing the possible colonization of his body by miniature green monsters.

"Little green men!" I warbled in my scariest voice, and laughed.

"*Aaagggh!*" Paul opened his mouth while waggling his fingers in pretend fright. But when he tried to towel the green off and discovered that it wouldn't budge, he started to look genuinely concerned.

"I think it's probably the chlorine, not anything like algae," I reassured him. "You move too much for algae. Blondes have to be careful their hair doesn't turn green in the pool. Maybe your gray hair is reacting the same way? I mean, you usually dry off in the sun instead of rinsing off. I've got some shampoo for chlorinated pools; let's try that."

And so we did, both scrubbing until he lost all of the green tufts.

"Mildred would have liked it," Paul said with a grin, referring to his Irish mother. "A big lad of shamrock green!"

For several days afterward, Paul kept inspecting his pelt and looking a little disappointed when he didn't find any more green. He liked briefly joining a race of reptiles and amphibians, he'd enjoyed the body pageantry. As a child, he'd always been fascinated by gargoyles, masks, totem poles, grotesques, war paint; then, as a young man, by the freak imagery of the Surrealists, and the prose high jinks of such writers as James Joyce and Samuel Beckett.

Mercifully, *word* pageantry kept returning to the household through the unlikeliest of routes. When he said funny things without meaning to, we all laughed—not *at* him but with him, at aphasia's comic side. Paul was growing comfortable enough in his own altered skin to laugh at himself, too, rather than just feel frustrated. This was good, I knew, not just any path out of the silent undergrowth, but a more comfortable one.

Working hard at my desk one afternoon, without thinking, I balanced my coffee mug on a foot-high stack of papers. Paul walked in, eyeing the mug with a look of concern—it was dangerously close to the computer and piles of my notes and books.

"Do you feel attached to that mug?" he asked. I smiled to myself, knowing he really meant: "Is it *safe* there?"

He seemed greatly concerned about my safety. Whenever I traveled, he always admonished me to mind my head on the low-ceilinged commuter planes, and take care to lock my hotel room door.

Just that morning he'd remarked: "Guard against precipitous motion," by which he meant: "Don't fall out of bed."

After which, Paul addressed me with the day's *piropo*: "Satrap of the Endless Sky . . ."

"*Ni-i-ice,*" I said, crinkling my nose in appreciation.

"They're talking about terminating the stars," he proceeded to tell me excitedly.

"Wow. That's quite a trick!" *Terminating the stars, holy smokes, that's a lot of celestial violence,* I thought. I pictured a lonely cold black sky. My mind set to work on his puzzle. *Maybe stars = going to the stars?*

"Do you *possibly* mean . . . ending the space program, stopping funds to NASA?"

"Yes!" he said, throwing up his hands, with a look that blared: *What a stupid decision they're making!* After years of amateur astronomy, roaming the galaxies in his imagination, scrutinizing close-up photographs of the planets, and savoring Hubble telescope images of deep space, he felt personally offended.

"Never mind," Paul said, quieting. "Is it sunny today?" Then, complaining about the long spell of cold rainy weather, he muttered: "April made me go insane." He yawned, and added by way of clarification: "A disheveled April is a really hard thing to sleep through." Then he chuckled, suddenly charmed by the silliness he'd uttered.

Despite his newfound pleasure in his own funny turns of phrase, it wasn't all skylarking. Some exchanges, so typical of aphasia, still frustrated him no end, like the time he casually said:

"Boy, do I have a story for you!"

"You have a story to tell me? What?" I asked.

"No, nothing," he said, dismissing it.

"You've decided not to tell me?"

After much confusion, he finally was able to explain that "Boy, do I have a story for you" had simply leapt out of his mouth against his will, even though it was actually the opposite of what he had meant: "I have nothing new to say."

Another aphasic icon continued to foil and frustrate us, too. Attempting to harpoon the right words, his mind would still occasionally produce nonsense, despite clearly wishing to say something important.

"Why don't you *smitch* the graffelklug on wentstodge?" he garbled one day while he was having breakfast.

"What did you say?" I asked in the even tone I aimed for on such occasions, trying not to make him feel self-conscious.

"Why don't you *smitch* the graffelklug on wentstodge?" he repeated in an irate whisper, clearly knowing what he meant to say.

"Take it slowly and have one more go."

After another aborted reply, he finally gave up and grew pensive. Then, with remarkable fluency and sadness, he reflected on his rubble of incoherent sounds.

"It's just the soft catechism of a great machine falling apart."

CHAPTER 31

OUT OF THE BLUE, PAUL REPORTED FEELING BOUTS OF calm euphoria, a mystical sense of all's-right-with-his-life-and-the-universe, a bright future in sight. He described it as a "swimmer's high," because in the past he'd felt the sensation only after spending several hours in the pool. I knew well the state of vigorous calm he meant, a frequent visitor throughout my own life.

His first episode took place late one night, while I slumbered and he sat on the end of the couch, sleepily watching television. As a veil of well-being swept over him, he "saw" his two old chums—Bryan and Alistair—friends from Newfoundland, where he'd held his first teaching job fifty-five years before. At eighty, Bryan now had multiple health problems; and Alistair had died the previous year. Yet in Paul's vision, or dream, or hallucination, they assured him that he was "doing everything right," the din of illness would abate, and all would be fine. He felt young and fit enough to run and hurl cricket balls once more. This blissful episode lasted about an hour, but the comforting memory remained, and when he told me about it the following morning, he looked almost serene. After a few hours the tranquillity melted away.

Four days later, he awoke early, scrambled out of bed, and shot to his study to begin writing, because his cantering mind was kicking up a dust cloud of ideas. Then he breakfasted, took his meds, and wrote again. Before grabbing a nap, he reported feeling the same calm euphoric "runner's high," whose spell veiled him as he slept.

I didn't tell him what I was thinking. I'd grown used to being wary of every new symptom, so I'm sorry to say that my initial response wasn't happiness for him but worry about what might be jolting his brain into euphoria. Lack of oxygen for some reason was a possibility. Or increased serotonin. Was the Zoloft, which he'd been on for four years, leaving his body more slowly than before? He'd been unusually creative of late, and in a different way: his recent fiction was still aphasic, but it was more purely imaginary than anything he'd written since the stroke, drawing less on real people and events.

For several days more, he woke with the muse on his shoulder, and wrote six to eight pages longhand in about two hours. Ashamed as I felt for begrudging him my free-spirited, wholehearted delight, I nonetheless worried. He was being the prophet, I the worrywart, he the one with the bedrock of peace, I the *agitata*. Being responsible for someone else's life had eroded my optimism. In the past, I mainly had my own health and well-being to keep tabs on. Now I had his, too. I had to be a reader of his signs, portents, and symptoms, a full-time savant of his well-being. Sometimes I felt like I was keeping him alive just for me, because I thirsted so for love, affection, and companionship. The primal warmth of being creatures together, loving mates, created its own powerful spell, even if he couldn't communicate as nimbly. This meant sometimes hovering over him as I might a child—because he wasn't quite independent, and his immune system was compromised by his diabetes and heart troubles—while also recognizing that he was not a child, and therefore giving him mental and emotional space to be an adult who made his own choices. A tough balancing act.

I was working in my bay window, while Paul was napping, when Liz came in for a consult. Her hair was now the color of tawny wheat at dawn in harvest season. Today's flips-flops were turquoise, and she was wearing a red spandex summer dress that clung in all the right places. It was unusual for her to interrupt my work, so my caregiver's antennae shot up. The way she stood aslant, with one foot crossed over the other, alerted me that she was worried about something, yet didn't want to worry me.

"Paul told me he's been feeling euphoric," she said. "That's nice, and maybe I'm being paranoid, but . . ."

As I slid the lap-desk forward on its shiny wooden pontoons, it glided over the window seat's woven tableau of swans and bull rushes. Liz had rigged up the makeshift sliding desk from a heavy oak breakfast tray and two polished wooden bowls.

"Yes, he told me, too, when he woke up," I said. "Should we worry? Do you think it's a symptom of something we need to keep an eye on?"

"Well, exactly," she said. "Could the euphoria mean less blood flow to the left side of the brain? Or, more optimistically, more blood flow to the right?"

We were both aware of Jill Bolte Taylor's account of euphoria and mystical visions when she had a left-brain stroke. This was Paul's second euphoric episode in a week. But other than the euphoria, he'd been stable, nothing out of the ordinary, except napping longer.

"He's been unusually creative of late," I thought out loud. "Writing with real gusto, hasn't he?"

"The pages he wrote today were strange for sure," Liz said, resting one hand on the counter, "odd and crazy, and I'm pretty darn sure that he's not getting these ideas from anyone else. He's dredging them somehow out of his own head. It's all coming from within that little skull!" She smiled in amazement, eyes wide in emphasis.

Liz's response amused me, because it was similar to what Paul's mother always used to say whenever he presented her with a new book: "I don't know how you think of it all!" But Liz was right, the way Paul was using his brain had changed since his stroke. At first he'd seemed mentally hollow, like an empty china cupboard—"Are you thinking?" "No, just sitting and staring." Slowly, over time, he began planting one thought after another, then extending thoughts, combining thoughts, noticing images, combining images. It was most visible in the record of his writing. In his dictated memoir *The Shadow Factory*, begun two months after the stroke, his sense of time and sequence were often confused. Most of it was based on actual events, not imagination. Then he'd written a careening novel about Goebbels, for which he had watched several documentaries and paged through a couple of books, but drawn mainly on details he remembered from his lifelong interest in WWII. I was frankly amazed by how much he recalled about WWII—while his brain had trouble remembering his own birthday and the names of commonplace objects and animals. The factual essay about coffee he wrote two years later—prompted by the narcotic smell of coffee, which he was no longer allowed, but whose aroma conjured up memories of buying it freshly ground with his mum when he was a lad—was based on tidbits Liz gleaned from the Internet for him. Then he wrote a novel set in Mongolia, in which he began to include many imaginary elements, some of which were based on stories of Liz's neighbor Gustaf, maps and guidebooks, and Internet research. Many essays and fictions followed.

Here he was in the midst of a sci-fi novel, and his post-writing naps lasted noticeably longer than before. Perhaps with the left side quieted, he was using the right side of his brain for language so much that it brought increased blood flow to the entire area, and since the right side is the wellspring of mystical experiences, it unloosed a few. Or was it a result of damage to his left parietal lobe, in the rear, at the top? This is where the brain divides the graspable from the nongraspable, the self from the world, delineating the many edges of the body, helping to orient us in space. Quieting that region—through deep meditation, or through damage—can sometimes belie the sense of inhabiting a body, and kindle vivid mystical experiences and feelings of transcendence. Paul still had trouble locating objects he meant to grasp, a hallmark of such an injury. That made the most sense, but why now, years later? He might have been sleeping more simply because he was using his brain more and exhausting it. Anxiously, I kept an extra-close eye on him, and the added vigilance gave me little rest.

The episodes of euphoria dissolved back into the mystery that spawned them, leaving us none the wiser. But a month later, Paul woke wheezy and breathless, bolting upright in bed, gasping for air. Paramedics rushed him to the hospital. One week later, after rounds of strong IV antibiotics, and the doctors never agreeing whether he'd had a heart or respiratory calamity, or both, Paul once again left the hospital for home. Adding yet another medication and a tank of oxygen at night, as if he were deep-sea diving while he slept, Paul soon said he felt better than ever.

Paul's brain was scanned upon admission to the hospital, showing no new stroke but a scarred and ravaged battlefield. In the ER, I watched pity creep over the doctor's face.

"What does the scan tell you?" I asked.

He pointed out the damage from the past stroke, in the temporal and parietal lobes, a large dead patch in the frontal lobe, and missing bits elsewhere.

"I'd assume this man has been in a vegetative state," he said with a soft humanity.

"Far from it. Would you believe he's written several books since then? That he's been aphasic but communicative, swimming a lot, living a much more limited life, but a happy and relatively normal one?"

His face flashed disbelief. "How is that possible?" he asked quietly, as if thinking out loud. Looking back at the scan's deadened landscape, and shaking his head again.

"Working the brain hard every day for four and a half years since the stroke."

"I'm so glad you told me this about him," he said thoughtfully. "It's important to know what's possible."

A STROKE SURVIVED, by definition, won't be the last emergency. How do you get over waiting for the other shoe to drop? Sometimes all you can do is stay busy, so that the waiting doesn't become

a conscious event, only background. Paul had a gift for losing himself in work; it spared him every day. He simply didn't dwell on his
illness or his several brushes with death. I envied him that. For me,
fear, uncertainty, and mystery remained. In the vest pockets of
time—walking down the hallway was long enough—I felt pangs
of worry. So, now and then, I powwowed with the different sides
of me, and tried to gather those terrified, loving parts together,
reach beneath the dread, and find gratitude for our still rich and
buoyant life.

Liz began taking more and longer vacations, and when she wasn't
around, Paul and I lived alone together, the paradox couples define,
and that was wonderful in its unique way. When she was present,
I had an articulate, high-functioning housemate, a crazy element
of verbal normalcy, a bridge to the loose wordplay of the past.

Much of our chatter still crested right over Paul, especially while
he was dawning. When Paul emerged, bleary-eyed, from the bedroom one morning, for instance, he found Liz and me in the
kitchen trying to remember the steps to old dances: the Monkey,
the Pony, the Locomotion, the Mashed Potatoes, the Twist, the
Swim. She'd been inspired by her Uncle Harold's antics, showing
off his successful double knee replacements at her recent fracas of a
family reunion.

"How about the Prairie Chicken?" I suggested, angling my arms
overhead like horns, trotting around the room, and scratching the
floor with one foot, while singing:

> Everybody's doing it, the Prairie Chicken,
> Come on baby, do the Prairie Chicken

Meanwhile Liz was doing justice to the Monkey with long-
armed, almost prehensile abandon. Tossing her now sangria-red
hair, she looked like the ghost of a red howler monkey.

We suddenly noticed Paul standing in the doorway, his face a
scene of intricate puzzlement.

"How much coffee have you two had?" he asked dryly, with just
a touch of nervous concern.

EPILOGUE

Iᴛ'ꜱ ʙᴇᴇɴ ᴏᴠᴇʀ ꜰɪᴠᴇ ʏᴇᴀʀꜱ ꜱɪɴᴄᴇ ᴘᴀᴜʟ'ꜱ ꜱᴛʀᴏᴋᴇ, ᴀɴᴅ ʜᴇ has re-loomed vibrant carpets of vocabulary and his speaking continues to improve. Last week, he started regularly making puns again, for the first time since his stroke.

"Those dollar bills look battered," he said, watching me assemble change for a foray to the farmers' market, then added with a smirk: "Battered and *fried*!"

Paul and I no longer worry about his "getting better," no longer regard aphasia as a process of recovery with stages. We unwrap one day at a time, treating it as a star-spangled gift. The pool is no longer the only place where Paul is happy. He often wakes up too early, finds me and says: "Come and cuddle." Then I'll crawl back into bed, enjoying the special radiant warmth of the already-occupied nest, slipping deep between the womb-like folds of the comforter, and we'll curl tight, linking our breaths. He'll call me his little *scaramouche* (a rascal or scamp), and we'll recall past times together, easy and hard spells, and some of the fun things we've done.

Nonetheless, there are times when his mind seems so different that I barely recognize him. As when he finishes breakfast and wipes his plate with balled-up Kleenex, round and round, and then places it on the draining board, insisting it is now "clean." I explain yet again that dishes need to be washed after a meal, but he just doesn't believe it. To his eye they look clean, even when clotted with egg, and I regularly find dirty plates on the draining board, ready to be reused. And sometimes the illogic really worries me, like when he asked if he could catch the flu by talking on the phone with a sick friend, because "the breath goes in one end and comes out the other."

And yet, and yet, the old spouse I know still inhabits his being. I often see him clearly through the storefront window of his face, his thoughts rapping to come out, and I hear him speaking in old familiar ways, crafting a new *piropo* with Whitmanesque flare, such as "O Parakeet of the Lissome Star." Or he will juggle his aphasia with an ease that quite startles me.

"That's a lovely anthology Anne-Laure sent you," I said the other day.

Paul swirled the pool skimmer like a butterfly net as he strode slowly around the pool, capturing tufts of cottonwood to jettison onto the grass.

"I wish they'd change their approach to painting," he complained, then quickly added, "by which I mean use bigger print."

I couldn't help laughing. "You've translated *yourself* for me? How funny is that!"

Fortunately, despite his left-hemisphere stroke (which too often results in severe depression, anger, or both), and a near-death pneumonia of ten months ago, he seems altogether happier than before, living more in the moment, grateful to be alive. Our life is different, but sweet, often devolving into hilarious charades as he tries to pin a word down, like a lepidopterist with a handful of oysters. Such funny word combinations can spill from an aphasic's mouth! So our days together still include many frustrations, but once again revolve around much laughter and revelry with words.

"The thing you put in the kitchen is void," he told me yesterday, and it was only when we went there and looked out the window that I understood he was trying to say: "The bird-feeder in the kitchen courtyard is empty." The finches were looking for their breakfast.

One recent afternoon, I mumbled with a yawn: "Why am I feeling so sleepy today?"

He replied with utmost sincerity: "Perhaps your mental encyclopedia has been requisitioned by a higher force."

Those were the words his brain had found to say: *Maybe you're worn out from having to concentrate so hard on looking after me.* I pictured the encyclopedia in my head and a big hand reaching in to grab a bunch of volumes.

After five years, I can finally share such word lore with Paul again. But aphasia still plagues him with its merry dances, and with its occasionally missed adverbs and verbs, its automatically repeated words or phrases. He can't use a computer, can no longer type, and has trouble reading his own handwriting. So he will always need an assistant.

On the other hand, when a French magazine recently emailed him a dozen interview questions about a newly translated novel of his, he answered them without a fuss. The novel is *The Place in Flowers Where Pollen Rests*, the title of which he had tried so hard to tell speech therapist Kelly, way back when he was nearly wordless.

Although his style has become less baroque, his creativity and flavor of imagining seem to have returned, as he's written three novels, proofed galleys, and published essays and fiction that he wrote after the stroke. Paul writes in longhand, Liz reads the pages through and types them up, marking the aphasic lapses. He takes the pages away and makes the corrections he wants. She retypes the pages. He rereads them. Reading is still very hard for him, because words on the right-hand margin often disappear, and a line can seem to jump up over the line above it. Nonetheless, he has trained his eyes to adapt. He has written and revised his pages, faithfully, for two hours, nearly every day for over four years. Recently, to his delight, he even wrote a book review—over the years, he'd written hundreds, mainly for *The Washington Post*, but this was his first since the stroke.

In the past, before manuscripts were submitted by computer, he rejected editing with a snip. Whenever he received edited pages, he'd get out a large pair of scissors and methodically cut off the margins, paste up the shorn pages, number them differently, Xerox the lot, and stubbornly return the clean copy to his editor. Now he welcomes Liz's proofreading and values my feedback. As of old, I rarely see a book of his until it's finished. Then I read it through, perhaps making suggestions in the usual way of a "first reader." However, I resist becoming his secretary, assistant, or scribe. It's important for me to remain a spouse, even if also a caregiver.

I can hear Paul shuffling papers at his desk right now, revising a sci-fi novel, *Now, Voyager,* whose main character 1/8 Humbly has a son named 1/16 Humbly. Apparently one of the characters is the Zoom Queen, a woman who can become unfathomably large or infinitely small depending on her mood. *Hmm. Wonder who that could be?* In *Now, Voyager,* the narrator shifts from first to third person, "I" to "he," and when I asked Paul if this was intentional, he said that he hadn't noticed. So perhaps the several voices in his head continue to take turns, or he simply forgets which perspective he's speaking from.

Liz kept a list of some unusually esoteric—but all legitimate—words in this latest manuscript:

termagant, revenant, pseudo-aphorism, aminadversions, foison, unhouseled, welkin, cicisbeo, bailiwick, propaedeutics, dystopia, carboniferous chondrites, captious, circumambient, tapeta, vedette, inanition, traduced, logomachy, capstan, fulvic acid, proprioceptors, misanthropy, palaver, chimerae, plosive, dispositive, pukka, pabulum, hadron, plutocrats, sylph-like, longueurs, latifundia, estaminet, synoptic, atrabiliousness

Not bad for a man who five years ago could only say the syllable "Mem!"

During his window of heightened fluency in the middle of the day, he can write, stringing together chains of regained words, or make phone calls, or lunch with friends. Not all three; he has to choose. But, to some degree, isn't that the same for all of us? I can write first thing in the morning, or I can answer a bunch of emails, or I can telephone a friend—I, too, have to choose where to spend my limited packet of mental energy.

Most often he enjoys writing letters, longhand, allowing the aphasic traces and cross-outs to remain, not being bothered by them, knowing that the recipients will understand and be happy he took the time to write, appreciative that he was holding them in his thoughts.

This morning, while working in my study, I heard the low whisking rumble of the bedroom door opening, followed by the steps of naked feet, then a tiny clicking which I knew to be the sound of Paul returning his ear stopples to their plastic case. I called to him with a *mrok*, to tell him where I was—in my bay window—and he *mrok*ed back, then appeared at my study door, naked as a wombat.

"Where's my cantilever of light?" he asked sleepily.

I smiled. This was a new one. "Do you mean . . . your velour jogging suit?"

"Yes."

"It's in the laundry room."

Why did his brain produce *cantilever of light* when searching for *velour jogging suit*? How or why or when might it seem to him a cantilever of light? Cantilevers are rigid, his jogging suit soft. Cantilevers support bridges. Unless he was thinking of his clothes as a bridge to the bright, wide-awake world? That seemed a reach. But the phrase captivated me, and I had to laugh when I realized that we'd been together so long I had instinctively known that *cantilever of light* meant *velour jogging suit*. Thank heavens for circumlocution . . . That dog can hunt.

Amid all the nonsensical verbal puzzles, living with Paul at times feels like living with a *koan*, one of those paradoxical dialogues, inaccessible to reason, that are taught by Buddhist sages as psychic knots for meditation. Even to begin to interpret a *koan* one has to shed the cords of logic, bend language, dismiss conceptual ways of thinking, and give oneself over to intuition. Talking with someone who is aphasic, one lives in a similar state of perpetually *realizing*, of enjoying the *aha!* moment of insight that comes with solving a verbal puzzle. Like creativity, it invites muscling into the world while simultaneously letting go. His stroke has changed him, but not all for the bad, and it has also changed me.

A caregiver is changed by the culture of illness, just as one is changed by the dynamic era in which one lives. For one thing, I don't have as much time in conversation with myself, and I feel the loss. Certainly I worry more about his death, and mine too, since I'm so much a part of the evolving saga of his health, which I have to monitor each day. But I've grown stronger in every aspect of my life. In small ways: speaking more directly with people. In large ways: discovering I can handle adversity and potential loss and yet keep going. I've a better idea of my strength. I feel like I've been tested, like a willow whipped around violently in a hurricane, but still standing, its roots strong enough to hold.

Coming to terms with being responsible for someone else's life, having to live with such decisions, took a long while, and I didn't like the struggle. At times it even felt like I might be breaking down. Overwhelmed, I feared I was either going to have to give up my career and just take care of Paul, or feel like a total monster and have my career but *not* take care of Paul. My challenge was to see beyond either/or, and find a way to be a loving caregiver of Paul while also nourishing myself.

As the immediacy and complexity of life changed, I struggled with it. At first I managed only by compartmentalizing—*my own life, his life, work life, play life, house life*—and then, finally, I learned to embrace it as a whole. Now, for the most part, it's become seamless, I'm just living *my life*.

As I've written this book, at the speed of one to three pages a day, I've read the pages to Paul, usually after dinner, and we've talked and reconstructed memories about what happened to him in the hospital and during his first years at home (little of which he *remembers*, because his brain wasn't storing memories well at the time). It has helped him understand himself better, what he went through, all he's accomplished since the stroke. Whenever I read passages about caregiving, about my stresses and worries, his face grows tender, and he says, "Little Thing, how hard that must have been." It has provided an opening for us to talk about my hurts and experiences, as well as his, and about our history and life together. A life like an intricately woven basket, frayed, worn, broken, unraveled, reworked, reknit from many of its original pieces. As a result, it has brought us much closer. Life can survive in the constant shadow of illness, and even rise to moments of rampant joy, but the shadow remains, and one has to make space for it.

I am in a phase of life with responsibilities I could not have imagined during my boy-crazy high school years in the heart of Pennsylvania, when Beatles tunes suggested that love was as simple as "I Want to Hold Your Hand." Like the teen years, this is also a passing phase. *Be fully awake for it,* I tell myself, *pay attention to all of its feelings and sensations, because this is simply another facet of being alive, of life on earth, and then there will be another era when Paul will be gone and you won't have these responsibilities and worries.* That has been the unthinkable thought. One that haunts each day, the worry of being left behind and alone that comes with having an older and/or sick spouse. It's no use telling myself that I worried needlessly for twenty-five years—though, in retrospect, I did—because now that Paul is eighty, the fear rings truer. I know there will most likely be a long spell without him. I tell myself that I will be fine. On my walk today, I sensed: *When Paul is gone, the trees and sky will still be beautiful, I will still be poignantly aware of life's transience, and how lucky I am to be alive on this planet in space. It's all part of the adventure. I will still cherish being alive, even though I will miss him fiercely. And, oddly enough, I will probably look back on these days as some of the happiest of my life, despite all the worries, frights, and impediments, because I've loved heartily and felt equally loved in return.*

The pet names and *piropos* continue to flow and flower, some funny, some romantic, some playfully outlandish—all a testament to how a brain can repair itself, and how a duet between two lovers can endure hardship. *This* is what we have made of a diminished thing. A bell with a crack in it may not ring as clearly, but it can ring as sweetly.

SOME LESSONS
LEARNED

I N THE FIFTH YEAR, I READ OF CLINICAL STUDIES WITH aphasics, using a number of the therapies that, sheerly by instinct, we had already adopted, trying all of them at once.

Immersion Training. Absolutely swamping Paul with language all day long and insisting that he talk, in pidgin if need be, just as if he were a settler in a foreign country who has to learn the local dialect as fast as possible to survive. He didn't want to do it at first, because it's so fatiguing, frustrating, and littered with embarrassments and missteps. Giving up, giving in to silence would have been easier, tending him without making verbal demands, as he crawled deeper into his shell.

Instead I engaged him in conversation nonstop, and spoke slowly, using clear, short sentences, and repeating important words and ideas. Gradually I ratcheted up the difficulty in tiny increments as he improved. Although I set up daily routines, I also encouraged yards of rest time. I allowed him plenty of time to speak and often asked for his opinion, helping him find words only when he got stuck. I praised his progress, no matter how small. Two weeks of speech therapy in a Rehab Unit, while essential, is nowhere near enough. The University of Michigan offers a top-flight intensive six-week residential aphasia program, which includes fifteen hours of individual therapy, five hours of group therapy, and three hours of computer-assisted training each week. Paul stayed home, but for the past five years has received the equivalent of about twenty hours of individual therapy per week, and ten hours of group therapy (talking with two or three people at a time).

A Corollary to the Above: Communication Partners. Speech therapists helped at first, but after a while it became clear that Paul would be living with aphasia for the rest of his life, and that it wasn't something any amount of medicine or instruction could "fix." The worst suffering came from lesions in everyday life. Beyond vocabulary and grammar skills, he had lost his social well-being, his connectedness to others, and that left him feeling marginalized and alone. The challenge was to restore a sense of normalcy, an intimate relationship with me, some responsibility and agency, and a willingness to socialize with others once again. Paul needed to be cajoled, tempted, led out, absorbed in chatting about everyday things, and surrounded by people who talked slowly to him but normally to one another. The latter was important because he naturally eavesdropped, wanting to know what people were saying, and he tried hard to follow. I found that one-on-one conversations with friends were easiest for him, and tried to minimize noise. It worked best to have people on hand who felt comfortable with his new speaking patterns, like his longtime friends Chris, Lamar, Jeanne, and Steve, whom Paul connected with and was inspired to pay attention to.

I'd watched as some words returned to him as cherished gifts, one by one after the stroke, especially the words Paul had learned as a professional. It's possible that other aphasics could understand and use equally esoteric vocabulary related to their own work or special interests, words a speech therapist or even a spouse might not recognize.

Adventures in Circumlocution. "Can you talk around it?" I'd ask whenever Paul couldn't think of a word he was trying to say. Liz would ask, "Is it a food? Postage? Have to do with writing?" etc. Getting his brain started on the right pathway seemed to help him focus on smaller subsets of words. He could usually describe it or find a rough synonym, which sometimes produced a parlor game of guessing. I praised his circumlocution, however far-fetched. The alternative was for him to take the easier route and fall silent or pantomime, or just make sounds, instead of trying to say what he meant. What he meant was interesting, and it certainly mattered to him, but my intent was to keep him talking and engaged.

Appreciation and Humor. Given my arty trade, I may be able to follow looser verbal connections between things more easily, but anyone can swing open their mental doors and consider the surprising poetry of what an aphasic might be saying. Such as Paul's using "This is the time of springtime reversal" when he clearly meant "Indian summer." Or "a cache of creepy crawlies," when he meant the annual brigade of ghost ants invading the kitchen. Laughter provides an indispensible spice during tragic times, and it's been essential to our well-being, inspiring Paul to collar words and speak, since he knows that we won't laugh *at* him, but *with* him about the normal high-jinks of aphasia. So he has nothing to lose— what he says might be amusing, even if it's wrong.

Constraint-Induced Therapy. To my surprise, Paul began his own Constraint-Induced therapy as soon as he returned home from the Rehab Unit, stubbornly refusing to feed himself with his good left hand, but insisting on somehow clutching a spoon in his partially paralyzed right hand. It took a while for me to recognize that he was doing this on purpose, not automatically, and that I shouldn't try to assist or correct him. In CI therapy, a patient wears his good arm in a sling, good hand in an oven mitt so that he can't use it, thus forcing him to use the weak hand, and also forcing his brain to rewire for it. In Paul's case, this meant that eating was slow-motion, spilly, and almost impossible at first, as the spoon sometimes swiveled upside down in his grip and food often splattered all around. But it was important to let him struggle and flail with his bad hand until he learned to subdue it. Now, despite the permanent droop of his outer two fingers, he holds cutlery or pen firmly in his right hand.

Ongoing studies at the National Institute of Neurological Disorders and Stroke (NINDS) are evaluating CI aphasia therapy, in which patients are asked only to use words to communicate, no gestures or other sounds. Paul mainly practiced this, and once declared: "There's nothing my mind resists more than the canceled half-sentence!" Frustrating to be sure. So he'd occasionally add his runic *templum* or make cheerful *mrok*ing sounds of greeting. But he mainly insisted on speaking, however long it took.

At nearly eighty, Paul chose not to take part in clinical trials of new drugs, implanting neural stem cells, electrical stimulation of the brain, or Botox injections into the flexor muscles of his clenched finger. And, because he already had its equivalent at home, he didn't wish to join the Aphasia Book Club, for people with trouble reading, which includes audiotapes and worksheets. However, these sound promising and might benefit others. NINDS, part of the National Institutes of Health (NIH), organizes such research and runs a host of clinical trials, with details available online.

Ignoring Timetables. People often talk about there being a "window of opportunity" in the first months after a stroke, during which one can learn most of what's possible, and after that the window closes and learning stops. As Oliver Sacks advised us early on, and we discovered for ourselves in time, that's simply not true. Learning is still possible at any stage or age. Years later, the brain can rewire itself. For example, just two months ago, Liz and I noticed that one aspect of Paul's vision and memory for words had improved. We were watching him compare two typed manuscripts—an original typescript and another one with Liz's corrections marked in red and her notes scrawled in red in the right-hand margin. He had to look from page to page, over and over, hold the words in mind, and compare the sentences—something previously hard for him to do. Now he was able to swing his eyes back and forth smoothly, quickly. This was new. After years of daily practice, his brain had finally rewired his vision for this specific skill. The result meant revising more fluently and also reading a little better. During his annual eye exam, five years post-stroke, he read the letters nimbly across each line—something he hadn't been able to do the year before.

Shared Narrative. In the beginning, it was important for Paul to dictate whatever he could remember about his stroke. Because the process required collaboration, he was forced to socialize more, which provided a bridge from his bottled-up interior to the outside world. It offered him mental shovels and gunnysacks during a time of frightening chaos. Sandbag by sandbag, sentence by sentence, he could rig up levees against the sea of nonsense words that kept threatening to spill in when he spoke. Some aphasia therapists help patients with a similar sort of recital, and refer to the "wounded storyteller" integrating his illness into the narrative of his life.

Building a Bridge to Before. Even if Paul hadn't been able to continue writing, I would have encouraged him to do something related to books, since they had occupied so much of his life before his stroke, and furnished such pleasure. Paul had many files of literary letters and papers to sift through, and several unfinished novels which he could take down from the shelf and tinker with. I might also have suggested he create in another medium—paint or collage—since he'd enjoyed both during an early period of his life.

I'll never forget the impact of going to a Matisse exhibit at the Museum of Modern Art and entering a room devoted to the artist's giant paper cutouts. Bedridden for the rest of his life after an operation, and unable to wield a brush—but still wildly creative— Matisse began scissoring shapes from paper and having helpers arrange them on the walls, building visionary landscapes. In one of my favorites, from his print collection *Jazz*, a black Icarus figure with a round red heart is dancing against a sapphire blue sky hung with giant yellow stars. Handless, footless, the figure none-theless conveys the hopeful, joyful abandon of reaching for the sun. Matisse had captured in cutouts the exact bend of thighs, neck, and arms that goes with that feeling, and felt it himself I'm sure, even though he was infirm. *What to make of a diminished thing?* Frost had asked. For Matisse the answer was a spectacular leap of invention, because the tools available to him had suddenly become limited.

Encouraging Creativity. How hard it is to fathom subtle changes in the brain after a stroke, when tests rely so heavily on the use of words, and favor linear thinking and syllogistic logic. IQ tests measure intelligence, not creativity, which is a different kettle of ghosts. How can creativity be measured, let alone nourished? One way is through simple mind-stretching games, such as the one we called Dingbats, asking: "How many things can you do with a shoe— other than wear it?" In his pre-stroke years, Paul was exceptionally good at that sort of creative puzzle, far better than I, he being the Rabelaisian fictioneer. After the stroke, he rarely joined in. However, inventing pet names taxed and excited his imagination in a similar way. As did the *Mad Libs.* I praised all attempts at speech, and encouraged him to write creatively. It was different from Dingbats, but still stretched his mental muscles, and provided him with a rich sense of satisfaction.

Time-outs. Caregivers need small oases, private moments of being. Creating—plunging into the world of *The Zookeeper's Wife* in WWII Warsaw, or writing about nature at dawn—offered me vital breathing space. Meditation provided another, gardening, biking, and swimming three more. Paul had his pool mysticism, I had mine. Reaching my arms long as I swam, with my chest opening wide and the water flowing continuously cool around my body, I felt like I was flying.

Some useful allies offer online help, support, and advice for care-givers: *Caring Connections* (caringinfo.org), *Share the Care* (sharethecare.org), *Well Spouse Association, Support for Spousal Caregivers* (wellspouse.org), *Family Caregiver Alliance* (caregiver.org). *The Eldercare Locator,* provided by the U.S. Administration on Aging, helps one find agencies in every community that can help with transportation, meals, home care, and caregiver support services (eldercare.gov; 800-677-1116).

Exercising the Brain. The more intellectual and verbal challenges one encounters, the more neurons and connections the brain will grow, so exercise is useful for either prevention or therapy. In a pinch, some of those may ward off dementia or compensate for neurons lost to a stroke by providing a mental reserve, spare brain goods in the cupboard. But one can create mental reserves at any age—even eighty—by challenging the brain and perpetually learning. It doesn't have to be a foreign language. The ideal exercise forces the brain to give up a tired, routine, habitual way of knowing and blaze a new perspective, however small. Crossword puzzles, watercolors, a Comparative Religions course, learning Braille or a musical instrument, or becoming a gardener. Taking a sensory walk in which you focus only on smell. Reversing your walking paths, indoors and outside. Driving a different route to work or school. Showering with your eyes closed and really experiencing the shower. Eating slowly and silently, with undivided attention. Volunteering with a telephone crisis line, a charity, an environmental organization.

Or maybe taking a "Mystery Trip"—a longtime household favorite—in which one person has a destination in mind, but the other tries to figure it out based on clues in the landscape. I took Paul on an aerial Mystery Trip for his birthday one year when I was teaching in Athens, Ohio, by renting a plane and flying us north about an hour to a small field hosting an Aercoupe convention (WWII airplanes Paul had a fetish for). After Paul's stroke, although he couldn't read well, he learned relentlessly by watching countless science (especially astronomy and animal behavior) programs on PBS, Discovery Science, and National Geographic channels. And, by year five, helping me do the easiest *New York Times* crossword puzzles most evenings after dinner.

"What's a four-letter word for a pitcher?" I sang out, stumped by a clue in the first puzzle we tried.

Counting four spaces in his mind, he had to hold those in memory, picture a pitcher, remember the image, search through his lexicon for possible words, choose a word, then attach sounds to it.

He scrunched up his forehead in thought until at last, twinkling with pride, he declared: "Ewer!"

"Ewer? What's a ewer?" Not a word I'd encountered.

"A pitcher. Roman."

He was right. Since then, with great excitement he's come up with the likes of *ethos*, *agora*, *trireme*, *jape*, and *olios*, and we've enjoyed playing with crosswords during our end-of-the-day kickback and relax time.

Living More in the Present. After the loss of someone I had years of relating to in a certain way, familiar as the air I breathed, I sometimes had to remind myself that life is a place where good things happen as well as bad. At times it's been hard to accept that life has changed irrevocably, and will never be the way it used to be.

Mind you, life will never be what it feels like at this moment either, because it's a whirligig flux all day long, as trillions of sensations bombard the brain, millions of ideas and feelings haunt the corridors of the mind. Less like a single tapestry, and more like spindrift spray blown by impetuous winds along the surface of the sea. All of those dramas adhere to the self, a quixotic animal that never stops revising and reimagining who it is, while changing second by second, as new sensations winkle in, new events challenge, new thoughts and feelings well up. Our lives together, our duet, also continues to evolve, and even if we can't go back to *how it was*, we're designing a good life for us, in spite of everything.

THE ONE HUNDRED
NAMES

Celandine Hunter

Swallow Haven

Spy Elf of the Morning Hallelujahs

Bow-Ribbon of the August Sky

My Little Spice Owl

The Epistle of Paul to the Rumanian Songthrushers

Summer Veil of Highest Honor

Dream Hobbit

Apostle of Radiant Postage Stamps

Ivory-billed Woodpecker of the First Rainwater

My Snowy Tanganyika

Little Moonskipper of the Tumbleweed Factory

Blithe Sickness of Araby

Divine Hunter of the Cobalt Blue Arena

Pong of the Pavilion Where Sweet Peas Go to Spoon

Parapluie of the Snowy Ecstasy

Golden Little Dreamer

Pavlova of the Morning Dew Line

Avatar of Bright April

My Little Bucket of Hair

Fierce Angel of the Marmalade Valley

Rheostat of Sentimental Dreaming

Southern Carmine Bee-Eater

Belle Dame of the Morning Pavilion

Romantic Little Dew-Sipper

Commendatore de la Pavane Mistletoe

Sugarplum of the August Faery

Edelweiss of the Blizzard Pink

Highest Massage of the Succulent Endearing Poach

Swan Boat of the Imperial Sun

Baby Angel with the Human Antecede Within

Fleet-footed Empress of Sleep

Buoyant Hunter of the Esteemed and Cosmological
Tsunami

Hummingbird of the Tricyclic Montevideo

Goddess of Abstract Conversation

Terpsichore Deladier

Delicious Pie of the Alternate Sheepfold

My Little Celestial Porcupine

Diligent Weather Sprite

Diligent Apostle of Classic Stanzas

Mistress of Wonderment

Sylvan Grove of the Endless Flare

Stanza Trance

Patient Priestess of Ever-afters

Lovely Ampersand of the Morning

My Billiard Table of the Decaying Gods
Anti-Gravity Drive of the Century
Autobiography of an Almond
Opalescent Rejoicing of an Eel
Salute to the Kitchen of Creation
My Hooray for the Atheist's Asylum
Super-driver of History Beyond Herodotus
Buoyant Eft
Carmine Postulant of the Pleasant Voice
She for Whom All Flowers Bloom Early
Goddess of Godspell, Saint of African Violets
O Rose of Sharon, I'm All Rosy
Book-Lover of Life's Infinite Volume
Satrap of the Endless Sky
Chasuble of the Evening-painted Cloak
Plethoric with Broken Limbs
Condor of the Light-footed Ridge
Soft Little Hummingbird Who Waits for Me
My Lawn Raider, Everlastingly Pure
Little Scarab of Delight
Lithe Swan, Why Do You Linger So Long?
Valley of the Uprooted Silver-tongued Nightingale
My Showy Sedum, My Sycamore Tree
O Singing Squirrel of the Antipodes
Elk of Bright Morning
Tumultuous Wren, Say When, When, When!
Dark-eyed Junco, My Little Bunko
Black-capped Chickadee Who Puts on Robes for Me
Skylark of the Perfect Trance

O Little Titmouse, Here in My House

Jocund Sprite of the Dew

Historic Shaman Sent to Propitiate

Moon Swivel

Flotation Ninja

My Poetic Little Starfish

Umbrella of Light

Celestial Elf

Delicate *Frisson* Enclosed in a Warm Bunnycuddle

Uxorious Bountiful

Inertia Canceled

Sweet Opalescent Centrifuge

My Remains of the Day, My Residue of Night

Star Equerry

Blessed Little Smile

Queen of Purple Emotions, Starlike in Their Crescendo

Telephone Fensterhorn

Betelgeuse of Bright Inquiry

My Hopi Planet

Foundling of the Here and Beyond

Pleiades of Starship Mine

Bobby-dazzler of the Golden Morn

My Moon Calf of Perpetual Ceremony

Little Flavanoid Wonder

O Parakeet of the Lissome Star

FURTHER READING

Amen, Daniel G. *Healing the Hardware of the Soul*. New York: Free Press, 2008.

Andreasen, Nancy C. *The Creative Brain: The Science of Genius*. New York: Plume, 2006.

Basso, Anna. *Aphasia and Its Therapy*. New York: Oxford University Press, 2003.

Beckett, Samuel, *Waiting for Godot: A Tragicomedy in Two Acts*. New York: Grove, 1994.

———. *Watt*. New York: Grove, 2009.

Bloom, Floyd, ed. *Best of the Brain from Scientific American*. New York: Dana Press, 2007.

Bogousslavsky, J., and F. Boller, eds. *Neurological Disorders in Famous Artists*. New York: Karger, 2005.

Bogousslavsky, J., and M. G. Hennerici, eds. *Neurological Disorders in Famous Artists*, Part 2. New York: Karger, 2007.

Bonet, Théophile. *Guide to the Practical Physician*. London: Thomas Flesher, 1686.

Damasio, Antonio. *Descartes' Error: Emotion, Reason, and the Human Brain.* New York: Grosset/Putnam, 1994.

———. *Looking for Spinoza: Joy, Sorrow, and the Feeling Brain.* New York: Mariner, 2003.

Doidge, Norman. *The Brain That Changes Itself: Stories of Personal Triumph from the Frontiers of Brain Science.* New York: Penguin, 2007.

Duchan, Judith Felson, and Sally Byng, eds. *Challenging Aphasia Therapies: Broadening the Discourse and Extending the Boundaries.* New York: Psychology Press, 2004.

Fehsenfeld, Martha Dow, and Lois More Overbeck, eds. *The Letters of Samuel Beckett 1929-1940.* New York: Cambridge University Press, 2009.

Gardner, Howard. *Art, Mind & Brain: A Cognitive Approach to Creativity.* New York: Basic Books, 1982.

Gazzaniga, Michael S. *Human: The Science of What Makes Us Unique.* New York: HarperCollins, 2010.

Heilman, Kenneth M. *Creativity and the Brain.* New York: Psychology Press, 2005.

Iacoboni, Marco. *Mirroring People: The New Science of How We Connect with Others.* New York: Farrar, Straus and Giroux, 2008.

Jaynes, Julian. *The Origin of Consciousness in the Breakdown of the Bicameral Mind.* Boston: Houghton Mifflin, 1976.

Lyon, Jon G. *Coping with Aphasia.* San Diego: Singular Publishing Group, 1998.

Paciaroni, M., P. Arnold, G. van Melle, and J. Bogousslavsky. "Severe Disability at Hospital Discharge in Ischemic Stroke Survivors." *European Neurology* 43 (2000) 30–34.

Rhea, Paul. *Language Disorders from Infancy Through Adolescence: Assessment and Intervention.* 3rd ed. St. Louis, Mo.: Mosby, 2007.

Rose, F. Clifford, ed. *Neurology of the Arts: Painting, Music, Literature.* London: Imperial College Press, 2004.

Sacks, Oliver. *Musicophilia: Tales of Music and the Brain.* New York: Vintage Books, 2008.

Salisbury, Laura. " 'What is the Word': Beckett's Aphasic Modernism." *Journal of Beckett Studies,* vol. 17, September 2008, pp. 78–126.

Sarno, Martha Taylor, and Joan F. Peters, eds. *The Aphasia Handbook: A Guide for Stroke and Brain Injury Survivors and Their Families.* Adapted from *The Stroke and Aphasia Handbook,* by Susie Parr et al. New York: National Aphasia Association, 2004.

Schwartz, Jeffrey M., and Sharon Begley. *The Mind and the Brain: Neuroplasticity and the Power of Mental Force.* New York: HarperCollins, 2002.

Siegel, Daniel J. *The Mindful Brain: Reflection and Attunement in the Cultivation of Well-Being.* New York: W. W. Norton, 2007.

———. *Mindsight: The New Science of Personal Transformation.* New York: Bantam, 2010.

Smith, Daniel B. *Muses, Madmen, and Prophets: Hearing Voices and the Borders of Sanity.* New York: Penguin, 2007.

Taylor, Jill Bolte. *My Stroke of Insight: A Brain Scientist's Personal Journey.* New York: Viking, 2006.

Tesak, Juergen, and Chris Code. *Milestones in the History of Aphasia: Theories and Protagonists.* New York: Psychology Press, 2008.

West, Paul. *The Place in Flowers Where Pollen Rests.* New York: Doubleday, 1988.

———. *Words for a Deaf Daughter and Gala.* Champaign, Ill.: Dalkey Archive, 1993.

———. *Portable People.* New York: Paris Review Editions, 1990.

———. *A Stroke of Genius.* New York: Viking, 1995.

————. *Life with Swan*. Woodstock, N.Y.: Overlook Press, 2001.

————. *The Immensity of the Here and Now: A Novel of 9.11*. New York: Voyant Publishing, 2003.

————. *Tea with Osiris*. Santa Fe, N.M.: Lumen Books, 2005.

————. *The Shadow Factory*. Santa Fe, N.M.: Lumen Books, 2008.

Yankowitz, Susan. *Night Sky*. New York: Samuel French, 2010.

Zaidel, Dahlia W. *Neuropsychology of Art: Neurological, Cognitive and Evolutionary Perspectives*. New York: Psychology Press, 2005.

ACKNOWLEDGMENTS

Heartfelt thanks to friends who drew even closer after Paul's stroke, especially Dava, Peggy, Jeanne, Dan, and Philip. Continued thanks to Alane Salierno Mason, my smart and savvy editor at Norton, for her encouragement and guidance. Jeanette Norden, director of the Brain and Behavior Module at Vanderbilt University, brought her expert eye and welcome insights. Dr. Ann's medical knowhow and generosity of spirit were a godsend. And I'm indebted to Paul and Liz, who read and listened to the manuscript in its many revisions, sharing invaluable memories, corrections, and suggestions. In *Rashômon* fashion, we've all experienced the same events, though from different angles.

ABOUT THE AUTHOR

Diane Ackerman was born in Waukegan, Illinois. She received an MA, MFA, and PhD from Cornell University. Her works of nonfiction include *An Alchemy of Mind*, a poetics of the brain based on the latest neuroscience; *Cultivating Delight: A Natural History of My Garden*; *Deep Play*, which considers play, creativity, and our need for transcendence; *A Slender Thread*, about her work as a crisis-line counselor; *The Rarest of the Rare* and *The Moon by Whale Light*, in which she explores the plight and fascination of endangered animals; *A Natural History of Love*, which celebrates humankind's oldest and most defining mystery; *On Extended Wings*, her memoir of flying; the bestseller *A Natural History of the Senses*, a poetic and scientific tour through the kingdom of the senses; and, most recently, *The Zookeeper's Wife*, a narrative nonfiction about one of the most successful hideouts of World War II, a tale of people, animals, and subversive acts of compassion.

Her poetry has been published in leading literary journals and in the books *Origami Bridges: Poems of Psychoanalysis and Fire*, *I Praise My Destroyer*, *Jaguar of Sweet Laughter: New and Selected Poems*, *Lady Faustus*, *Reverse Thunder: A Dramatic Poem*, *Wife of Light*, and *The Planets: A Cosmic Pastoral*. She also writes nature books for children: *Animal Sense, Monk Seal Hideaway,* and *Bats: Shadows in the Night.*

Ms. Ackerman has received many prizes and awards, including a DLitt from Kenyon College, a Guggenheim Fellowship, the John Burroughs Nature Award, the Orion Book Award, and the Lavan Poetry Prize, as well as being honored as a Literary Lion by the New York Public Library. She also has the rare distinction of having a molecule named after her—the dianeackerone. She has taught at a variety of universities, including Columbia and Cornell. Her essays about nature and human nature have appeared in the *New York Times, Smithsonian, Parade, The New Yorker, National Geographic,* and many other journals. She hosted a five-hour PBS television series inspired by *A Natural History of the Senses.* She divides her time between Florida and upstate New York.